Minority Rights

Recent Titles in Contributions in Political Science
Series Editor: Bernard K. Johnpoll

Neighbors Across the Pacific: The Development of Economic and Political Relations Between Canada and Japan
Klaus H. Pringsheim

International Dynamics of Technology
Ralph Sanders

Party Politics in Israel and the Occupied Territories
Gershon R. Kieval

The Strange Career of Marihuana: Politics and Ideology of Drug Control in America
Jerome L. Himmelstein

French Communism in the Era of Stalin: The Quest for Unity and Integration, 1945-1962.
Irwin M. Wall

North Korea in Transition: From Dictatorship to Dynasty
Tai Sung An

The Harmonization of European Public Policy: Regional Responses to Transnational Challenges
Edited by Leon Hurwitz

The Press and the Rebirth of Iberian Democracy
Edited by Kenneth Maxwell

Domestic Policy Formation: Presidential-Congressional Partnership?
Steven A. Shull

Communications Policy and the Political Process
Edited by John J. Havick

Abortion: A Case Study in Law and Morals
Fred M. Frohock

The State as Terrorist: The Dynamics of Governmental Violence and Repression
Edited by Michael Stohl and George A. Lopez

Minority Rights

A Comparative Analysis

Jay A. Sigler

CONTRIBUTIONS IN POLITICAL SCIENCE, NUMBER 104

GREENWOOD PRESS
Westport, Connecticut . London, England

Library of Congress Cataloging in Publication Data

Sigler, Jay A.
Minority rights.

(Contributions in political science, ISSN 0147-1066 ;
no. 104)
Bibliography: p.
Includes index.
1. Minorities—Legal status, laws, etc. I. Title.
II. Series.
K3242.S57 1983 342'.087 83-5580
ISBN 0-313-23400-0 (lib. bdg.) 342.287

Library of Congress Catalog Card Number: 83-5580
ISBN: 0-313-23400-0
ISSN: 0147-1066

First published in 1983

Greenwood Press
A division of Congressional Information Service, Inc.
88 Post Road West, Westport, Connecticut 06881

Printed in the United States of America

10 9 8 7 6 5 4 3 2 1

To Ian and Niall

Contents

Preface

THE acceptance of the ideal of individual human rights has spread all over the globe since the end of World War II. President Jimmy Carter's emphasis on human rights violations highlighted American concerns with the rights of other peoples. The United Nations has long championed the cause of individual human rights. Indeed, as a result of the Helsinki Agreements, the Soviet Union has acknowledged the importance of individual human rights. Nonetheless, the progress of individual rights since 1945 has not been accompanied by a greater interest in minority rights. On the contrary, with the exception of a heightened concern with certain minority groups in the United States, India, the United Kingdom, and Belgium, minority rights have been low on the agenda in many nations and actively discouraged in others. This book is an effort to sort out the main features of minority rights in order to provide an awareness of collective or group rights in addition to the much more familiar rights of individuals.

It is impossible to do full justice to the vastness of the topic. Yet it is worthwhile to reexamine standard thinking about rights in order to incorporate the genuine needs and concerns of various groups of people around the world. Palestinians have more than a mere political claim to decent treatment. Kurds, Copts, Sikhs, and Basques have expressed their minority group claims with violence. Others have passively endured what they regard as majority oppression. We should be prepared to understand the basis of these claims in a context other than the familiar, Western, individualistic version of human rights.

We live in an age of vast transformation, but one of the greatest changes has been mass population movements on a scale unparalleled in recorded history. This has occurred in the past few decades as a part of the termination of Western colonialism following the two world wars. The result of these mass population movements has been to increase tensions among groups. The breakdown of the homogeneity of some older states and the fragility of newer states has exacerbated numerous group conflicts. Minorities confront majorities in most parts of the world but with little effort to understand the positions of one another. For this reason too, there must be a clarification of minority rights.

A modern view of minority rights must partly be based upon history. For this historical perspective, I am grateful to James Muldoon, a medieval historian whose insights were indispensable to the conceptualization of this book. In addition, chapter three is largely a product of his efforts.

Yet the disciplines of law, political theory, sociology, geography, and economics were also necessarily examined for their contributions to understanding minority rights. A selective approach to these materials was taken, and the most practical contributions were blended for the uses that I believed were appropriate. In the process some technical issues were simplified, some broad generalizations were made, and some broad conclusions were reached for which I accept full responsibility. Some errors may also have crept into a work of this ambitious sweep. In the spirit of cooperative scholarship, I would appreciate receiving helpful suggestions for improvements from those specialists who have an even more exact understanding of aspects of this prismatic subject.

I am convinced that minority rights problems are here to stay and are growing in salience. Those pioneering efforts in the United States, India, the United Kingdom, Belgium, and the Union of Soviet Socialist Republics deserve our attention. Partly on that basis I have sketched out what I believe to be the basis of a viable provisional theory of minority rights. I hope others will improve upon and refine this theory. The topic deserves to be rescued from the neglect of serious scholars and statesmen.

The harder task that lies ahead is the reconciliation of minority rights with individual rights. Issues such as affirmative action, which have generated much heat but little light, could be better resolved if the competing and complementary aspects of group and individual rights were fully grasped.

I recognize a substantial intellectual debt to Inis Claude and J. A. LaPonce, who have examined minority rights before me. I hope that I have done justice to them in extending their efforts. At another level I am indebted to Mary Archibald, who patiently helped produce and cleanse the manuscript. Deciphering the meaning of clumsy handwriting was as difficult as has been my task in weaving together complex strands of scholarship.

Finally, I should apologize to those advocates of women's rights who may have expected to receive support from this book. I have chosen to exclude women's rights from the coverage of minority rights not because women do not deserve better recognition but because the topic did not fit the scheme of analysis that was adopted.

Minority Rights

1

Defining the Minority

AN adequate understanding of minority rights hinges upon a simple concept or definition of a minority group. Unfortunately, no sufficient definition has yet emerged. Leading sociologists have made little headway, noting that "like everything else that is social, minority groups must be socially defined as minority groups, which entails a set of attitudes and behaviors," whatever that may mean.[1] This vagueness in social science literature remains a current difficulty as scholars grope for a proper approach to minority groups.[2] But the real needs of minority groups cannot wait indefinitely for sociological description. Minority rights claims abound, and they can only be appraised by first establishing the nature of the minority group.

The very existence of minority groups is often denied by political leaders of nation-states. This refusal to acknowledge the presence of a minority group is an easy way to deny that group any claims of right. A definition cannot change this evasiveness of some political regimes, but it can make evasion much more difficult.

United Nations definitions of minority groups have varied from time to time in an effort to safeguard the sensibilities of political leaders. At times, race, ethnicity, or nationality have been removed from the list of minority group attributes. The Universal Declaration of Human Rights, adopted in 1948, lists "race, colour, sex, language, religion, and national or social origin as impermissible grounds for unfavourable treatment."[3] However, the United Nations Covenant on Civil and Political Rights refers only to "ethnic, religious, or linguistic minorities."[4] Does the elimination of race, color, sex, and nationality mean that national or racial groups have no rights unless they are also ethnic or linguistic minorities?[5] The Covenant on Civil and Political Rights does not provide the answer. Only a clearer definition of the nature of minority rights can do so.

Francesco Capotorti of the UN Sub-Commission on Prevention of Discrimination and Protection of Minorities has attempted to draft a definition of minority groups that will be acceptable to most UN members. After reviewing various unsuccessful efforts toward defining minorities, Capotorti, as Special Rapporteur, offered his own. This definition, while unofficial, remains the leading example for this topic and deserves serious attention. Boiled down to its essentials, Capotorti defines minorities as groups "numerically inferior to the rest of the population of a state, in a non-dominant position, whose members—being nationals of the state—possess ethnic, religious or linguistic characteristics differing from those of the rest of the population and show if only implicitly a sense of solidarity, directed towards preserving their culture, traditions, religion, or language."[6]

This definition was drawn up to be consistent with the United Nations Covenant on Civil and Political Rights. It does not extend far beyond Article 27 of the Covenant and excludes various kinds of groups that might otherwise have been considered as legitimate minorities. Because of their numbers, such majority groups as blacks in South Africa or women are excluded. The definition excludes aliens from its coverage by its limitation to "nationals of the state." Thus guestworkers, refugees, and immigrants, in general, are not covered. Because the definition has a subjective element in including a minority's wish to preserve its individuality, there is, as Capotorti admits, a risk that "any state wishing to evade the rule might justify its refusal by claiming that the groups themselves did not intend to preserve their individuality."[7] Indeed, it would be most difficult to establish what a group willed.

The narrowness of Capotorti's definition is based upon the suspicion of minority rights claims that is prevalent among the United Nations member states. The collapse of the minorities regime under the League of Nations and the use of the Sudeten Germans as a Trojan horse for Nazi German expansionism give good ground for suspicion. Added to these historic factors is the fragility of many of the states formed after World War II. Capotorti notes that there is a need to safeguard the integrity of the state and to avoid separatism, but he observes as "a matter for regret that concern to avoid weakening the integrity of the state or opening the door to separatist tendencies sometimes presents an obstacle to the adoption of special measures in favour of individuals belonging to minority groups."[8] Fortunately, this study is not bound by the current fears and attitudes of member states of the United Nations and can adopt a more generous and logical definition. Nor are we compelled here to follow the recent United Nations emphasis upon a right to self-determination that excludes "ethnic, religious, or linguistic minorities."[9]

While the United Nations appears to have retreated from its post-World War II view of minority rights, there was an initial willingness to look at the problem of protection of minorities as a general universal conception,[10] as noted previously. However vague and imprecise the meaning of the term "minority," it is possible to strive for a commonsense definition that meets the ordinary expectations of ordinary people. This definition goes beyond the earlier UN statements. Surely we can exclude from our definition the problems of the left-handed, the disabled, the old, the rich, and the Ph.D.'s. These may have their claims to make, but they should not be considered as groups in the same way as race, caste, language, culture, ethnic, religious, national or similar groups, which share recognizable, common disadvantage. *In its simplest form we can regard as a minority any group category of people who can be identified by a sizable segment of the population as objects for prejudice or discrimination or who, for reasons of deprivation, require the positive assistance of the state. A persistent nondominant position of the group in political, social, and cultural matters is the common feature of the minority.* Into this definition fall various groups whose condition derives from race, religion, language, ethnicity, nationality, caste, and culture. Aliens, refugees, and immigrants might fall into this category at various times and places, but Ph.D.'s would not. While no definition will satisfy all critics, this one is based upon the evident inadequacy of earlier definitions in this field of study.[11] Subordinate status and low self-esteem are the chief features of minority groups. As a sociologist recently observed: "The crucial aspect of a minority group is not that it has proportionately fewer members than other groups in a system, but that it is inferior or is thought by other groups, and often by its own members, to be inferior in a hierarchical system."[12] Our definition meets the standards of current sociological wisdom and the expectations of thoughtful observers of human rights.

One of the difficulties in applying the definition is in determining whether it includes women. Are women the objects of prejudice or discrimination? Sometimes in some places, surely.[13] The issue about including women is not whether they have not suffered in many nations and cultures but whether they are a sufficient "group category of people" to constitute a minority group. The decision is made arbitrarily here and in the negative. For the purposes of this study, women are not regarded as members of a minority group on the ground that they do not comprise a group. While some women are feminists, others are not. Women share biological similarity but whether that similarity confers "groupness" upon them assumes that all or most women are socially perceived in much the same prejudiced way, a point which can be made against a male-oriented society but which cannot be shown to be similar from one society to another. Women are a social category but not a "group category" for the purpose of this analysis of minority rights. Advocates of greater rights and protections for women have a very strong case to make in most nations, but that case is not advanced by treating women as a minority.[14]

IDENTIFYING THE GROUPS

Since groups have the capacity to make claims and some of these claims may mature into rights, the central issue is to identify those groups that may legitimately or appropriately make claims. All red-headed persons within a territory do not comprise a group, but all dark-skinned people may. Skin color is one of the most common differentiating factors used in human affairs. What accounts for group status? An organized and formal structure, a subjective feeling of membership, or official recognition by the state? Many governments refuse to recognize the existence within their territory of separate ethnic or linguistic groups. The political consequences of attaining official status may actually be so great that a government's stability may be endangered by the recognition of a group. Since national governments are often committed to integration of the state and society, they are prone to discourage recognition of separate groups. On the other hand, if group existence is dependent upon the will of government, group claims of right are inherently untenable, since one of the functions of group rights is to restrain the government or to gain its favor and support.

The right of a group to exist and survive seems to be most fundamental. Only if groups are permitted to persist, can they hope to assert their claims. If the government disperses a group or prevents its expression of cultural identity, the group may be destroyed. Plainly, the two-tier theory of rights that pits the individual against the state is inadequate to meet this situation of group claims.[15] To some extent, the question of which groups possess rights is different from the question of which groups are entitled to claim rights, but by examining the first category, we may learn of the second. Rather than impose a broad theory of group rights, it might be best to survey which groups have attained rights in order to understand how the process works.

Group life is one of the oldest features of human experience. The family, the clan, and the language group all antedate the state. Has the creation of the modern state resulted in the decline of the significance of these and other groups? Probably so, but groups persist and the swift-moving currents of world affairs appear to be eroding loyalties to the state. All the more reason why the identification of significant groups is politically important.

In order to cut through many of the ambiguities that surround the term "group," the focus here will be upon minority rights as an aspect of group rights. Minorities are better understood and more clearly identified than more amorphous kinds of groups. A minority has been defined as "a group of people who, because of their physical or cultural characteristics, are singled out from the others for differential and unequal treatment" and "the existence of a minority in a society implies the existence of a corresponding dominant group with higher social status and greater privileges."[16] In addition, we should include in our definition not only the feature of inequality of treatment, but also the denial of distinctive features of collective identity. So, a United Nations subcommission defines minorities as "those nondominant groups in a population which possess and wish to preserve stable ethnic, religious, or linguistic traditions or characteristics different from the rest of the population."[17]

Minority groups often are victims of discrimination and prejudice. Their members are often denied access to jobs, education, housing, and other social goods because of their minority affiliation. In addition, the minority groups may wish to keep and preserve their culture and ways of life. Their claims of right may arise from their being denied rights available to other citizens or denied the right to live differently from other citizens. Gypsies, for example, are seldom thought of as a minority group. Yet they speak their own language and preserve their own culture. They often wish to avoid the schools, homes, and factories of the societies through which they wander. Yet, they are a distinct minority group according to our definition, even if many societies try to compel gypsies to abandon their ways and to conform to majority practices.

In many modern nations there are several minority groups living within the same territory. Hierarchies sometimes develop among minority groups, and the majority may play off minority groups against each other to enhance majority domination. In a most perverted form minorities may dominate larger groups by treating them as though they were minorities. Afrikaners have engineered a policy of apartheid, of strict racial separation, as a means of securing power over blacks, coloureds, Asians, and other groups in South Africa. Though small in number, this white minority has been able to keep the larger entities at bay by treating them as though they were minorities and blocking their efforts to organize for obtaining political power. In any event, each nation has its own constellation of minority groups, with the Soviet Union and India having the largest numbers of different minorities.

Minorities are generally subordinate segments of complex states (save South Africa and Rhodesia until 1979). The minority groups are self-conscious units that share similar traits, culture, language, or even physical attributes. Religion may not be enough to bind a group into a coherent minority, although small sects such as Copts, Jehovah's Witnesses, or Zoroastrians frequently are perceived as minority groups.

Minority group membership is rarely voluntary. Minority status is usually determined by descent or inheritance. Marriage and family life are usually confined within the fold of the minority. Intermarriage tends to be discouraged by the minority and by the majority because it breaks down the group identification of the minority.

In continental Europe the term minority usually refers "to a group of people living on soil which they have occupied from time immemorial, but who, through change of boundaries, have become politically subordinate."[18] These minorities are historical and cultural minorities. Some have lost their political autonomy, such as the Latvians, Estonians, and Lithuanians. Some rarely had it, such as the Ukranians and Armenians. Some have gained it in this century, such as the Czechs and the Slovaks.

This narrower use of the term "minority group" does not account for African experience, where tribal affiliations are so important. Nor does it account for religious splits that are significant in the Muslim world. Race is clearly absent from this European-style definition. However, rampant minority nationalism among the Basques, the Flemings, the Welsh, and the Scots has been an increasing feature of European political life, and it is appropriate to see nationality groupings as paramount in Europe, if not in other parts of the world.

Minority status does not require a numerical minority. Bantus comprise around 80 percent of the population of South Africa but are in a subordinate position by virtue of their treatment and self-perception. Furthermore, groups are not naturally differentiated into majority and minority status. Social definition creates minority status, rather than racial, linguistic, or cultural differences. Minority groups are perceived as somehow unlike other groups or else, regardless of size, they are not minority groups. Mass communication, by the printed word, by radio, and television, has heightened our awareness of minority differences and conditions. As a result there seem to be more minorities in the world today than ever before.

Minorities are conflict groups. They are sources of unrest and social dissatisfaction. Unless suppressed or discouraged, they help precipitate social change. Minorities often form their own political parties or join dissident factions of a ruling party. They hope to improve their lot by agitating from within the government, when permitted, or against the government, if need be. On the other hand, the need of the majority to repress minorities may freeze the political structure and cause stagnation. Again, South Africa is a fine example.

Access to the majority group may be quite difficult for members of the minority. The factors that differentiate the majority from the minority tend to increase over time if the minority is isolated from the majority. A few minority members may cross the line, but they may be in a no-man's-land between the majority and the minority left behind. This is often the position of the black American who joins the middle class or who enters the professions. To a different extent Jews fall into this marginal category when they intermarry with Christians. Barriers always exist between the majority and the minorities, although some permeability also exists.

The political and social relationships between the majority and th minorities have varied in different places and at different times.[19] Dominant groups have often preferred to attempt to assimilate their minorities. Assimilation could be forced, as in Tsarist Russia and Nazi-occupied territories, or peaceful, as in the blending of races in Brazil or the so-called melting pot in the United States of America. Peaceful assimilation may be promoted by various governmental policies, but it is best advanced in an open society with free access for minorities to jobs, housing, education, and other social goods. Obviously, assimilation is always incomplete and some minorities remain unabsorbed.

For minorities that do not want to be assimilated, *pluralism* is the preferred policy. The fear of losing minority group identity may be so intense that minorities may wish little more of government than protection against the incursions of majority culture and values. A pluralist policy would encourage and promote the development of minority cultural institutions. Diverse languages would be used in the schools. Religious differences would be tolerated. Switzerland has practiced pluralism most extensively. Differences among the French, German, and Italian cantons persist and are encouraged. Canada has had much more difficulty with its French-speaking population. Belgium is working toward a set of pluralist political compromises. Pluralism may be expressed in legal documents, such as constitutions, treaties, and statutes. There is a strong worldwide trend toward legal guarantees to support pluralist policies.[20]

Population transfer is a more drastic solution to minority problems. Dominant majorities may hope to reduce tensions by physically moving dissident minorities to other, more hospitable, territory. In the 1920s the governments of Greece, Turkey, and Bulgaria made a reasonably satisfactory population exchange. Yet the minorities involved did have difficulty adjusting to the new conditions. Many individuals were driven from their homes to satisfy these treaties.

The Nazis pursued a vicious, vigorous policy of population transfer over subjugated areas. Today, population transfer is pursued by the South African government homelands policy, which forces blacks to obtain homes in certain regions of the country deemed appropriate to their tribal group. Since many blacks work in the cities and mines far away from the homelands, this policy has the effect of splitting families. The importation of labor is an economic means of population transfer. This is how Chinese and Japanese were originally attracted to America and how Indians and other groups found their way to Africa.

As a last resort, dominant majorities may adopt a policy of repressing minorities. Minority group activities may be closed. Minority group practices may be outlawed. Minority group leaders may be jailed. Access to education, employment, and housing can be curtailed. Such a policy may end in expulsion of unwanted minorities (Indians in Tanzania) or genocide (Jews in Germany, natives in Tasmania, Amerindians in the United States).

RACE AS A GROUP CONCEPT

The word "race" was not used to classify peoples until late in the seventeenth century. Until the European voyages of discovery to America and Africa, the concept of race as a physical category did not exist. European contact with Indians in America and with black Africans gave rise to speculation about human differences. In spite of the fact that European nations were themselves composed of peoples from different sections of the world and in spite of the fact that European nationalities had developed physical differences, race as a group concept did not arise until after European contact with so-called barbaric societies. The origins of racial thinking suggest the artificiality of racial groupings.[21]

Today, modern physical anthropology denies that individuals can be separated into strict distinctive racial groupings, although an attempt was made by American anthropologist Carleton Coon, who devised an elaborate and rigid description of different racial types.[22] Anthropologist J. Z. Yang has said of Coon's efforts that "the attempt has been a major feature of man's naive study of himself and still is so in spite of the demonstration that it is scientifically impossible and socially dangerous."[23] Yang and others accept that there are regional groupings of genes that cause differences in skin color, hair, noses, and lips. But there are many combinations and variations of these features. Some of them are environmentally conditioned. The human species is exceedingly variable, and racial classification can only be made in the crudest terms. Extensive isolation of a particular group may result in reproductive isolation and a very distinct appearance among that group of people. However, wherever cultural conditions have permitted contact with other groups, distinctiveness breaks down and racial groupings lose their validity. The distinctiveness of peoples may be produced by cultural and political conditions as much or more than by any inherent genetic differences. Plainly, there are physical differences visible among peoples, but cultural and political factors have contributed heavily to these differences. A prominent anthropologist reduces the explanation of human differences to two principles:

> (a) Whenever two populations persist over time in separate environments and there is no remixing of individuals, racial difference will tend to increase from generation to generation.
>
> (b) Whenever individuals from racially distinguishable populations are mixed up in the same environment, racial distinctions within the mixed population will tend to decrease from generation to generation.[24]

When the Europeans came to the New World, they found a number of different Indian societies. Some, such as the Mayas, the Aztecs, and Incas were quite advanced in the arts of civilization. Others lived in primitive, nomadic conditions. The gulf between the civilized Indians and the wandering hunters was as great as that which had existed between the Romans and the barbarians. All this was shattered by the arrival of the Europeans. Moreover, the differences among the various groups of Indians was virtually meaningless for the Europeans who rapidly destroyed Indian societies.

After being conquered many Indians were reduced to slavery, which proved impractical as thousands died from European diseases and excessive toil. As a result, African slaves were imported to cultivate the valuable sugarcane fields and coffee plantations. The Portuguese and Spanish Catholic clergy did not protest against the enslavement of Indians and Africans. In fact, many had slaves themselves, and slavery was morally justified because it provided religious converts. The church at least demonstrated some concern for the Indians, while remaining indifferent to the lot of the Africans. Much racial thinking has its roots in these events.

Slavery in the United States had a quite different history and development than in Latin America. Black African slaves were in the minority in every state except South Carolina at the time of Independence, while in Brazil and Latin America whites were very much in the minority. So small was the white labor force that intermarriage was frequently tolerated and free Negroes and free mulattoes came to outnumber the slaves. Strict separation of the "races" was the rule in the United States prior to the Civil War, but racial mixing was the rule in Latin America, especially in Brazil. Even today, racial identification in Brazil and Latin America is much less socially significant than in the United States. In the United States a man or woman who is even slightly tainted with Negro ancestry is a Negro. Coffee-colored people are considered blacks and are treated as such. Racial mixing is so prevalent in Latin America that race is less salient and racial identity less significant, except for many of the Indians who remain isolated from the rest of the society.[25]

Yet class and race are factors in Latin American life. In some nations, such as Ecuador, the white minority dominates the nonwhite population. But by and large it is economic class, not race, that determines social position and conveys political power in Latin America. In most nations racial lines are too blurred and class distinctions too rigid to rely on race as a powerful force.[26] By contrast, race retains powerful significance in the United States in spite of Supreme Court rulings and national legislation to protect and benefit American blacks. Housing and schooling are still infected with racial hostility, especially in the North.[27]

Race counts more than class for the American black (or brown or tan).

Race categories are often adopted for reasons of administrative convenience. Many forms require the identification of individuals by racial category. The word "Caucasian" has passed into usage as a euphemism for white. Nonwhite, Oriental, and Spanish are categories used on various official American governmental forms. The category of "other" seems to embrace Indians and Filipinos, but not Jews, who seem not to be regarded as a race in America. The 1960 census treated as "Negro" persons of mixed Negro and white descent and those of mixed American Indian and Negro descent. American Indians are those, according to the 1960 census, who have at least one-fourth Indian blood. Thus, racial groupings can be made arbitrarily to suit governments regardless of the will of the individuals themselves.

Some groups could be arbitrarily classified either as races or ethnic or linguistic entities. Jews seem to be an ethnic group, although some would assign them a racial status. Gypsies share a common language and culture and often bear physical similarities after centuries of inbreeding. Now that gypsies are organized internationally, they have sought to send delegates to the United Nations Economic and Social Council.[28] The question is what entity is being represented, since gypsies lack a homeland. Racial groupings may have unhappy consequences, too. The Crimean Tatars were all exiled from their homelands and sent to Siberia in 1944 for having collaborated with German occupation forces. Doubtless, there were many who did not collaborate, but just being a member of the group earned a ticket to Siberia. Even after their rehabilitation in 1967, the Crimean Tatars were denied permission to return to their homeland.

Legal rights are often allocated according to group status. The current English Race Relations statute is aimed at the protection of minorities in the United Kingdom.[29] However, if a particular minority is not regarded as a race, it is unprotected by this statute. The act is not concerned with discrimination on the grounds of religion, language, sex, or political belief, although the UN International Covenant on Civil and Political Rights does cover all these forms of discrimination. Hence Jews and gypsies may not come under its protection unless, perhaps, the discriminator treats them as a racial group. English courts have been unwilling or unable to declare Jews a racial group.[30] The act does not appear to cover a Sikh who was dismissed from his job for wearing a beard in an ice cream factory.[31] Members of minority religions such as Muslims and Hindus are not covered by reason of their religion but may be covered by reason of their race.

For legal purposes, then, only some groups are accorded official status. Most nations avoid problems of group rights by simply not recognizing the status of the group. This book does not accept that a group must be legally defined before it can have legitimate claims.

NOTES

1. Arnold M. Rose, "Minorities," *International Encyclopedia of the Social Sciences* 10 (1968), pp. 365-71. Rose says that "much of the literature soon becomes irrelevant because it is limited to description and because of the value orientations guiding the research" in sociology.

2. See Christen T. Joanssen, "Toward a Standardization of a Conceptual Scheme for Minority Group Research," *Ethnicity* 8 (1981), pp. 121-26.

3. Universal Declaration of Human Rights, adopted December 10, 1948, Art. 2, GA Re 217A, UN Doc. A/810 at 71 (1948).

4. Article 27, International Covenant on Civil and Political Rights, GA Res. 2200A, 21 UN GAOR, Supp. (No. 16) 52, UN Doc. A/6316 (1966).

5. See the Draft Convention on the Rights of Nationalities and Protection of Minorities (Internationales Institut Für Nationalitätenrecht und Regionalismus, Munich, 1978). The United Nations has also attempted to develop a Declaration and Convention on the Elimination of Religious Intolerance and Discrimination but has had little success with this effort.

6. Francesco Capotorti, *Study on the Rights of Persons Belonging to Ethnic, Religious and Linguistic Minorities*, UN Doc. E/CN 4/Sub. 2/384Rev. 1 (1979), p. 96.

7. Ibid.

8. Ibid., p. 98.

9. Aureliu Cristescu, *The Right to Self-Determination*, Report prepared for Sub-Commission on Prevention of Discrimination and Protection of Minorities, UN Doc. E/CN 4/Sub. 2/404/Rev. 1 (1981), p. 41. This recent study represents a severe setback for minority rights advocates because it seems to limit claims to self-determination largely to former victims of colonial or foreign domination, while virtually denying the possibility of minority group repression from other sources, which could be severe enough to justify a claim for separation or even greater autonomy. This report seems heavily influenced by dominant "third world" forces that advocate only a limited form of group activism in the form of anti-colonial activity. Yet this report does encourage social and cultural development for minorities.

10. See T. H. Bagley, *General Principles and Problems in the International Protection of Minorities* (Geneva: Imprimeries Populaires, 1950), p. 9.

11. The best known recent attempt is by J. A. LaPonce, who makes a vague distinction between "minorities by force" and "minorities by will," which adds little clarity to the definition, and seems, in fact, to have an assimilationist bias. See J. A. LaPonce, The *Protection of Minorities* (Berkeley: University of California Press, 1960), pp. 12-13. LaPonce's brief discussion of "border" and "enclosed" minorities has a descriptive value and some political sophistication but is not definitional in nature (pp. 11-12).

12. Jonassen, "Toward a Standardization of a Conceptual Scheme," p. 122.

13. Most certainly in the Arab world. See Nawal Gl Saddawi, *The Hidden Face of Eve: Women in the Arab World* (London: Zed Press, 1980). Sexual mutilation, sexual aggression, slavery, and physical abuse are recanted.

14. The fairness of this approach may be disputed, but the facts demonstrate that minority women have been considerably worse off than white women in America. See U.S. Department of Labor reports on minority women workers for a consistent demonstration of this fact in the employment field. Unemployment figures are especially significant indicators of deprivation for minority wonem. minority women.

15. Vernon Van Dyke, "Human Rights and the Rights of Groups," *American Journal of Political Science* 18 (1974), pp. 725-41.

16. Louis Wirth, "Minorities," in *The Science of Man in The World Crisis*, ed. Ralph Linton (New York: Columbia University Press, 1945), p. 347.

17. UN Subcommission on Prevention and Protection of Minorities, *Yearbook on Human Rights*, (New York: United Nations, 1952), p. 490.

18. Richard Schermerhorn, "Minorities: European and American," *Phylon* (1959), p. 179.

19. See George Eaton Simpson and J. Milton Yinger, *Racial and Cultural Minorities*, 3d ed. (New York: Harper and Row, 1965), pp. 20-25.

20. See Arend Lijphart, *Democracy in Plural Societies: A Comparative Explanation* (New Haven: Yale University Press, 1977).

21. Michael Banton and Jonathan Harwood, *The Race Concept* (New York: Praeger Publishers, 1975), pp. 13-42.

22. Best summarized in Carleton S. Coon, "The Taxonomy of Human Variation," *Annals of The New York Academy of Science* 134 (1966), pp. 516-40.

23. J. Z. Yang, *An Introduction to the Study of Man* (Oxford: Clarendon Press, 1971), pp. 3-4.

24. Edmund R. Leach, "Cultural Components in the Concept of Race," in *Racial Variation in Man,* ed. F. J. Ebling (New York: John Wiley and Sons, 1975), p. 31.

25. Marvin Harris, *Patterns of Race in the Americas* (New York: Walker and Company, 1964).

26. See the survey by Charles W. Anderson, "The Concepts of Race and Class and the Explanation of Latin American Politics," in *Race and Class in Latin America*, ed. Magnus Mötner (New York: Columbia University Press, 1970), pp. 231-55.

27. See Karl G. Taeuber, "Housing, Schools and Incremental Segregative Effects," *Annals of the American Academy of Political and Social Science* 441 (1979), pp. 157-67. In the same issue, see Franklin D. Wilson, "Patterns of White Avoidance," pp. 132-41.

28. Reported in *New York Times*, February 8, 1979, p. A10.

29. Race Relations Act of 1976. (1976 C. 74). This is the third English race relations statute. The acts of 1965 and 1968 were inadequate to meet the growing tensions of race in the United Kingdom.

30. Clayton v. Ramsden, A. C. 320 (1943); re: Tannpolsk Barclays Bank, Ltd. v. Hyer, 3 All E. R. (1958); Lindo v. Belisario, 1 Hag. Con. 216 (1975); re: DeWilton, DeWilton v. Montefiore, 2 Ch. 481 (1900).

31. Singh v. Lyons Maid Ltd., 1 R. L. R. 328 (1975).

2

The Gap Between Fact and Explanation

FOR the most part the prevalence of minority groups within most of the nations of the world is a residue of history. Historic population movements have resulted in the current distribution of smaller groups within the larger society. The movements are still taking place on a scale as great as any known to history, giving rise to new minority issues, especially in the wake of moribund Western colonialism.

In spite of the evident facts that give rise to minority problems, no satisfactory theory has emerged to explain the proper role of minorities within modern societies. The rights of minorities and the duties they owe have been frequently discussed, but no overall rational approach has yet emerged. Thus there is a gap between the facts and their explanation. We will review both here.

THE FACTUAL BASIS OF MINORITY PROBLEMS

Population movement is the root cause of minority problems. Mass migrations have sometimes been peaceful but often have led to conflict, war, and conquest. Incursions of unlike peoples have brought in their train conflicts of culture, religion, language, and race, which have remained unresolved for centuries. The gradual mingling of unlike peoples has produced such relatively homogeneous nations as Ireland, Korea, Denmark, Japan, and Germany, but most of the world's nations have not been as fortunate and contain within their borders substantial groups that remain unlike the bulk of the population.

In distinctive ways Western colonialism brought acute problems of racial and cultural conflict. Colonialists from Western Europe served as a ruling minority throughout Africa and in large portions of Asia and Latin America. The breakdown of Western colonialism and the withdrawal of the minority elites did not end the clash of cultures. Instead, most newly independent nations are subject to stresses and strains produced by conflicts among minorities and are saddled with minority grievances.

For most of human history, population movements have brought dissimilar peoples into the same territories. Intergroup conflict has been the rule, not the exception. In the modern age there have been more rapid migration shifts than ever before. As a result, a heightened awareness of group differences has arisen, and this expresses itself in the form of claims for minority rights. Even those few examples of apparent successful intergroup accommodation show signs of decay, such as is evident in Belgium and Canada. Close examination of most nations reveals the prevalence of group frictions and differences. For most minority group members, there are only two choices: adaptation or "a struggle against assimilation which takes place through the formation of a group, and the attempt to recreate something of the original milieu in the midst of the new environment."[1] Of course, a conquering minority has a third choice—to compel others to adapt its practices on its own terms.

As the next chapter demonstrates, religious differences during and after the Reformation racked Europe in the sixteenth century. Religion became the most salient social and political factor in Europe, and the position of religious minorities was more sensitive than those of the various linguistic and ethnic groups of the newly emergent European nations. Only in the nineteenth century did nationalistic sentiments become important features of minority group identification.

During the nineteenth century European colonialism reached its heights, transmitting the dual (but ambiguous) heritages of minority domination and nationalistic ideals. European nationalist ideas and the population changes wrought by the practices of European colonialism in the non-European world combined to provide the bases for eventual rebellion against colonialism and also for the unresolved minority rights problems of the postcolonial era.

The Ottoman Empire which by 1500 had acquired provinces in Europe and Asia, also encountered minority problems because of its diverse population. Some of these problems remain today. At its late sixteenth century maximum, the Empire included much of the Near East, most of North Africa, and nearly the whole of the Balkans, with a total population of somewhere near 30 million people. But the Ottoman Empire did not spread the gospel of nationalism and did not spur a sense of minority group sentiment until the nineteenth century when it lost its remaining grip on alien peoples. World War I destroyed the Empire, and in its ashes were constructed successor states of portions of Eastern Europe, each with acute minority problems. The final decay of the Ottoman Empire was a precursor of the decay of European colonialism after World War II. Both left fragile new nations with unresolved minority problems.

At the same time, the history of the United States suggests that a post-colonial nation can be built largely of migrants. Yet there have been large population elements that have not adapted easily. These undigested racial, linguistic, and cultural groups consider themselves as minorities holding rights against the government and other citizens. These minorities include the indigenous Indians, the offspring of imported slaves, and more recent migrants from Mexico, Puerto Rico, and other parts of Latin America. While America has been in the forefront of the struggle for democratic liberties, it has only recently acknowledged the true condition of its undigested minorities. America's policies toward its minorities are a belated recognition of essential features of its heterogeneous population. Any understanding of minority rights in America must begin with an appreciation of its population mixture. The same holds true for most other nations.

In 1492 the whole native population of North America consisted of fewer than 1 million people. As late as 1600 only a few hundred Spaniards had arrived in what is now Florida and New Mexico. English settlement brought a population of somewhat less than a third of a million people to North America by 1700. This can be considered a major transatlantic migration. About 10 percent of these migrants were African slaves. Natural increases of population brought the white population to 4.3 million and the black population to about 1 million by 1800. There were many more white men in America than Indians or blacks. This was the root of America's minority problems. The subsequent migration of other Western Europeans after 1820 and of Eastern Europeans after 1890 only added to the minority status of blacks and Indians. Many European immigrants adapted to white society. Only a few blacks were able to do so.[2] Post-World War II migrations from Puerto Rico and Mexico have led to the emergence of another kind of minority, one of language and culture rather than race. The fate of these undigested American Hispanics may resemble that of blacks and Indians. The nonadaptation of many of these people seems to require the formulation of minority rights or at least minority protections against discrimination.

Historical demography is a powerful explanatory tool for interpreting minority situations. Population changes over the centuries have had a potent influence upon power relationships within a geographic area. In the Americas as a whole, a total transformation has taken place. In 1500 the populations were entirely Amerindian, with minority problems arising only within an inter-Indian context. Vast Indian empires rose and fell as various Indian groups dominated others. After the arrival of the Europeans, a rapid set of changes were put in motion so that within four hundred years a totally new constellation of ethnic, racial, linguistic, and religious differences had arisen, creating minority problems of a new and as yet unsettled character.

The reduction of the Indians to minority status has been more or less complete. Smallpox and measles took their toll, but guns and horses were used as well by Europeans to break the Indians' resistance to the occupation of their lands. In the Caribbean the Indian natives were virtually wiped out by disease and killing.

The introduction of African slavery into the hemisphere followed different phases, depending on the varying policies of the European colonialists. Although considerable racial mixing has taken place over the past two centuries, the essentially inferior status of Indians, blacks, and their descendants is the preeminent feature of social life in the Western Hemisphere. Of course, there are other minority groups, but in most countries of North and South America these are the most notable minorities, and unless greater intermingling takes place in the future, they will remain the major sources of minority grievances in the hemisphere barring some other great demographic event.[3]

In Europe most of the great demographic events took place prior to the fifteenth century. The huge population transfers that effected the settlement of the Americas, Australia, New Zealand, Africa, and parts of Asia transformed the population structures of the non-European world. Europe itself has many sharp divisions based on language, religion, nationality, and race.[4] It has exported these differences to other regions of the world by settlement policies since the fifteenth century. Now that Europe is no longer the center of population exportation and redistribution, its own minority problems may become accentuated.

European minority problems have helped precipitate two world wars. The shots fired at Sarajevo were more than a mere pretext for general European war. The assassination of Austrian Archduke Ferdinand by a Serbian terrorist was linked to the unresolved minority conflicts of central and eastern Europe. German dismemberment of Czechoslovakia was based on Nazi minority policies and invited the later invasion of Poland, which sparked World War II. While the possibility of great power conflicts over minority issues has largely disappeared, minority problems persist. World War I destroyed the remnants of the Ottoman Empire and resulted in the dismemberment of Austria-Hungary. The successor states led to the minorities regime of the League of Nations.

No such concern for minority rights emerged from World War II although the demographic and political changes were even more sweeping. In fact, the nature of minority problems has been magnified by the termination of European colonialism after World War II due to the arbitrary colonial borders in Africa, Asia, and the Americas, which took little account of racial, ethnic, or tribal groups. While various United Nations documents express concern for cultural and religious rights, the political status of minorities no longer enjoys widespread support in spite of the increase of minority group problems since World War II.[5]

Major population movements have continued in the past century, and significant international migrations are still taking place, creating new forms of minority group problems. After the end of World War II, German minorities were expelled from Poland, Czechoslovakia, Hungary, Rumania, and other portions of Eastern Europe, thus ending a source of minority tension in those nations. In Israel some 1.5 million immigrant Jews arrived, which resulted in the Palestinian Arabs becoming a minority within the new state. The creation of Israel also drained many Jews away from European and Arab states where they had been significant minorities.

The independence of India (August 15, 1947) and the partition of Pakistan caused a transfer of more than 17 million people. About 10 percent of the original Pakistan population were refugees from India. The subsequent establishment of Bangladesh in 1971 led to the flight of 10 million people to India.

One estimate of the migrations of the past 25 years places the figure at about 100 million people, one of the greatest population movements in history.[6] This total includes a large Chinese and Indian emigration and a sizeable Japanese movement. Taken together, the population movements of the past twenty-five years are at the same levels as or higher levels than the vast European emigration of similar time spans in the nineteenth century. While European emigration has slackened, Western Europe has imported large numbers of foreigners from Turkey, Yugoslavia, Greece, and Southern Europe during the twentieth century. These temporary immigrants form a major form of cheap labor for Western Europe but they also form a new aspect of minority group relations in the postcolonial era.[7]

Interstate migration is a continuing and growing condition. The West has seen a noticeable ethnic resurgence in the past few decades caused by civil wars, the breakdown of empires, and the migration of manual laborers. The existence of the European Economic Community (EEC) and Commonwealth passport regulations has enhanced geographical mobility. Although the twentieth century has seen an attempt to clean up the ethnic map through genocide, expulsions, and semivoluntary population movements, minority group consciousness seems to be at new heights.[8] Unfortunately, there seems to be no coherent theory to account for these claims of minority rights.

CONSTRUCTING AN EXPLANATION OF THE FACTS

While there appears to have been a gradual willingness to accord certain protections to minorities, it is not possible to conclude that "the stages in the development of minorities were similar to those in the development of the rights of the individual."[9] Unfortunately, this comforting observation does not accord with experience since World War II. In fact, there has been a sharp decline in concern with the development of minority rights theory at the same time that human rights have expanded. Individual human rights have grown in theory and practice. Minority rights theory has not developed, although minority problems have increased since World War II.

Classical political theory did not neglect group theory altogether. Aristotle observed that the Greek city-state grew out of two more elementary associations, the family and the village (which was an extension of the family group).[10] Aristotle distinguished sharply among the status accorded citizens, noncitizens, aliens, and slaves.[11] He is also a source for a pernicious doctrine of justification of slavery on the ground of natural inferiority. Inferior souls and a lack of the faculty of deliberaton were organic causes of group deficiency. Women, too, were regarded as deficient as a group in goodness, deliberative capacity, temperance, and fortitude.[12]

Individualism, the social and political theory which emerged first in seventeenth century England, emphasized the supreme value of the individual as an end in himself and posited the moral equality of all persons. Individualists perceived society as merely a collection of individuals. In a negative sense, individualism opposed state controls over the person. Liberty was often defined by individualist philosophers as the absence of restraints by the state.

John Locke, the leading English political philosopher, held that government is a trust whose principal purpose is to secure a citizen's person and property. Lockean rights were individualistic and preceded the establishment of the state. For Locke, life, liberty, and property were most fundamental because these three rights were held by all individuals by virtue of their birth and "the supreme power cannot take from any man any part of his property without his own consent."[13]

Few liberals questioned Locke's justification of majority rule. Locke's position was that the principle of equality dictated the majority principle as opposed to any form of minority rule. Majority rule was based upon convenience and the superior strength of the majority. Jean Jacques Rousseau adopted it with the important addition that more than a bare majority should be required for all important political decisions. Jeremy Bentham, too, accepted majority rule without qualms.

In America, James Madison feared unadulterated majority rule. He proposed a division of governmental powers that would frustrate any permanent majority by breaking up authority "into so many parts, interests and classes of citizens, that the rights of individuals, or of the minority, will be in little danger from interested combinations of the majority."[14] Madison's distinction between individuals and the minority was not developed by other American political thinkers, although his view of competing interests did emerge as an important aspect of pluralist democratic theory in the twentieth century.

John Stuart Mill was aware of the risks of extreme forms of majoritarian democracy. In his major work, *Considerations on Representative Government*, the decline of individuality and the growing weight of mass opinion led Mill to a fresh view of voting and representation. Mill advanced his ideas regarding proportional representation as an institutional means of safeguarding minority interests. Plural voting was also proposed and federalism explored. Although Mill did not believe that free institutions were possible in a nation made up of different nationalities (including race, religion, and language), he held differently in his more famous work, *On Liberty*. In that book Mill argued that small minorities have as much right to express their views as do large majorities. Still, in most respects the minority that Mill seeks to safeguard often seems to be one based upon education, training, and intellect, not race, religion, or ethnicity.

In the early twentieth century, the English political theorist J. N. Figgis looked at liberal democracy and asserted that freedom required a pluralist foundation in small groups which could thrive apart from the "all-devouring Leviathan of the whole."[15] The existence of groups helps ensure freedom of thought and action for the individual. Religious toleration in England was the by-product of religious animosities. Freedom of religion and religious toleration were due to the failure of any group to predominate sufficiently to crush the others. Group diversity was a source of individual rights. Figgis and others contributed to liberal thought by demonstrating that group freedom and individual liberty were linked. Unfortunately, the exact nature of the linkage was only dimly perceived.

Many social theorists of the turn of the century regarded society as composed essentially of groups, not of separate individuals. This was the view of Herbert Spencer and Sir Henry Maine, but both theorists failed to convert these ideas into a group theory of rights.[16] On the other hand, French sociologist Emile Durkheim may have overemphasized the group as a source of independent will and action. But Durkheim did warn of the risks of a collectivist political regime that failed to give due attention to group loyalties.

The idea of group personality, the belief that group life is genuine, became a central notion of the English political pluralists of the early twentieth century.[17] Harold Laski insisted at one point that a group possesses personality with a character of its own.[18] G.D.H. Cole was also concerned with collective personality and even went so far as to use the term "group soul."[19] Yet the groups Laski and Cole had in mind were trade unions, clubs, churches, and families, not racial, ethnic, or linguistic groups.

The English pluralists portrayed the state as composed of diverse groups and subordinate organizations, not merely as individuals. The state was different from all the member social groups in that it had the authority to regulate and control the groups, although not to the point of destroying them. A group may be recognized by the state, but even if it is unrecognized or banned, it may continue to live on. Groups, then, have rights but these are not unlimited. The state may reconcile conflicting claims among groups. Theorist J. N. Figgis concluded that there are groups that exist in their own right and not by the mere fiat of the state, but he failed to specify which groups had rights or to what extent the state could interfere with those rights.[20] This failure to describe the nature, scope, and extent of group rights is still a great weakness of political theory. These pluralists also failed to understand that there might be a tension between individual freedom and group rights. They also failed to account for the possibility that group rights claims could endanger the state.

One of the perversions of group rights theory is the idea of corporatism and functional representation. The corporate state of Fascist Italy was grounded, in part, on ostensible representation of important groups in a functional assembly. Corporatism thrived for a time in Portugal and Spain as well as in Latin America and parts of Eastern Europe. Some remnants persist in many nations. Still, it is not possible to agree with the leading theorist of corporatism, Mihail Manoilesco, who once declared that "the twentieth century will be the century of corporatism just as the nineteenth was the century of liberalism."[21]

The core concepts of corporatism are hard to describe unless pejorative terms are avoided. The best known corporate state is Fascist Italy. In December 1928, following the destruction of constitutional democracy in that nation, the world's best known corporative parliament was established. In place of the old Chamber of Deputies, a 400-member body was created representing not local constituencies or individual voters, but official groups named by the government. Employers and employees were represented in six separate federations (industry, commerce, agriculture, sea and air transport, land transport and inland navigation, and banking). There was also a single federation of independent artists, artisans, and professional men. In addition, the corporative parliament contained representatives of over twenty nonincorporated organizations, such as the National Association of State Employees, the Disabled Soldiers Association, the universities, and the National Association of Primary Schools. The principle of representation was occupational. Economic groups were the basis of the legislative system, replacing representation of individuals with the principle of representation of salient economic concerns. This was the fascist reply to socialism and communism. The one legal political party, which fixed the quotas of representation, also ran the elections, but the elections were confined to choices among preselected occupational representatives.[22]

The fascist scheme of representation was a thin disguise for the absolute dictatorship of Benito Mussolini. Nonetheless, the idea of reducing group friction and combat by encouraging the articulation of the different needs and values of economic groups was a new and different way of looking at the problem of individual participation in political life. After all, nonvoting in the democratic United States of America has reached epidemic proportions, based largely upon a sense of the meaninglessness of voting in representative elections. Clearly, the fascists had a point to score on the subject of proper representation of individuals through appropriate groups.

Corporatism is not necessarily fascistic, although it has been associated with nondemocratic regimes. Salvador Allende attempted to establish a left-wing, unicameral, corporativist legislature in Chile, until unseated by a right-wing coup. Corporatism is a lively idea in Peru, Cuba, and other Latin-American nations and is by no means confined to reactionary or fascist regimes. Indeed, Mexico, Argentina, Ecuador, Bolivia, the Dominican Republic, and other authoritarian and nonauthoritarian nations are experimenting with variations upon corporate schemes of representation.

In its essence corporatism can be defined as a "system of interest representation in which the constituent units are organized into a limited number of singular, compulsory, noncompetitive, hierarchically ordered and functionally differentiated categories, recognized or licensed (if not created) by the state and granted a deliberate representational monopoly within their respective categories in exchange for observing certain control on their selection of leaders and articulation of demands and supports."[23] This definition is based upon the actual practice of many modern states. The definition does not exclude the possibility of other forms of representation with the same regime; thus corporate institutions need not be unique and may be paralleled by representation of territories or other entities. But the ideal of corporatism is to bring harmony among the social classes by providing an institutional, governmental means for economic and class expression and, at the same time, to encourage economic groups to legislate for their own members. Corporatism seems to provide a middle ground between capitalism and communism. Small wonder that it retains some appeal for nations unpersuaded by either economic system.

Group representation by economic interest seems to be possible only in a nondemocratic setting.[24] Whatever rights may flow from such group representation, they are of little direct concern to the minorities mentioned in the first chapter. Corporatism holds no remedies for denial of minority rights because it is not concerned with minority groups, only economic groupings.

American political theory has also failed to explain minority rights.

American political theorist Andrew Hacker has said that "a serious effort must be made to understand the variable character of minority groups" and "one way to do this is through a discussion of rights."[25] Yet there has been no such discussion. At best, American social scientists have produced a native variant of pluralism, resting largely on interest groups. This has been done with little attention to English pluralism and little consideration of the experiences of other pluralist societies.[26]

Contemporary American political science is constructed upon a pluralist foundation. In America, as in no other nation, an effort has been made to provide a theoretical and empirical explanation for the operation of democracy. Pluralism provides both an explanation and a justification for the continuation and, perhaps the superiority of the democratic political system. Empirical, democratic pluralism seems to be a source of rights, liberties, and freedoms as well as a source of regime stability.

In its narrowest form political science analysis has emphasized the important role of interest groups in the formation of public policy. In 1935 American political scientist Harwood Childs made a distinction between groups based upon "fundamental differentials" such as occupations and those "existing merely to further special ideas or groups of ideas."[27] Economic groups remain the central focus of interest group analysis to sort out under this dichotomy. Shared attitudes may provide the link.[28] Interest group analysis is accepted as appropriate in virtually all regimes, and interest groups influence upon the formation of public policy is an important discovery of political scientists, although the distinctions between party and interest group are quite blurred.[29] A few ardent democrats have wondered whether interest group activity is inherently non- or anti-democratic. After all, groups pursuing their private interests may prevail over the public good, in spite of majoritarian electoral practices.[30]

Most political scientists are convinced that interest group pluralism is perfectly consistent with democracy. At the same time dedicated American political scientists, having carefully examined the native scene, seem to have become convinced that the competing interest groups and other groups in that society inhibit the growth of dominant political elites and prevent the rise of totalitarianism in any of its forms. Robert Dahl, a leading spokesman for this point of view, has concluded that there are multiple centers of power in America, none of which is wholly sovereign. Most groups have access to power to benefit their members since "few groups . . . who are determined to influence the government—certainly few if any groups of citizens who are organized, active, and persistent—lack of the capacity and opportunity to influence some officials somewhere in the political system in order to obtain at least some of their goals."[31] Competition among groups is the lifeblood of democracy, and policy compromises are the inevitable outcome of a stable, pluralist system. A democratic system is receptive to "any active and legitimate group," and democratic pluralism is efficient in "reinforcing agreement, encouraging moderation, and maintaining social peace."[32]

But democratic pluralism does not guarantee or necessarily advance minority rights. The very slow advancement of American blacks provides vivid evidence of the group impotence of blacks and the inadequacy of the pluralist system in recognizing their needs. Dahl is forced to admit that American pluralism has not aided minorities such as blacks and Indians. He is forced to conclude that the case of the black minority is atypical, an "extreme one." The political compromises of 1820 and 1877 which, among others, adversely affected black rights, are criticized by Dahl but seem to be a normal product of a group process from which blacks were effectively excluded.[33] The best that can be said for democratic pluralism, then, is that minority groups must organize to present their claims. If they organize effectively, they may win some of them. If not, they can return another day to enter the group conflict. Group rights have no independent existence in pluralist America. Unlike individual rights, there is no theoretical justification for protecting blacks, Indians, women, Catholics, Chinese-Americans, or any other group. This is an interesting lesson, not only for America but for all nations—if it is a valid lesson.

The significance of American political experience is quite limited. Many nations have such severe social cleavages that group conflicts are quite intense. In certain societies, those which are impelled by divergent ethnic groups whose concerns persuade the whole policy-making process, class and economic interests are subordinated to the primordial interests of well-established communal groups. The "subcommunities of the plural society have permanent and separate histories, separate social institutions, customs and practices, and separate leaders."[34] Separate communal groups encourage the development of communally based politics.[35] Class and economic divisions are not so salient in Cyprus, Indonesia, or Malaysia. Parties and interest groups both pursue communal goals.[36] Obviously, American-style pluralism simply does not operate in these nations. Less obviously, minority groups may be less mobilized and more vulnerable in less democratic nations.

Nathan Glazer has perceived that American ideals of equality of treatment were inadequate to the needs of its multi-ethnic majority. He saw the society as torn between two competing principles: the quest for the achievement of the value of "fraternity," a more homogenous society, and the need to treat people according to their race, color, or national origin in order to overcome persistent inequalities. The latter principle supports affirmative action programs and preferential treatment of individuals on the basis of their membership in disadvantaged groups. Glazer asserts that this minority group approach will only be overcome by the notion of a larger American fraternity to overcome the smaller scale fraternities of the racial and ethnic groups. He fears that every group will be quick to claim special treatment unless his view of fraternity is adopted.[37]

While America struggles for a rational justification for affirmative action, most of the world confronts more intense conflict among groups within societies. Glaser's notion of fraternity holds little appeal even for America. It holds little meaning for many states with deeper divisions among their groups. There appears to be little available within the liberal, Western tradition to explain or justify the role of significant groups.

Some other nations acknowledge the existence of collective or group rights without explaining why they do so. West Germany accords some of its groups political status and a certain amount of rights or representational authority. A German theorist could say that "from the recognition of the fact that man is a social being, one can derive a special category of group rights" although "these rights but take their place beside them [individual rights]."[38] This insight suggests that continental theorists are aware that individuals are not replaced by parties, interest groups, occupational groups, or other groups, but a whole rights-enriched life somehow blends the individual's rights with his collective rights as a member of a group.

The same observation was made by Bronislaw Malinowski, the eminent anthropologist, who insisted upon a realistic definition of freedom—one based upon actual human experience. Malinowski states that "the instrumentalities of freedm we find in the political constitution. of a community, its laws, its moral norms, the distribution of its wealth, and the access to such benefits as health, recreation, justice and religious or artistic gifts of culture."[39] Malinowski concludes that "to scour the universe for possibilities of freedom other than those given by the organization of human groups for the carrying out of specific purposes, and the production of desirable results, is an idle philosophic pastime."[40] Rather than indulge in idle pastimes, we shall see how group rights arise out of the recognized claims of particular groups within multinational societies. We shall demonstrate that, bit by bit, group rights concepts have crept into fundamental documents, constitutions, and laws and that available individual rights theories do not adequately account for this development. The theoretical significance of group rights and their relationship to individual rights will be treated in the concluding chapter only after surveying the evidence that clearly points to the twentieth-century expression of group rights in addition to (or perhaps, at odds with) individual rights.

The only other writer who has attempted to grapple with this topic in analytic terms is Vernon Van Dyke. Van Dyke has attacked recent efforts to update the liberal, individualistic rights theories of John Locke. The much acclaimed *A Theory of Justice* of John Rawls has certainly restated contractual, individual rights theory for the modern age. Van Dyke attacks Rawls for omitting or ignoring the shortcomings of Rawl's theory of "justice as fairness" when it neglects to develop group rights concepts. As Van Dyke observes, "in practice groups often enjoy legal status and rights that are not accounted for, either in Rawls's theory of justice or in any other."[41] Van Dyke points out that three types of group rights policies can presently be observed: (1) the special protection of weak groups; (2) compensatory policies for groups which have been victimized by discrimination; and (3) special status and rights intended to enable some groups to survive.[42] Elsewhere, Van Dyke has sketched in a few facts which indicate that "groups identified by various characteristics including race, language and religion, in fact have rights."[43] Van Dyke does not indicate which groups have rights or the justifications that may legitimatize group claims of rights. He has scratched the surface of a very important topic. Later chapters will assemble detailed factual examples of group rights from which, it is hoped, a clearer foundation for group rights theory may be constructed. In addition, the relationships between individual rights and group rights will be shown. The minority-majority struggle for dominance is the root of minority rights issues. This, too, will be illustrated subsequently.

NOTES

1. J. Beaujeu-Garnier, *Geography of Population*, 2d ed. (Longman: London and New York, 1978), p. 238.

2. On American migration, see E. P. Hutchinsen, *Immigrants and Their Children* (Washington, D.C.: Government Printing Office, 1956). The best brief summation is J. Potter's, "The Growth of Population in America, 1700-1860" in *Population in History: Essays in Historical Demography,* ed. D. V. Glass and D.E.C. Eversley (New York: Aldine Press, 1965).

3. Of course this generalization does not explain all situations in the Americas. Argentina and Chile are composed of sharply different population groupings in spite of their close proximity to each other. Argentina is a largely white country composed largely of European immigrants with only a 10 percent Indian or mixed-ancestry population. Chile is divided almost equally between whites and Indians or those of mixed descent. In both countries only a few pure-blooded Indians are left. The minority problems of Argentina and Chile are quite different because of different population mixes. Nonetheless, it is clear in both countries that Indians are at the bottom of the heap and those of mixed Indian blood are regarded somewhat more highly.

4. European concepts of minority rights began with the religious struggles of the Reformation. Minority rights issues arose as a result of territorial changes,

such as a cession of territory. For example, consider the Treaty of Oliva of 1660, by which Poland the Great Elector ceded Pomerania and Livonia to Sweden. The inhabitants of the ceded territory were guaranteed their existing religious liberties. Sweden, the victor in battle, promised to permit its new subjects their religious "rights, liberties, and privileges," (Article 2 [3], Treaty of Oliva. Not until 1815 in the Final Act of the Congress of Vienna did issues of nationality become a significant feature of minority rights in Europe.

5. The United Nations seems willing to support a "right of self-determination of peoples" but not to agree upon a definition of "peoples." See Aureliu Cristescu, *The Right to Self-Determination* UN Doc. E/CN 4/Sub. 2/404/ Rev. 1 (1981) and memorandum prepared by Secretary-General of the United Nations: Definition and Classification of Minorities, UN Doc. E/CN 4/Sub. 2/85 (1949).

6. See Beaujeu-Garnier, *Geography of Population*, p. 181.

7. Switzerland is highly dependent upon imported labor, as is West Germany. Approximately 15 percent of the Swiss population consists of alien workers.

8. See Uri Ra'anan, *Ethnic Resurgence in Modern Democratic States* (New York: Pergamon Press, 1980).

9. Arthur de Balogh, *La Protection internationale des minorités* (Paris: Les éditors internationals, 1930), p. 28.

10. Aristotle, *The Politics*, Book I, chapter 2.

11. Ibid., Book III, chapter 5.

12. Ibid., Book III, chapter 13.

13. John Locke, *Of Civil Government,* Everyman's Library (London: J. M. Dent & Sons, 1924), p. 187

14. James Madison et al., *The Federalist Papers* (New York: Modern Library, 1961), p. 301.

15. J. N. Figgis, *Churches in the Modern State* (London: Longmans, 1913), p. 101.

16. See David Nicholls, "Positive Liberty, 1880-1914," *American Political Science Review* (March 1962), pp. 114-28.

17. David Nicholls, *The Pluralist State* (New York: St. Martin's Press, 1975), p. 60.

18. Harold Laski, *A Grammar of Politics* (London: Allen & Unwin, 1925).

19. G.D.H. Cole, *Labour in the Commonwealth* (London: Swathmore, 1918), p. 38.

20. J. N. Figgis, *Churches in the Modern State*, p. 90.

21. Mihail Manoilesco, *Le Siècle du Corporatisme*, rev. ed. (Paris: F. Alcan, 1936), p. 7.

22. See Howard J. Wiarda, "Corporatism and Development in the Iberic-Latin World: Persistent Strains and New Variations," in *The New Corporatism Social Political Structures in the Iberian World*, ed. Frederick P. Pike and Thomas Strich (Notre Dame, Ind.: University of Notre Dame, 1974), pp. 3-33.

23. Phillipe C. Schmitter, "Still the Century of Corporatism?" in ibid., pp. 93-94. Schmitter is the leading contemporary scholar of corporatism.

24. But there are elements of functional or corporatist representation in some democratic states, most notably Sweden, Switzerland, the Netherlands, Norway, and Denmark.

25. Andrew Hacker, "Freedom and Power: Common Men and Uncommon

Men," in *Liberty, Nomos IV,* ed. Carl J. Friedrich (New York: Atherton Press, 1962), p. 322.

26. David Nicholls, *Three Varieties of Pluralism* (New York: St. Martin's Press, 1974), p. 24.

27. Harwood Childs, "Pressure Groups and Propaganda," *The Annals of the American Academy of Political and Social Science* 179 (May 1935), p. xi.

28. The view of the classic American study: David Truman, *The Governmental Process* (New York: Alfred A. Knopf, 1955).

29. See Joseph La Palombara, "The Utility and Limitations of Interest Group Theory in Non-American Field Situations," *Journal of Politics* 22 (1960), pp. 29-49.

30. See E. E. Schattschneider, *The Semi-Sovereign People* (New York: Holt, Rinehart & Winston, 1960), for a balanced view of this threat to democracy.

31. Robert A. Dahl, *Pluralist Democracy in the United States: Conflict and Consent* (Chicago: Rand, McNally & Company, 1967).

32. Robert A. Dahl, *A Preface to Democratic Theory* (Chicago: University of Chicago Press, 1956), pp. 149-50.

33. Robert A. Dahl, *Pluralist Democracy*, p. 297.

34. Richard Schermerhorn, *Comparative Ethnic Relations* (New York: Random House, 1970), p. 64.

35. Robert Melson and Howard Wolpe, "Modernization and the Politics of Communalism: A Theoretical Perspective," *American Political Science Review* 64 (1970), pp. 1112-30.

36. K. J. Ratnam, "Constitutional Government and the Plural Society," *Journal of Southeast Asian History* 2 (1961), pp. 1-10.

37. Nathan Glazer, "Liberty, Equality, Fraternity and Ethnicity," *Daedalus* 105 (Fall 1976), pp. 115-27.

38. Peter Schreider, "Social Rights and the Concept of Human Rights," in *Political Theory and the Rights of Man,* ed. D. D. Raphael (Bloomington, Ind.: Indiana University Press, 1967), p. 93.

39. Bronislaw Malinowski, *Freedom and Civilization* (London: Allen and Unwin, 1947), p. 95.

40. Ibid., p. 96.

41. Vernon Van Dyke, "Justice as Fairness: For Groups?" *American Political Science Review* 69 (1975), p. 610.

42. Ibid., p. 612.

43. Vernon Van Dyke, "Human Rights and the Rights of Groups," *American Journal of Political Science* 18 (1974), pp. 725-41. Quote at p. 740.

3

James B. Muldoon

The Development of Group Rights

THUS far we have discussed minority rights in broad theoretical terms, focusing on modern statements of the issues involved and on examples of the problems that minority groups face in the modern world. Before moving to an extended discussion of the variety of situations in which minority groups find themselves in the modern political environment, a look at the historical development of minority group rights will be useful in order to appreciate the relative novelty of such ideas. The opinion that a minority within a society possesses special group rights has been a matter of political and legal concern only for the past two centuries. The reason for this is paradoxical. Until modern political thinkers, beginning with the philosophes of the eighteenth century, developed the notion of majority rule, there was no need to define minority rights at all because there was no perceived adversarial relationship between majority and minority that required resolution.[1] Likewise, the notion that a state should be the political expression of a culturally homogeneous society has been generally accepted only since the eighteenth century. As a result, until modern times there has been no reason to assert the unique claims of minority groups.

The assertion that the majority should rule and that the minority group (or groups) should conform to the will of the majority, ideas springing from eighteenth century political thought and first implemented by the French revolutionaries, remains, even in the twentieth century, a predominantly Western European idea. Elsewhere in the world, states exist that contain a variety of linguistic and cultural groups, often joined together only in a very fragile way and dominated by one of the minority groups that comprises the entire body. In this form of society there is no perceived adversarial relationship between the dominant minority and a dominated majority. The conflict is among the various minority groups, each one seeking the dominant position. The groups that have lost the struggle for domination do not see themselves as forming a majority that shares a common body of interests with the other minorities in the same position. Indeed, even within western Europe, where the modern notion of the homogeneous state developed, the theory has neever been totally implemented even in the smallest political unit. Even as the philosophes and the revolutionaries of the eighteenth century were bringing the concept into being, the early theorists of nationalism were beginning to emerge, and with them came the notion that the individual cultural and linguistic traditions of the various European peoples deserved to survive in the face of growing pressures to become assimilated into the majority culture.

The contemporary world generally recognizes that within any large society there are groups, usually linguistic, cultural, or religious, that do not accept the values of the majority of the population. These differences are not simply what are defined as political differences, reflected in the existence of political parties. Rather, these differences reflect distinct outlooks on life, codes of values, and unique customs and traditions that are threatened, implicitly or explicitly, by pressures stemming from the majority. Spokesmen for minority groups demand legal protections for their groups, ranging from official recognition of a particular religion, through the establishment of public schools using the minority language, to the creation of a regional homeland and a fixed share of political power guaranteed to members of the minority. Their claim is that the minority groups have a right to exist, and so they demand a heterogeneous society in place of the homogeneous society that the majority's pressure seems to demand.[2] In a sense they are demanding a return to the sociopolitical structure of pre-eighteenth century Europe. By the standards of modern political thought, these spokesmen are reactionaries, although they do not see themselves as such. Their call for the rights of groups echoes the criticism of majority rule made by eighteenth-century spokesmen for the traditional corporate groups that composed medieval and early modern European society.

HISTORICAL BACKGROUND

In general, the political theory and practice of the ancient and the medieval Western world did not deal with the issue of majority rights versus minority rights. The assumption upon which ancient and medieval societies operated was that a society consisted of a variety of groups that dwelled within its geographical borders but that the right to participation in political life did not automatically follow from birth within the borders. Even in the smallest Greek city-state, citizenship was a jealously guarded privilege enjoyed by only a small percentage of the total population, even though the unenfranchised members of the population were usually linguistically and culturally indistinct from those who were citizens. In the largest city-state, Athens, there were about 400,000 inhabitants in the midfifth century B.C., of these, about 168,000 men, women, and children were Athenian citizens, while 200,000 were slaves.[3] The remainder consisted of aliens, usually citizens of other cities, who were permanent residents of Athens.[4] Furthermore, although Athens had the reputation of granting citizenship comparatively easily to foreigners who were likely to make important contributions to Athenian life, by modern standards at least, citizenship was granted only rarely.[5] In addition, Athens was unusual in the comparatively high ratio of citizens to noncitizens. Contemporary Sparta, for example, had at most 10,000 citizens who ruled over a much larger population of slaves and free inhabitants.[6] The Spartans were able to dominate their subject population only by forming a garrison state whose members were constantly on the alert for signs of rebellion among the helots, the state slaves who did the manual labor in Spartan society.

Complete political equality existed within the body of citizens in a city-state. The fact of citizenship transcended economic and social barriers that otherwise differentiated the citizens of a city such as Athens. Equality was the product of a long history of internal political conflict, as Aristotle's *Politics* demonstrated.[7] It was also constantly threatened by those who preferred government by an even more limited segment of the population. Sparta was more egalitarian than Athens in that the citizens were economically and socially equal as well. Furthermore, they were required to live the greater part of their lives in barracks and to eat at communal tables.[8] While the Spartan citizens formed a body of equals, they did not view the helots and the resident freemen, the *perioeci*, as in any way their equals. One historian has described the helots as "socially and morally the most submerged class in all Greece."[9] The harsh military life-style that the Spartans adopted was rooted in the need to protect themselves from the helots. Elsewhere in Greece there was a general sense of Greek superiority. The barbarians, that is those who were not Greek in culture, were presumed to be naturally inferior to the Greeks. Aristotle was even able to argue that the Greeks were fit by nature to rule other men because of their innate superiority.[10]

The city-state form of government continued to flourish in the ancient world even after the rise of empires. The Roman Empire was essentially a federation of city-states at the apex of which was the city of Rome itself.[11] Each city-state that the Romans conquered retained its local governing elite and political structure. The conquering Romans recognized that the stability of their empire depended upon the cooperation of the conquered. As a result, the Romans won the support of those whom they defeated by making peace treaties that allowed local elites to continue governing in their traditional fashion with a minimum of interference from Rome.[12] As long as taxes were paid and Roman subjects did not wage war with one another or with Rome, the conquerors were satisfied. In addition, the Romans made slightly different treaties with neighboring states in order to prevent the development of a common body of grievances against the Romans. In other words, even the conquered did not form a majority in the sense of a body of people with a broad base of common interests that differentiated them clearly from the Romans. Rather, each conquered society's leaders saw themselves as sharing to some degree in ruling the empire and possessing a special relationship with the imperial government. Furthermore, the Romans held out full Roman citizenship as the ultimate reward for those who supported the conquerors, making the members of the local elites partners in the elite that ruled the entire empire.[13] When the Emperor Caracalla granted Roman citizenship to all freemen in 212 A.D., however, he did not create a democracy in which a true majority determined imperial policy. There remained a large number of slaves and other persons who were not citizens. Furthermore, real power within the empire remained in the hands of a small number of individuals who formed the imperial elite.[14]

Although the political history of the Middle Ages differed greatly from that of the ancient world, ancient and medieval political structures were similar in that power remained divided among a variety of local power centers rather than centralized as tends to be the case in the modern Western world. The cities of the western Roman Empire gradually disappeared or were markedly reduced in size from the fourth to the tenth century A.D. Only during the eleventh and twelfth centuries did cities and towns reappear as important political and economic units.[15] Elsewhere, political power devolved into a variety of hands and institutions during the same period, only to coalesce gradually into rudimentary kingdoms. Even within these kingdoms, no matter how small, kings shared power with a variety of groups and individuals. When medieval writers described the nature of a society, they tended to do so functionally. That is, they saw society as composed of three functional groupings, those who pray, those who fight, and those who labor.[16] These groups obviously did not reflect equality of numbers. The great bulk of the population labored, but political power was restricted to the groups that fought and prayed. Only gradually did a fourth group appear to claim a place within this functional structure. This occurred when the growth of trade and the rebirth of urban life on a significant scale gave rise to the bourgeoisie, the city dwellers who functioned as merchants and bankers.

The functional nature of the medieval political outlook appears most clearly in that most medieval of institutions, the parliament. While the particulars of such assemblies varied from kingdom to kingdom and from century to century, medieval parliaments shared certain characteristics. In the first place, the existence of such an assembly reflected the general assumption that a king required the advice of certain segments of the population if he wished to rule effectively.[17] He was bound to request advice from those who possessed power, by which was meant economic, military, or moral power. In England, for example, the early parliaments had representatives from the clergy, the greater nobility, the lesser nobility, and the wealthier urban dwellers. By the end of the thirteenth century, the clergy as a bloc had withdrawn from Parliament, to meet separately as the Clerical Convocation, leaving the bishops and abbots of some large religious houses to attend the House of Lords in their capacity as landlords and royal vassals, just as the secular lords did. The division of the Parliament into a two-house assembly led to the union of the lower ranks of the landholding, warrior class, represented by the Knights of the Shire, with the representatives of the chartered town, the burgesses. Although other parliamentary bodies had as many as four branches, or estates as they were often termed, the principle of functional, not numerical, representation persisted. In addition, each of these estates had its own laws and judicial practices. The clergy answered to canon law, merchants to the law merchant, and nobles to the laws and courts of their own estate. Magna Carta in 1215 demonstrated the importance of these various legal systems as they functioned in early thirteenth-century England.[18] The first chapter explicitly guaranteed the rights and privileges of the church, while chapter thirteen did the same for the city of London and "all other cities, boroughs, towns, and ports" as well. Individuals were to be tried by their peers because only a man's equals knew the laws that governed his behavior. "Earls and barons shall not be amerced except by their peers," while no "freeman shall be taken or imprisoned or disseised . . . except by the lawful judgement of his peers or by the law of the land."

Below the politically enfranchised segments of medieval English society, no undifferentiated mass existed that could be described as a majority in the modern sense. The numerical majority of medieval Englishmen existed legally within the various categories of the unfree or serf class. Each degree of serfdom had its own rights and obligations.[19] Furthermore, every feudal manor and village had its own laws and customs, which regulated the behavior of those who lived there. The establishment of shires administered by the sheriff, a royal official responsible for collecting royal revenue, overseeing military affairs, and administering justice, led to the linking of the basic units of local government, the village and the hundred, to royal government. Periodically, the sheriff, accompanied by travelling royal judges, visited each village and hundred to inquire into administrative and judicial matters.[20] One historian has described the result as "self-government at the King's command."[21] Local laws and customs, suitable for parochial interests, were eventually supplemented by the common law, which had general application, unlike local laws and customs, which were "particular, extraordinary, special."[22] The common law and the handful of royal officials who enforced it formed the framework of government within which the estates, the hundred courts, boroughs, and so on functioned. The king, the law, and the sheriff formed a coordinating layer, a dominant minority, that directed English society, a society composed of numerous distinct groups.

Although the English political structure was the only one to survive the end of the Middle Ages largely unchanged, it was not unique. Every other European kingdom was administered in roughly the same fashion as modern comparative studies of medieval government emphasize.[23] The major difference between the English experience and that of the continental kingdoms is that the medieval English system of government survived the general move to centralized government associated with the rise of absolutism in the seventeenth century. Even so, throughout the eighteenth century absolutist states, of which France was the best example, retained many distinctive legal practices and political privileges for inhabitants of particular regions or members of different estates.

With the Enlightenment of the eighteenth century, however, the notion that a society should be legally and politically homogeneous became widespread in intellectual circles. Instead of a patchwork quilt of estates, communities, and associations, each with its own laws and customs, the philosophes wanted uniformity and order. In a sense, the philosophes wanted to revive the ancient notion of citizenship with each person possessing the same political and legal status.[24] The French Revolution put the ideas of the philosophes into practice, at least in the initial stages of the Revolution. The Preamble to the Constitution of 1791 summed up the goal of the new government this way:

> The National Assembly . . . abolishes irrevocably the institutions which were injurious to liberty and equality of rights.
>
> Neither nobility, nor peerage, nor hereditary distinction of orders, nor feudal regime . . . any longer exists.
>
> Neither privileges nor exception to the law common to all Frenchmen any longer exists for any part of the nation or for any individual.
>
> Neither *jurandes* nor corporations of professions, arts, and crafts any longer exist.[25]

Although the revolutionaries did not create absolute equality overnight for all the inhabitants of France and although the status of citizen was not automatically granted to anyone born in France, the French Revolution pointed the way to the modern notion of political equality.

With the end of what the French revolutionaries termed the "feudal regime," the problem of minority rights gradually began to emerge concurrently with the concept of the national majority that claimed the right to direct society's destiny. In spite of increasing linguistic, cultural, religious, and economic pressures, some lesser groups within the overall society refused to accept the values and practices of the dominant majority. Nineteenth century romantic nationalists stressed the importance of preserving the cultures of these submerged groups that appeared on the way to extinction. With the calls to retain traditional cultures and dying languages, there also emerged calls for political structures that would defend the threatened ways of life.[26] At this point, the rights of minority groups became a public issue with the official majority position of assimilation being defined as oppressive of a minority's right to its own way of life.

One final point remains for discussion. What is a right? The entire issue of minority status is bedevilled by that one word. The contemporary meaning of the word *right* is the result of the philosophical, legal, and political debates of the seventeenth and eighteenth centuries. A recent textbook on American governmental policies concerning rights stated that "a claim which is recognized and accepted by authoritative decisionmakers (courts, legislatures, governors) can grow into a right. . . . A right does not exist, except as a moral abstraction, unless someone or some group is prepared to make a claim for its implementation. . . . In a nutshell a right is a valid claim."[27] This pragmatic definition avoids dealing with the problems involved in the long history of philosophic debate about the nature of rights. At the same time, we must recognize that this functional definition of what constitutes a right is a very modern approach to the question.

Before the eighteenth century, those who concerned themselves with these issues that we would view as rights issues, the lawyers, philosophers, and theologians, rarely spoke of rights, that is the rights or validated claims of individuals or groups. Generally, they described the existing social order, suggested remedies for abuses, and considered society as a whole within which individuals sought their moral well-being. The ancient Roman lawyers, for example, pointed out that according to natural law, all men were free and all property was to be held in common. In practice, however, according to the *ius gentium*, the law of nature that is the actual practice of mankind, slavery and private property existed and were part of the normal order of things.[28] While the lawyers concentrated their attention on the situation that actually existed, philosophers and theologians focused on the moral purposes of society and on the moral qualities that the virtuous ruler should possess, accepting as given the basic social order.

In part at least, ancient and medieval writers did not think in terms of individual rights as we understand them because they did not assume an adversarial relationship between the individual and society. Like Aristotle, they assumed that men were naturally social and political animals and that man's nature required that he live in community, as part of a group, in order to become a fully developed human being.[29] The realities of medieval life reinforced this view. To live outside of a well-organized group was to place oneself at the mercy of anyone or any group that was stronger. In the Middle Ages, the term "outlaw" literally meant the person who was outside of the protection provided by a group and its law. The freest person in medieval society, paradoxically to the modern mind, was the person who was enmeshed in the greatest number of legal relationships. The feudal system of government made this point very clear in the homage ceremony, which demonstrated before witnesses the contractual relationship that created mutual responsibilities for lord and vassal. The contract specified certain rights and privileges that each party possessed. The more such relationships into which a man entered, the more rights he possessed and the more protection he received. While the most obvious example of this sort of right was the possession of land, the fief, it extended to a wide range of other items as well. One could possess the right to hold a court and share in the fines it assessed, be exempt from a particular court's jurisdiction, collect a particular tax, or be exempt from being taxed.[30] One observer noted that in the Middle Ages an individual possessed not rights in the modern sense, broad claims rooted in a general sense of how the world should function, but a bundle of specific and concrete rights that could be added to or subtracted from according to circumstances.

During the eighteenth century, the philosophes completed the development of a new theoretical basis for understanding rights. Parallel with their rejection of the group as the basic unit of society, they stressed the rights of the individual without regard to his membership in any group. In the Declaration of the Rights of Man, the French Revolutionaries turned the philosophes' theories into political reality. The assumption that each and every individual possessed the same fundamental rights underlaid the Declaration. The purpose of government was to protect these rights. In one sense, this view continued the medieval concept of government as being contractual in nature. It was different, however, in that it assumed that each individual had precisely the same contract with the government, not a unique contract based on status differences. Instead of assuming that natural law referred to the general principles that directed a just society, the philosophes pointed to a natural law that guaranteed inalienable rights to individuals.

Because of the great changes in political theory and political practice that took place during the eighteenth century, it might seem that the medieval political scene would bear no significant relationship to the modern scene. This would seem to be especially true where the question of minority rights is involved because of the shift from the group to the individual as the basic unit of society and the bearer of rights. This assumption would not, however, be accurate. The issue of minority rights exists in the modern world precisely because the withering away of groups claiming distinctive status within a society has not occurred. By attributing rights to individuals, not to groups, eighteenth-century thinkers believed that they would effectively destroy groups as the loci of rights. What they did achieve was the destruction of certain kinds of groups; the clergy, the nobility, and the guilds being the most prominent of these. By the early nineteenth century, however, spurred on by romanticism and nationalism, new groups, usually cultural and religious groups, were demanding political and legal recognition from the dominant majority. In effect, these groups were asserting that the inalienable rights possessed by individuals also belonged to groups. The difficulty was that while the rights assigned to individuals were comparatively straightforward, life, liberty, and property as John Locke put it, the rights claimed by groups were often vague and even divisive, threatening the cohesive social and political order that the revolution had created. One group might demand political and legal protection for an agricultural way of life that faced extinction as national policy required industrialization and urbanization. Yet another group might insist upon the use of its own language, a minority tongue, in courts and public schools. In both cases, the wishes of the dominant majority for the society as a whole would be frustrated if the minorities had their way.

The modern problem of minority rights has some analogues with medieval society in a minority group's demand for political and legal recognition that differs in some important ways from the cultural life of the dominant majority. The analogy is not, however, with the medieval secular government, which, as we have seen, clearly recognized the right of groups to exist. The comparison must be to the medieval Christian Church. Like the modern nation-state, with its core of common values and beliefs expressed through the public schools and various other institutions, the medieval church was not simply an institution but a way of life that was the highest expression of human life. The medieval church provided a common core of beliefs that lay at the heart of society. As the nation-state asserts the superiority of its cultural values over all others, so the medieval church claimed that it alone possessed religious truth superior to all other religions. When a minority culture in a modern nation-state exempts itself from the claims of the dominant culture and demands recognition of its right to exist free of interference, it makes the same claims against the dominant culture that medieval heretical groups made against the claims of the Christian Church.

The comparison of the nation-state with the medieval church is difficult to accept at first because of the modern assumption that religion is a matter of private conscience, not a matter of public policy. In medieval Europe, however, as J. N. Figgis noted long ago, the

> state had one basis of unity denied to the modern [state]—religion. Baptism was a necessary element in true citizenship in the Middle Ages and excommunication was its antithesis. No heretic, no schismatic, no excommunicate has the rights of citizenship.[31]

Being a matter of public interest, religion was of concern to secular officials as well as to ecclesiastical ones. The result was the close and necessary relationship between the temporal and the spiritual powers that is often seen as characteristic of medieval Europe. Figgis described the relationship bluntly: "[In] the Middle Ages the Church was not a State, it was the State; the State or rather the civil authority . . . was merely the police department of the Church."[32] While this statement somewhat overstates the realities of medieval political life, it certainly reflects the way in which many medieval ecclesiastical thinkers saw the relationship between church and state. Secular rulers at least mouthed spiritual goals when they took coronation oaths in which they promised to protect the church from its enemies and to advance spiritual goals.

Religion, Catholic Christianity to be exact, played a role in medieval society that the national culture and language play in a modern society legally composed of individuals, not groups. As the medieval church employed the secular power to achieve its ends, so the modern nation uses the state as the vehicle for achieving its goals. For this reason numerous minority groups in the modern world have demanded the right to establish their own states so that not only the individuals who compose this group will survive, but that the distinctive national culture will also survive as something apart from the individuals who share it. Furthermore, both the medieval church and the modern nation represent not only the dominant groups in their respective societies, they were—and are—numerical majorities as well. In theory, of course, the power of the medieval church was attributed not to its majority status but to its essential truth. Likewise, modern nationalists often attribute spiritual value to the "spirit of the nation" that transcends sheer numbers. Thus, when the church or the nation faces opposition from a numerical minority, they see such opposition as a conflict not only between groups but between truth and error, an even more important issue. Thus, to a significant extent, the contemporary debate about minority political rights is quite similar to the medieval and early modern debates about religious toleration.

The question of religious toleration is one that is virtually unique to

Christianity and stems from its assertion that it alone possesses the truth about God and the meaning of human existence. Other doctrines are not only wrong, they are positively dangerous to spiritual health and well-being. Modern nationalism, sometimes described as a "secular religion," differs from medieval Christianity in that each nation occupies only a small part of the earth's surface and population, while the church claimed a universal mission and expected eventually to include all men everywhere.[33] In each case, however, the Christian and the nationalist asserts not only the superiority of his own values but the inferiority, not to mention the subversive nature, of competing values. Those who reject the language and culture of the nation-state are heretics in a secular sense.

RELIGION IN THE ANCIENT AND MEDIEVAL WORLDS

Generally speaking, the problem of the rights of religious minorities did not exist in the ancient world. Just as ancient political society consisted of a congeries of political units headed by a dominant minority, so too ancient religion was pluralistic. Each political unit had its own religion that symbolized its sense of community. In turn the political unit, such as the city-state, comprised various groups, associations, and families, each of which had its own divine protectors and related cults. In *The Ancient City*, Fustel de Coulanges described the city this way:

> Several tribes might associate together, on condition that the religion of each should be respected. The day on which this alliance took place the city existed. . . .
>
> We must remark, also, that when the different groups became thus associated, none of them lost its individuality, or its independence. . . . In religion there subsisted a multitude of subordinate worships, above which was the established one common to all; in politics, numerous little governments continued to act, while above them a common government was founded.[34]

At the political apex of the Roman Empire was the emperor ruling over the network of conquered states. At the apex of the religious system was the goddess Roma who ruled over the conquered gods of the conquered peoples. Below the emperor, local governments continued to function in subordination to the Romans and so did the local cults. The city-state rulers saw no difficulty with the continued existence of a variety of cults associated with tribes, families, associations, and so on, as long as the members of these cults also participated in the public rituals honoring the city's patron deity. Likewise, the Roman emperors interfered little in the religious practices of the conquered peoples unless such practices meddled in the common worship of the Roman gods.

By some later standards, the ancient city was broadly tolerant in religious matters, just as it was in political matters. At the same time, this does not mean that the rulers of ancient cities were necessarily tolerant on principle in the way that modern liberal states profess to be. Ancient society recognized common religious practice as the fundamental element that unified diverse groups into a community with common goals and interests. It was simply natural, without further analytical elaboration, for groups to possess their own religious cults. While intellectuals occasionally theorized that there was but one god and that the various local cults reflected one or another aspect of this god's qualities, this was a minority opinion. Much more common was the belief that each people or nation had its own experience with the divinity that was then reflected in its formal religious practice. In a sense, the religious structure of a nation was identical with its political structure. Religion was the ultimate characteristic that differentiated one society from another. This meant that any group of people had a natural right to express its unity by whatever religious rituals and practices that were traditional among its members.[35] Describing acceptance of divergent religious practices as a natural phenomenon did not mean that ancient thinkers developed a theory of religious toleration based on comparative study of various societies. Neither does it mean that in the ancient world the concept of a right as a valid claim existed. Natural in this sense simply meant traditional or customary practices of any society that were considered the normal mode of behavior and expression for members of that society. Such behavior should be tolerated unless there was some specific reason for not so doing.

The major exception to the general Roman policy of religious toleration concerned the various mystery cults that entered the Roman world from Egypt and Asia. Unlike the traditional cults found in the city-states, cults that stressed external forms demonstrating the bonds linking the citizens together, the mystery religions stressed individual experience with the divine. The devotees engaged in practices designed to give the worshipper immediate contact with the god or goddess, not a communal experience stressing social unity. From the conservative Roman perspective, the cultists were engaging in bizarre practices that were abhorrent and even dangerous to the social order.

> Consider the sacred rites of the mysteries; you will find tragic deaths, dooms, funerals, mourning and lamentations of woebegone gods. . . . Shaven priests, mourning, bewailing, and searching . . . miserable votaries beating their breasts. . . . These old Egyptian rites have now found their way to Rome, so that you may play the fool.[36]

Furthermore, the Romans feared religions whose adherents met privately rather than holding their ceremonies in public. Mystery cults often met after dark in wooded areas or in caves out of public view. Roman officials feared that such meetings signified the unwillingness of the cultists to open their beliefs to public scrutiny because behind the facade of religion they were actually hatching plots to subvert the empire. In 270 A.D., for example, the Roman government banned Manichaeism, a mystery cult that originated in Persia, Rome's long-time enemy to the east. One Roman observer described this cult as a "perverted doctrine" and another example of the Persian threat to Rome.

> We have heard that these men have but recently sprung up and advanced . . . from the Persian people, our enemy, to this part of the world, where they are perpetrating many outrages, disturbing the tranquillity of the people and also introducing the gravest harm to the communities.[37]

The Romans banned Manichaeism because of its mixture of secrecy and potentially subversive activities, not because of any particular intolerance of the doctrines themselves. That is, it was the social and political consequences of Manichaeism that the Romans opposed.

Roman religious toleration was, however, a two-way street. The Romans expected that the peoples whom they conquered would accept the formal rituals of Roman civic religion as a sign of Roman domination. While most conquered societies were willing to add Roman gods to their local pantheons, not all were willing to do so. The Jews and then the Christians were the most notable exceptions to Roman expectations about reciprocal religious toleration. Both groups asserted that their cult alone was the one true religion. All others were false, thus making reciprocal toleration impossible. The Romans responded to the claims of these two groups in interestingly different ways that reflected Roman ideas about the nature of religious toleration.

Basically, the Romans tolerated what they perceived to be the strange and stubborn behavior of the Jews in refusing to accept the forms of Roman civic religion.[38] Although on occasions the Roman government did consider affronting Jewish religious sensibilities, the traditional Roman policy of seeing a religion as an integral part of a national culture won out. It is not quite accurate to say that the Romans believed that the Jews had a right to their religious customs, at least not a right in law. Neither would it be accurate to see the Romans as recognizing a valid claim of the Jews to practice their own religion even if it meant rejection of a Roman cult. What the Romans saw was a collection of practices and attitudes that were strange, even seemingly anti-social by Roman standards, but a collection of traditional national customs nonetheless.

What the Romans did oppose very firmly were Jewish attempts to assert political independence from Rome. The Romans were not at all tolerant of that sort of activity. Roman toleration of Jewish stubborness in religious matters was influenced by Roman awareness of the close links between Jewish religious and political life. A proposal to place a statue of a Roman god in the temple at Jerusalem as a sign of Roman domination was rejected when the Romans recognized that the political and military consequences of such an action would cost more than the effort involved was worth.[39] The destruction of Jerusalem in 70 A.D. by the Romans was not for religious reasons but for political and military ones. The Jews had rebelled, so the center of their cult was destroyed as punishment. Their religion, however, was not banned, so that Jews dwelling within the Empire continued to practice their religion.

Roman toleration of Jewish religious beliefs did have some limits. In the first century A.D., an imperial edict forbade Jews living outside of Palestine from making converts from among their non-Jewish neighbors. From the Roman perspective, this edict did not violate the tradition of religious toleration. It was, rather, the Jews who were violating traditional standards by proselytizing in order to add members to their religious community who were not part of the Jewish nation. In addition, the Romans feared the growth of any religious group whose membership transcended national boundaries. The only international group that the Romans encouraged was that composed of those, Roman and non-Roman by birth, who possessed full Roman citizenship with its important legal and social rights. Roman citizenship was held out as the reward for those among the conquered who collaborated with the conquerors. The men from various nations who composed this international elite shared common interests that contributed to the empire's cohesion. If the Jews were successful in their proselytism, they might create an international group that, in Roman eyes, could compete with the Roman citizens for control of the empire.

This Roman fear of religious doctrines that were not restricted to a single identifiable national group led the Romans to their eventual confrontation with the Christians. As the Roman experience with the Jews demonstrated, the Romans would tolerate unpalatable religious ideas as long as they were not subversive of the social order and restricted to a single group. When unpalatable ideas became linked to a religion that transcended national boundaries, then the Romans reached the limits of their toleration. The Christians, though Jewish in origin, insisted that their religious teaching was directed to all men, not simply to a small number of Chosen People. Furthermore, as if to underscore Christianity's universal message, the Christians had no cult center of their own, as the Jews and others did. Neither were they a nation because they had no land of their own. Furthermore, the Christians at the outset shared with the despised mystery cults a tendency to meet behind closed doors, thus conjuring up the traditional Roman fear of subversion by secret societies. In addition, Christian doctrinal absolutism, international membership, and strange beliefs all combined to make Christianity appear to be a dangerously subversive movement, one that did not fall into the category of tolerated cults. Finally, like the Jews, the Christians rejected participation in Roman civic cults, which demonstrated to the Romans exactly how wicked the Christians were.

At first the Romans could not distinguish the Christians from the Jews, and so the early Christians benefitted from the toleration accorded the Jews. The increasing number of converts from among the non-Jewish population of the Roman world, however, meant that the Romans eventually did come to distinguish the two groups and to single out the Christians as a potentially dangerous group. The Emperor Nero (A.D. 54-68) was even able to use the Christians as scapegoats on whom to lay the blame for the great fire that destroyed much of Rome in A.D. 64. The historian Tacitus wrote that the Christians were really convicted "not so much for incendiarism as for their anti-social tendencies."[40] What Tacitus meant was that the Christian refusal to join in the great public rituals of the civic religion struck their fellow Romans as a serious form of anti-social behavior and as such worthy of harsh punishment, lest others be encouraged to withdraw from society as well. Elsewhere, the Romans termed the Christians "atheists" because they denied the existence of the pagan gods whose cults were at the heart of the civic rituals.[41] From the Roman point of view, to deny the gods was not only a religious statement, it was a politically subversive one as well.

Until the middle of the third century, however, the Roman government interfered only occasionally with the activities of the Christians. As the threat of barbarian invasion from without and economic collapse from within grew, persecution of the Christians increased. The purpose of the persecution was political, not religious. The imperial government was anxious to strengthen the sense of loyalty to Rome that the traditional rituals of civic religion were designed to encourage. The imposition of emperor worship, a product of Roman expansion into the Middle East, was designed to do the same in those parts of the empire where ruler worship was common.

The Christians did not see civic religious practices and emperor worship as being public or political functions. They saw them as worshiping false gods. Like the Jews, the Christians were clearly not syncretic in their approach to religion and so appeared subversive of the Roman order. In addition, the Christians' refusal to participate in the civic religious ceremonies could not be seen as the peculiar custom of a particular nation because the Christians were drawn from all segments of the Roman world. In A.D. 303, when the Emperor Diocletian unleashed the most extensive persecution of Christians that the Roman world had seen, he did it for political reasons, not religious ones. His goal was to insure the survival of the Empire and, if necessary, by forced conformity, of all those who lived there. Forcing all the inhabitants of the Roman world to indicate their loyalty by requiring them to perform the rituals connected with emperor worship was, presumably, in Diocletian's mind, not an invasion of private religious conscience but only a necessary part of public behavior.[42] To demand that all his subjects perform some nominal ritual before his statue was of a piece with his edicting freezing wages and prices. Both actions were designed to stabilize Roman society even at the expense of making it rigid. Neither policy worked, however, so that when Diocletian retired in A.D. 305, he left an empire that was in worse condition than when he had taken office.

Following a period of civil war among a series of contenders for Diocletian's throne, Constantine assumed the imperial office and initiated a policy that, while superficially the reverse of his predecessor's with regard to religion, was in reality quite similar. In A.D. 313, Constantine issued the Edict of Milan that gave legal standing to the Christian faith and provided for the return of Christian property that had been seized under Diocletian's persecution.[43] Contemporary Christian apologists attributed Constantine's reversal of Diocletian's policy to his having had a religious experience on the eve of his final battle in the civil war. While such an explanation cannot be dismissed out of hand because divine intervention in human affairs was taken for granted in the Roman world, other explanations can also be advanced. Although the Christians formed only a minority of the Empire's total population, they were found in large numbers in the great trading cities of the Near East, the region that Constantine was most determined to protect. In that sense, Christianity may have appeared to Constantine as a well-organized group whose support might make the survival of the Empire easier. If granted legal status, the Christians would presumably be grateful and anxious to show their gratitude by wholeheartedly supporting the Empire against its enemies.[44] At the same time, it is important to realize that Constantine did not make Christianity the official religion of the Roman Empire, as is often believed. He only gave the Christians the same legal recognition that other cults possessed.

The legalization of Christianity was not a response to a claim to religious toleration that the Christians presented. It was a recognition of the role that they might play in the effort to maintain the Roman Empire in its time of crisis. At the same time, the Christians themselves had long asserted a claim to legal recognition. From the middle of the second century, Christian writers occasionally tried to point out to the government that they did deserve toleration. Their argument was not that religious toleration was a good thing, but that the Christians practiced precisely the virtues that the Romans themselves traditionally praised. Furthermore, the Christians also pointed out their loyalty to the empire.[45] Christianity was after all founded within the Roman Empire, and its leader was not associated with the Jewish groups that sought to overthrow Roman domination of Palestine. In addition, the Christians were not associated in any way with the various enemies the Roman Empire was facing.

During the remainder of the fourth century, the status of the Christian Church within the Empire gradually rose. By the end of the century, the Christian Church was the sole legal religion in the Empire. In A.D. 382 the last vestige of the old civic religion passed from the Roman scene when the statue of Victory, which had stood in the senate house, was removed by order of the Christian Emperor Gratian. For centuries senators had placed a bit of incense on the flame that burned continuously before the statue. Even Christian senators engaged in this practice until the emperor ordered the statue removed because of its identification with the ancient pagan religion.

The removal of the statue of Victory provided an opportunity for the surviving pagans to pose the question of the rights of a religious minority within a Christian society.[46] Symmachus, Prefect of the City of Rome, a pagan belonging to an ancient senatorial family, protested the emperor's action and contrasted the Christian and the pagan attitudes toward religion. He pointed to the antiquity of the Roman state and the apparent connection between the traditional Roman religion and the success of Roman arms. Furthermore, he wondered how the Christians could be so certain that theirs was the sole true religion.

> The divine mind has distributed different guardians and different cults to different cities. As souls are separately given to infants as they are born, so to peoples the genius of their destiny. . . . Since our reason is wholly clouded, whence does the knowledge of the gods more rightly come to us, than from the memory and evidence of prosperity? . . .
>
> We ask, then, for peace for the gods of our fathers and of our country. . . . What difference does it make by what pains each seeks the truth?[47]

In response to Symmachus's plea for toleration, St. Ambrose, Bishop of Milan and an advisor to the emperor, presented the Christian view of the nature of religion and of its role in society. Like Symmachus, Ambrose was a member of an ancient Roman family that had played an active role in political life, and he had also been an imperial provincial governor before becoming a bishop. His credentials as a Roman, in other words, were as good as those of Symmachus. He can be presumed to have understood exactly what Symmachus was defending. As a result, his rejection of the prefect's position was not simply that of an unsophisticated Christian exulting in his religion's victory over the old Roman cult. In Ambrose's opinion, the wicked religious practices of Symmachus's ancestors and of his own as well were of no interest. He flatly rejected the ancient view that a variety of paths led to knowledge of the gods. There was only one god and one path to him. The other so-called paths to god were false and could not claim any right to exist in a Christian society. In other letters Ambrose asserted the independence of the church from secular authorities on the grounds that the church's spiritual mission was superior to the secular government's mission to maintain physical peace and order.[48]

Ambrose's rejection of Symmachus's arguments marked the beginning of a new approach to the question of religious rights. Symmachus and his fellow pagans continued to take the position that absolute religious truth could not be known so that toleration was a reasonable policy. The pagans stressed that a religion should be judged by its antiquity and by its political or social successes. Finally, Symmachus's apologia for the old ways reflected the traditional opinion that every people has a religion that reflects its unique historical experience. For a committed Christian, as Ambrose surely was, truth was not a matter of historical experience or imperial success. Truth was absolute and could be known by those who wished to know it. It was not subject to the kinds of tests that Symmachus mentioned. Being untrue, the traditional Roman cult was a danger to the spiritual well-being of the Empire's subjects and should be abolished. A Christian emperor would have to take a different approach to religion than his pagan predecessors had taken. Ambrose and those who followed his line of argument gradually reshaped the role of religion in society. Where religion had once been a means of identifying a particular society and then linking its individual members together through communal rituals, religion in the Christian era became a means of achieving individual salvation, with the secular power playing a significant, but subordinate, role in the work of salvation. Thus, while religious toleration could be seen as good and even necessary in pagan society because it enabled divergent peoples to live together in harmony, toleration in Christian society was wrong because it harmed the possibility of salvation for individuals. Christianity, in other words, reversed the roles of religion and the political order, making religious goals, not political ones, the primary end of human society. In so doing, it destroyed the traditional basis for religious toleration.

The victory of the Christian Church over Roman paganism was only one part of the great transformation, not to say revolution, in conceptions about government that occurred as Roman Christianity came to replace Roman paganism. The universal Christian religion replaced the hierarchy of local civic cults that had previously dominated the European religious outlook. At the same time, the universal Roman political order broke up to be replaced not by another universal political order but by the feudal order in which political power was widely decentralized. Attempts to maintain or to re-create the pagan Roman Empire as a Christian Roman Empire failed. The city-state was replaced by the manor, a small, self-sufficient agricultural unit, except in Italy where urban life remained in existence although on a much smaller scale. Baptism into the Christian Church, not Roman citizenship, became the badge of membership in medieval society. Membership in the church was a prerequisite for participation in public affairs. As a result, there was no problem about the political rights of those who were not members of the Christian Church—they had none. On the other hand, the question of the right of a religious minority to exist was a separate issue and one that required a more complex answer.

The nature of the medieval Christian response to the presence of nonbelievers within Christian Europe varied according to a number of circumstances. In the first place, Christianity took a long time to penetrate the religious and cultural fabric of the peoples who outwardly became Christians from the fourth to the tenth centuries in the wake of the barbarian invasion of Europe. Pagan religious practices, sometimes under a Christian veneer, continued to survive, especially in rural areas. In addition, there were Jewish communities of long standing scattered throughout Europe. Rome, for example, was the home of a Jewish community dating back to about 200 B.C. In Spain there was a large Muslim population composed of those who remained there as the Christians proceeded to reconquer the peninsula from the Arabs who had conquered it in the eighth century.

From the fifth century until the late eleventh century, the Christian Church lived at comparative ease with residual paganism, Judaism, and Islam. The pagans were gradually converted, at least nominally. As for the Jews, although Christian Spanish rulers had begun to persecute Jews and to limit their role in public life before the Arabs invaded Spain in the eighth century, early medieval society elsewhere was generally tolerant of Jewish religious practice, although not to the extent of allowing Jews the right to participate in political life. The Muslims who remained in Spain after the Christian reconquest were also allowed to practice their religion publicly, even though church leaders, especially in the thirteenth century, objected to the policy of religious toleration.[49]

Starting in the late eleventh century, however, European Christian attitudes began to harden against religious toleration. To some extent, this change appears connected with the crusading movement that began in 1095 A.D. in an attempt to restore the Holy Land to Christian hands. Not only were the distant Muslims seen as a threat, the Jews living in Europe were also identified in the popular mind as secret supporters of the Muslims. Attacks on Jews were especially noticeable in those parts of northern Europe where crusaders gathered to begin the journey to the Near East. Cologne, a major mustering point for crusaders, was the scene of one of the earliest of these attacks as potential crusaders gathered to travel down the Rhine.[50]

Ecclesiastical and secular rulers often, but not always, opposed these acts of violence, not because they believed that the rights of the Jews were involved, but because they disliked the random, unofficial violence involved or because they believed that baptism should not be forced upon the unwilling. In 1215, the Fourth Lateran Council of the church mandated distinctive dress for Jews and required that they reside within a designated region of the towns they inhabited. This was the origin of the ghetto.[51] In Church law, the Jews were allowed to live among Christians, admittedly under restrictive conditions. Some secular rulers would not even allow that much. Jews in northern Europe generally came under the special personal protection of the rulers. This protection could be lifted at any time and for any reason or for no reason. In 1290, Edward I of England ordered all Jews out of his kingdom, a decision that was not reversed until Oliver Cromwell formally invited them to return in the midseventeenth century.[52]

In Spain, where the largest concentration of Muslims living in the Christian world could be found, the condition of the Muslims was roughly equivalent to that of the Jews elsewhere. There were restrictions on their activities, and at least some attempts were made to restrict aspects of their religious life. Popes occasionally complained about the fact that in Spanish Christian cities the cries of the mullahs calling the faithful to prayer could be heard to the scandal of Christians. Nevertheless, the role of the Muslims in the economic and professional life of Christian Spain effectively insulated them from persecution. Here again there was no formal legal right to practice an alien religion. Toleration was a practical necessity, not a theoretical ideal. Limits or restrictions on the religious practices of Muslims and Jews were not perceived as an invasion of their right to religious freedom. Instead, the Christian position was that these religious practices, though tolerated for practical purposes, were always a potential danger to Christian souls.[53] Periodically, efforts were made to convert Jews and Muslims to Christianity. In that way, the skills of these peoples would not be lost to their Christian masters, but the danger to the souls of Christians would be eliminated.

Muslims and Jews presented one test of the Christian reaction to the nonbeliever. Heretics, those who were members of the Christian Church but who objected to one or another of its doctrines, provided another test. Here again, the eleventh century was an important turning point in Christian attitudes toward those who did not conform in matters of religion. Before the eleventh century, heresy was generally seen as an individual matter. Increasingly, however, it became a social issue as distinct groups of dissenting believers appeared who rejected Church doctrine and even advocated what amounted to radical social change. From being an individual posing a threat to the souls of his neighbors, the heretic was transformed into a sinister member of a subversive cult desirous of overturning the entire social order. Heretics of this sort generally accused the church of having abandoned the poverty of the early church in favor of an alliance with temporal wealth and power. Almost as if to prove the truth of the allegation, church councils in 1179 and 1215 issued decrees asserting the need for cooperation between ecclesiastical and secular officials in order to rid Christian society of those who wished to subvert its spiritual and its temporal well-being. It should be noted that the heretics themselves were not demanding toleration. They, like the dominant papally led church, believed that they possessed the truth and were as willing to persecute nonbelievers as was the pope whom they criticized.[54]

The most emphatic statement of the relationship that should exist between church and state in these matters appeared in a decree of the Fourth Lateran Council 1215: "Convicted heretics shall be handed over for due punishment to their secular superiors." A secular ruler who "neglects to fulfill the demand of the Church that he shall purge his land of this contamination of heresy" risked excommunication and even loss of office. The Christian ruler who was appointed to replace a recalcitrant heresy hunter "shall exterminate the heretics, possess the land without dispute and preserve it in the true faith.[55]

Secular rulers saw no difficulty with their assigned role as executioners of heretics. As early as the sixth century, Christian Roman emperors at Constantinople had issued legislation designed to eliminate heresy by eliminating the heretics. One law stated that at the very least it "is just to deprive of their worldly goods those who do not worship the True God."[56] Other laws ordered the death penalty for heretics. Although the implementation of these laws varied from reign to reign depending on the realities of Byzantine politics, the principle was clear—heretics had no rights at all, not even the minimal toleration that Jews and Muslims enjoyed.

The first medieval secular ruler in Western Europe to issue legislation concerning heretics was the Holy Roman Emperor Frederic II (1220-1250). Between 1220 and 1239 he issued a series of decrees for his various possessions that provided a scale of punishments for heretics ranging from public recantation of error to the death penalty. In 1231 he issued the Constitutions of Melfi for the administration of his southern Italian possessions. In the constitutions he asserted the secular ruler's responsibility for eliminating heresy and specified burning as the proper punishment for convicted heretics. The opening chapter of the constitutions explained the importance of eliminating heresy this way.

> Heretics try to tear the seamless robe of our God. . . . They are violent wolves, but they pretend the tameness of sheep until they can get inside the sheepfold of the Lord. . . . They are sons of depravity. . . . Therefore, we draw the sword of righteous vengeance against them. . . . We have decided in the first place that the crime of heresy and these condemned sects should be numbered among the public crimes as it was promulgated in the ancient laws. . . . Committed to the judgment of the flames, they should be burned alive in the sight of the people.[57]

These laws in turn became the model for similar decrees issued by other Christian rulers over the next two centuries.

The medieval blending of spiritual and temporal interests into a definition of what constituted the common good meant that there could be no justification for heresy. As Thomas Aquinas (1225--1274) put it, "if forgers of money or other malefactors are straightway justly put to death by secular princes, with much more justice can heretics . . . be not only excommunicated but also put to death."[58] The analogy is striking because it compares the coining of false money with its implication for the temporal economy with the impact of false doctrine on the spiritual economy.

During the thirteenth and fourteenth centuries, special church courts, the courts of the Inquisition, searched out and extirpated heresy in Europe. By the early fifteenth century, these courts had fallen into disuse because of their success in eliminating heresy. At the same time, however, secular rulers continued to be vigilant where heresy was concerned. In 1401, Henry IV (1399-1413) of England issued a statute ordering the burning of convicted heretics.[59] This was a reaction to the appearance of a movement associated with the ideas of the theologian John Wycliffe (1320?-1384). Like earlier reformers, Wycliffe had demanded a purified church, one that gave up its lands and political power. His insistence upon purging the church of its wealth was attractive to some, especially nobles, who hoped to benefit materially from the process of divestiture that Wycliffe proposed. On the other hand, Wycliffe's argument that sinners could neither administer the sacraments nor hold public office legitimately was less acceptable. Wycliffe's ideas were condemned by the church, first at a synod of English bishops and then by the Council of Constance (1414-1417).[60] Henry IV's statute on the punishment of heretics made it clear that Wycliffe's teaching had significant social and political implications that had to be checked. It was not only Wycliffe's theological ideas that were dangerous, it was the fact that his followers "made unlawful conventicles and confederacies, they hold and exercise schools . . . and, as much as they may, excite and stir [the people] to sedition and insurrection and made great strife and divisions among the people." These activities result in "not only the greatest peril of souls" but "many other hurts, slanders, and perils . . . which, God forbid, might come to this realm" unless the spread of heresy was halted.[61]

The medieval identification of heresy with social and political unrest found its greatest crisis in the sixteenth century as the Protestant Reformation produced large-scale heretical movements that possessed strong political and military support. At the beginning of the Reformation, the identification of the religious community with the political community was firmly in place. By the end of the Reformation, there was strong evidence that the two communities could be distinguished, though intellectual support for this opinion was still weak. Once the existence of two or more religious communities within a single political community became theoretically possible, the problem of minority rights became an important one for political and legal thinkers. community became theoretically possible, the problem of minority rights became an important one for political and legal thinkers.

Two events in the sixteenth century paved the way for reconsidering the relationship of minority groups to the larger society in which they lived. The first of these was the Protestant Reformation that ended the Roman Catholic Church's monopoly of religion in Europe. There emerged as a result a multiplicity of Christian denominations, each asserting that it alone possessed Christian truth and each possessing strong political support that prevented Catholic authorities from eliminating it. The second event was the discovery of the non-European world and the subsequent debate about the rights, if any, that indigenous peoples possessed in the face of their potential conquest by Europeans. These events did not, strictly speaking, concern majority-minority relations. The Reformation was a debate about religious truth, not a debate about religious toleration. The debate that broke out in sixteenth century Spain about the conquest of the Americas concerned the right of a Christian minority to conquer a non-Christian majority in the name of religion. Nevertheless, both of these events contributed at least indirectly to the development of modern theories of minority rights.

Protestants as well as Catholics in the sixteenth century believed in the absolute truth of their version of the Christian religion. In the opinion of the leading Protestant reformers, the problem with the dominant Catholic Church was not simply that individual churchmen were corrupt or immoral. Rather, Martin Luther, John Calvin, and the other preachers of reform declared that the Church of Rome was teaching false and perverted doctrine, which, if followed, would lead men to eternal damnation. Luther, Calvin, and their followers were not asserting their right to practice a competing version of Christianity, they were demanding that secular rulers act to reform the practice of the Christian faith within their realms under the direction of reformed clergy. Inasmuch as secular rulers had long accepted a role in securing the spiritual as well as the temporal well-being of their subjects, the call by the reformers to impose reformed religious practice in their lands was acceptable to many rulers. For a ruler who took his spiritual responsibilities seriously, the problem was not whether he should interfere in religious practice but what religious doctrines and practices he should impose on his people.[62]

An unforeseen and unintended consequence of the Reformation was the emergence of policies granting limited toleration for religious minorities. This was not due to a revival of ancient skepticism about religious truth, but because of the inability of a single religious denomination to dominate Europe as a whole in the way that the Catholic Church once did. Even within the individual European kingdoms, rulers found it impossible to eliminate minority religious groups completely. The rulers of France and Germany in particular found themselves forced to authorize limited religious toleration and even to extend political rights to members of minorities in order to maintain the integrity of their kingdoms. The choice was for some form of religious toleration, usually for only one religious minority, as the price for ending a destructive civil war.

The religious civil wars that broke out in Germany during the 1520s resulted in the first attempts to use religious toleration as a basis to resolve potentially destructive conflicts. After facing two serious wars that were closely linked to the religious crisis, the Knights' War in 1522 and the Peasants' War in 1524-1525, some of the German nobles met at Speier in order to develop a solution to the seemingly endless series of wars that the Reformation had spawned. The nobles who attended the meeting proposed as a temporary solution that each secular ruler within Germany be allowed to determine the religion to be practiced within his domain. This would mean that the king of Germany and Holy Roman Emperor Charles V (1519-1555), a staunch defender of the Catholic Church, could not legitimately interfere in the religious life of any of the approximately 300 political units that composed Germany unless that unit was a part of his own family's personal domain. This solution was based on traditional principles about the rights and privileges of the German nobles. Throughout the Middle Ages they had acquired for themselves much of the power that in other kingdoms remained in royal hands. In spite of a late fifteenth century attempt to provide at least some rudimentary institutional forms that would unify the 300 political units in Germany, the central authority was virtually nominal. In this case, the local rulers took upon themselves the traditional royal responsibility for the spiritual well-being of their subjects. The result was the policy of *cuius regio eius religio*, his land, his religion. The ruler of the land could choose the religion of his people.[63] Even this formula did not give unlimited freedom to the nobles to select a religion. The only allowable choices were Catholicism or Lutheranism.

After another series of wars in which neither Catholics nor Protestants were able to win the upper hand permanently, another meeting was held, this time at Augsburg in 1555, to seek a permanent resolution to the crisis. Here again, the *cuius regio eius religio* formula was accepted as the basis of a solution. This time, Charles V assented to the solution so that either Catholicism or Lutheranism could be imposed by a noble on his subjects with imperial blessing. No other forms of Christian religion were permitted to "enjoy their religious beliefs, liturgy and ceremonies as well as their estates and other rights and privileges in peace" within Germany.[64] The Peace of Augsburg was the result of political exhaustion, not the result of any growing awareness that religious minorities possessed rights that should be respected. The best evidence of the Peace of Augsburg's essentially intolerant substance was its explicit rejection of all religious denominations other than the two denominations, Catholicism and Lutheranism, that possessed significant political and military power: 'However all such as do not belong to the two above-mentioned religions shall not be included in the present peace but be totally excluded from it.[65] Even as the peace was being signed, Calvinism was beginning to make significant inroads in areas that had been Lutheran previously, thus paving the way for a new round of religious violence and requiring a new solution that would incorporate a third denomination.

In the long run, the fissioning of the Protestant movement during the last half of the sixteenth century undermined the Peace of Augsburg. The failure to develop a theory of society that would reconcile the conflicting claims of competing religions meant that the growing number of religious minority groups could only make the situation worse, possibly leading to even harsher efforts to repress heresy. In 1618, the Thirty Years War, a three-sided religious war in Germany engaging the Calvinists along with the Catholics and the Lutherans, broke out. The Thirty Years War became the turning point in the history of the role of religion in Western society.[66] Ostensibly, the war began as a religious war involving the three major denominations in Germany. During the course of the war, however, it became clear that the war had provided an opportunity for neighboring states, regardless of their religious position, to acquire land and power in Germany even at the expense of their coreligionists. The rulers of Denmark, Sweden, and, above all, France supported one or another party in Germany in order to advance their own political ends. Eventually this led to the Catholic king of France providing the bulk of foreign support for Protestant rebels against the Catholic Hapsburg rulers of Germany. The reason for this was that French political interests would be best served by a weak German monarchy. Inasmuch as the Hapsburg monarchs were Catholics, it was rational for French policy to support the Protestant nobles who were in rebellion against the Hapsburgs. In matters of foreign policy, the French government was distinguishing between religious and political interests. The focus was upon achieving political goals that would enhance the stature of France even if the results would be detrimental to the Catholic Church elsewhere. The Peace of Westphalia which ended the Thirty Years War settled the religious issue in a few words.

> The Reformed [Calvinists] are to have equal rights in Religion and other matters with the other states and subjects.
> . . . but besides the religions named [Catholic, Lutheran, Calvinist] above, no other shall be accepted or tolerated in the Holy Roman Empire.[67]

This peace, in other words, only gave legal recognition to those religious groups that were too strong to be destroyed. Persecution of small Protestant sects such as the Anabaptists continued in the lands controlled by the three legally recognized religions. The Anabaptists were unable to win recognition because they were often pacifists and therefore unwilling to use force in their own defense. Thus they were fair game for the stronger powers that saw persecution of heresy as their religious duty. In the final analysis, the Peace of Westphalia simply reiterated the approach to religious minorities and to religious toleration that had been used ineffectively in Germany for over a century. Religious toleration, if indeed that is even the term for it, was available only to those groups who possessed political and military might.

The series of religious wars in Germany made it increasingly clear that religion was becoming a divisive force in society instead of the unifying force it had once been. The problem was now how to deal with religion in this new context. The traditional Christian opinion that there was only one true faith and that it was the secular ruler's responsibility to insure its position in the state was no longer viable. As political reality revealed a wide variety of competing religions, each claiming the privileges and position of the medieval church, the secular rulers found themselves in an increasingly complicated dilemma. A handful of people on the fringes of the Reformation movement, such as the Anabaptists, proposed separating religion from government and allowing each man to worship as he pleased so long as he did no harm to anyone. This solution was not acceptable to Catholics or to most Protestants because they continued to believe that toleration was fundamentally destructive to the purposes for which government existed in a Christian society.

Although Germany had the worst outbreaks of religious violence, it was France that produced the most extensive discussions of a theory of religious toleration.[68] In addition to problems arising from the religious crisis of the sixteenth century, France was also undergoing serious internal conflict involving the various political, economic, and social subgroups that composed the kingdom and their relationship to one another and to the monarchy. More than any other kingdom in Europe, France reflected the complex nature of medieval social structure as it survived into the early modern world. The request for religious toleration in France came at the same time as the monarchy was making strenuous efforts to eliminate group autonomy in favor of national uniformity. By the midsixteenth century, France was the scene of a series of religious civil wars pitting the Catholic monarchs against the Huguenots, the French term for Calvinists. The Huguenots had strong support from among the ranks of the nobles and from the urban commercial class, two groups that the monarchy aimed at bringing under tighter control. Thus, when the Huguenots demanded religious toleration, they were demanding a kind of autonomy in religious matters that the kings were anxious to eliminate in other spheres of French life. The religious civil war was then given special urgency because of its implications for the future of the French kingdom. Would the kingdom be unified and centralized under the king or would it be decentralized with a great deal of power remaining in the hands of the nobles and the middle class? By the 1580s it was clear that neither side could win a complete victory over the other and that the only victor would be the king of Spain, who was gaining influence in France through his support of the Catholic party in the wars.[69]

Faced with the possibility that France might be significantly reduced in power as a consequence of the religious wars, a group of important public officials, both Catholics and Huguenots, began to develop a basis upon which the existence of the French kingdom, with a Huguenot minority within it, could be assured. This group, known as the *politiques*, was headed by Michel de L'Hôpital, chancellor of France. These men were important political figures who were in a good position to weigh the consequences of the continuation of the religious wars on the future of the kingdom as a whole. In their opinion, the religious claims that the wars incorporated undermined the purpose for which government was established, that is peace and order. L'Hôpital was pragmatic in his approach to toleration and to the issue of minority rights. As a traditional Christian, he was opposed to religious toleration because of its detrimental effects on the souls of the king's subjects. On the other hand, he and his fellow *politiques* concluded that when the spiritual ends of society cannot be obtained except at the price of destroying the very political structure that was necessary to insure the achievement of these goals, then the spiritual goals became unrealizable and therefore must be subordinated to the needs of public order and security.

With the accession to the French throne of King Henry IV in 1594, the ideas of the *politiques* became political reality. Henry IV had been a leader of the Huguenot party who, because of the biological accidents of royal life in the sixteenth century, became the leading heir to the French throne. Reputedly saying that "Paris is worth a Mass," he reconverted to Catholicism, the religion of his earlier years. This made it possible for him to accept the throne. His public return to the Catholic Church made him acceptable to the Catholics, while the Huguenots recognized the necessity of the reconversion and accepted it. As king, Henry IV issued the Edict of Nantes in 1598, granting a number of legal privileges to the Huguenots while maintaining the Catholic Church as the official state religion.

> The Catholic, Apostolic and Roman faith [shall] be restored and re-established in all those districts and places of this our Realm . . . in which its exercise has been interrupted, there to be freely and peaceably exercised.

In return for agreeing not to interfere with the practice of the majority's religion, the Huguenots, numbering about 10 to 15 percent of the French population, were granted permission to exist.

> We permit those of the so-called Reformed Religion to live and abide in all the towns and districts of this our realm . . . free from inquisition, molestation or compulsion to do anything in the way of Religion, against their conscience . . . provided that they observe the provisions of this Edict.[70]

Here again, the basis for toleration, that is, for granting the right to exist and to participate in public life, rested not on a theory of rights but upon acceptance of political reality. There were so many Huguenots and they could muster so much political and military might that they could effectively bring much of the kingdom's life to a halt if they were not granted legal recognition. Like the Lutherans in Germany, the Huguenots forced the government to grant them legal status as the price for their allowing public life to function uninterruptedly. Only the Huguenots in France benefitted from this grant, however. It was not extended to any other Protestant sect. Under Henry IV's successors, the rights granted by the edict and its accompanying acts were gradually whittled away until Louis XIV revoked the Edict of Nantes in 1685. The Huguenots were then required to convert to Catholicism or to emigrate. From the royal perspective, the revocation was designed not only to save the souls of the Huguenots, but also to eliminate a group that opposed royal centralization of power in France.

The experience of the Huguenots was a microcosm of contemporary

European ideas about the role of religion in society and about the role of minority groups. When Henry IV issued the Edict of Nantes, he was responding to an immediate crisis in a traditional manner, that is, granting legal privileges to a corporate body that could not be eliminated. The Huguenots were simply being treated as other such groups, the clergy, the nobility, various economic groups, and chartered towns were being treated. Even as Henry IV was doing this, however, the tide was running against the conception of a kingdom as a federation of groups, each with its own rights, privileges, exemptions, and status. Under Louis XIII (1610-1643) and Louis XIV (1643-1715), the monarchy embarked upon a policy of limiting the powers of those groups that posed a threat to royal control of the entire kingdom.[71] The power of the church had been significantly restricted in the early sixteenth century when Pope Leo X granted to King Francis I the right to make all major ecclesiastical appointments in France.[72] By the terms of this agreement, the Concordat of Bologna, even the decrees of church councils, such as the Council of Trent (1564), could not be published in France without royal permission.[73] The powers of the nobles were limited less directly. More and more nobles came to rely upon positions in the royal service and other forms of royal largesse for their income. To insure obtaining a share of royal money, a noble was forced to attend permanently upon the king. Louis XIV capped this development when he constructed the great palace at Versailles as a stage on which he produced, directed, and starred in a continual pageant that kept the nobles occupied while royal officials carried on the supervision of government at the local and regional levels, a task that the nobles had traditionally performed.[74]

During the eighteenth century, there was a reaction against this policy of reducing the powers of the interest groups in order to strengthen the power of the monarchy.[75] Groups and their interests flourished during the eighteenth century as a line of weak French kings was unable to continue the policy of exalting the monarchy at the expense of the groups. On the eve of the French Revolution, there was even what has been termed an aristocratic reaction against a century of royal attempts to control the nobility. The attempt to bring peace and order to France by controlling the groups that possessed rights and privileges that caused division within the kingdom and to replace these group loyalties with total reliance upon the king's personal willingness to rule justly, that is the policy of royal absolutism, ultimately failed. The groups were too well-entrenched and the tools available to the government too weak to make absolutism possible. What all these efforts did demonstrate was that groups, whether based on religion, economic position, or hereditary status, could be destructive of national unity, to use a modern phrase. Some new basis for constructing a society using a basic unit other than interest groups would be required.

The new basis upon which modern societies were to be built was the autonomous individual who possessed a body of rights rooted in natural law, rights that preceded the creation of the state. The purpose of the state in this theory is to protect the rights of the individuals who compose the society. The religious wars of the sixteenth and seventeenth centuries were not sufficient in themselves to force the development of a theory of individual rights. What gave added weight to the pressure to discover a new basis upon which to construct governments was the European encounter with quite different societies in the wake of Columbus's momentous voyage. By the middle of the sixteenth century, European intellectuals had begun to debate the legitimacy of the European conquest of the non-European world that was beginning. The issue boiled down to what, if any, rights did non-European societies possess in the face of European conquest. In raising this question, however, the intellectuals were asking fundamental questions about the nature of society and of government. The discovery of societies that functioned along lines different from European states when joined to the demand for reconsidering the nature of religion's role in European society meant that it was possible to construct theories of society that did not rely upon the European experience alone.

The problem of the rights of non-Christians *vis-à-vis* Christians centered on the question of whether or not the Christian Church's obligation to preach to all men transcended a society's right to exclude foreigners and to govern itself according to its own laws without any outside interference. According to this line of argument, Christians could not legitmately invade non-Christian lands simply in order to convert the inhabitants to Christianity. In general, however, the writers who took this position, recognizing the natural right of men to select their own rulers and to live as they saw fit, also tended to admit an important exception to the right of a society's members to live as they pleased. If these people lived according to laws and practices that violated natural law, then it was permissible for European Christians to conquer them, not to convert them, but to force them to abide by the natural laws that bound all men.[76] In practice, violations of the natural law meant that the people practiced cannibalism or had unacceptable sexual mores. Under these circumstances, a Christian invasion was justified in order to punish crimes against the natural order.[77] The underlying assumption here, of course, was the notion that all men know, or could know, a basic set of principles governing human behavior.

As Europeans encountered an ever widening circle of different societies, ranging from very primitive aboriginal peoples to the very sophisticated Chinese and Japanese societies, they found it necessary to reconsider their attitudes toward non-Europeans. In addition, once the process of reevaluating the rights of non-Christians began, it was not possible to stop further analysis of minority groups within Europe as well. If non-Christian, non-European peoples had certain rights to govern themselves that were rooted in natural law applicable to all men, how could it be denied that minority groups within Europe also possessed the same rights? The ultimate goal in this line of thought was the concept of a world order based not on religious principles but upon rational assumptions about the nature of man and society that all men could accept. In the seventeenth century, Hugo Grotius presented the European world with his *On the Law of War and Peace*, a discussion of an international legal order based on the "law of nature . . . comprising alike that which is so called in a larger sense, proceeding as it does from the essential traits inplanted in man." This "essential trait" comes from God who has "willed that such traits exist in us."[78] Grotius spoke in terms of rights as legal capacities, not the philosophical notion of natural individual rights as they came to be understood in the eighteenth century. Nevertheless, Grotius played an important role in the development of those later ideas.

During the eighteenth century, attacks on the existing European hierarchical social and political order, combined with a deeper awareness of the great variety of social and political orders that existed elsewhere and a revival of interest in the republican thought of ancient Greece and Rome, all contributed to further reconsideration of the nature of political life. One result was a view of society based on egalitarian assumptions. That is, eighteenth-century intellectuals concluded that all men are equal by nature and possess the same basic rights so that in a just society everyone would be equal before the law and in the realm of public affairs. In differing but related ways, the American Declaration of Independence and the French Declaration of the Rights of Man expressed this new approach to political life. For the Americans, it was "self-evident, that all men are created equal, that they are endowed by their Creator with certain inalienable rights," and that "to secure these rights, governments are instituted among men." The rights that individuals possess spring from nature itself, not from law or from historical experience. This statement was, of course, inconsistent with a number of aspects of American colonial life at that point, slavery and property restrictions on voting being the most obvious contradictions. Nevertheless, the American thinkers at least recognized the conflict between their theories and the political realities.

Developing an egalitarian society was easier for the American colonists than it was for the Frenchmen who led the revolution that ended the *ancien régime* in 1789. The American colonies did have the rudiments of a hierarchical society, but such a society was comparatively undeveloped. Above all, there were few groups that possessed traditional or legal rights in the way that such group rights existed in Europe. When the French revolutionaries came to the problem of creating a new society, they had first to destroy the remains of an old and well-entrenched society. The revolutionaries drew up a constitution that made all men legally and politically equal. Rights belonged to individuals without regard to what, if any, groups to which they belonged. Groups became private matters, not matters of public law. In effect, the state became the sole legal group to which individuals belonged. It also became the guarantor of the individual's natural rights.

Since the eighteenth century, the theory that society is composed of groups that are bearers of legal or civil rights has battled with the theory that the individual is the only bearer of rights and that the state exists only to protect these rights. The basic terms of this battle were set down by Edmund Burke in his *Reflections on the Revolution in France*. Burke argued that natural and civil rights were different. Furthermore, he also argued that the historical experience of a society cannot be summarily dismissed by a committee of constitution-writing intellectuals. Thus, the claims of long-standing groups to special status cannot be rejected out of hand.[79] To a great extent, Burke's criticism of the French revolutionaries was that they failed to appreciate human psychology, that the sovereign individual of their theories not only did not exist, he could not exist. The response of the French revolutionaries and those who subsequently accepted their views was that the state should form the individual who would then take up the burden of these individual rights. The public school, along with the body of common law and the sole officially recognized national language, was to be the means of creating the new man. The problem of minorities was then to be eliminated by a process of social homogenization.

The expectations of the French revolutionaries about the new man who would be the model citizen of the new society were frustrated in a variety of ways even before the century was over. The pressure on the subordinate groups within France was resisted. Under Napoleon the Christian religion that the original revolutionaries ousted in favor of the Cult of Reason was restored, along with religious toleration for Protestants and Jews. Napoleon even created a class of noblemen when he created the Legion of Honor to recognize merit. The greatest threat to the ideals of the Revolution came, however, not from a betrayal of its principles in France, but from their extension throughout Europe. Romantic nationalism, a result of revolutionary ideas about society, spread throughout Europe, encouraging every linguistic and cultural group to desire its own sovereign state in order to protect its unique way of life.[80] The subsequent history of European political life has revolved to a great extent around the conflict between theories of individual rights and the demands of groups that their rights be recognized as well.

NOTES

1. The development of modern nationalism has led to the idea that a state is the political form that a nation, that is, a culturally distinctive people, takes in the

political order. Those who belong to the nation and share its culture and values form the dominant majority. Those who reject this culture and its values form the minority or minorities that are at odds with the majority. For a recent survey of nationalism and its effects, though without any discussion of majority-minority rights, see Boyd C. Shafer, *Faces of Nationalism: New Realities and Old Myths* (New York: Harcourt Brace Jovanovich, 1972). The standard older works on nationalism are: Carlton J. H. Hayes, *Essays on Nationalism* (New York: Macmillan, 1926); and Hans Kohn, *The Idea of Nationalism*, reprint ed., (New York: Collier, 1967).

2. Within Europe, the successor states of the Austrian and Ottoman empires in eastern Europe have had the most difficulty in reconciling the conflicting interests of minority groups. See Oscar I. Janowsky, *Nationalities and National Minorities* (New York: Macmillan, 1945).

3. N.G.L. Hammond, *A History of Greece to 322 B.C.*, 2d ed. (Oxford: Clarendon Press, 1967), p. 329.

4. Albert A. Trever, *History of Ancient Civilization*, vol. 1, *The Ancient Near East and Greece* (New York: Harcourt, Brace and World, 1936), p. 292.

5. Raphael Sealey, *A History of the Greek City States, ca. 700-338 B.C.* (Berkeley: University of California Press, 1976), p. 299.

6. Trever, *History of Ancient Civilization*, 1, p. 181.

7. Aristotle, *Politics and Poetics*, trans. Benjamin Jowett and Thomas Twining, reprint ed., (New York: Viking, 1957), pp. 25-41.

8. Ibid., pp. 46-47.

9. Trever, *History of Ancient Civilization*, 1, p. 181.

10. Donald Kagan, *The Great Dialogue: History of Greek Political Thought from Homer to Polybius* (New York: Free Press, 1965), p. 235.

11. Harold Mattingly, *Roman Imperial Civilization* (London: Edward Arnold, 1957), pp. 84-85.

12. Ibid., p. 96.

13. Albert A. Trever, *History of Ancient Civilization*, vol. 2, *The Roman World* (New York: Harcourt, Brace, 1939), pp. 52-53; 335-37.

14. Ibid., pp. 636-37.

15. Christopher Brooke, *Europe in the Central Middle Ages, 962-1154* (New York: Hold, Rinehart and Winston, 1964), pp. 78-79.

16. Edward Peters, *Europe: The World of the Middle Ages* (Englewood Cliffs, N.J.: Prentice Hall, 1977), p. 271.

17. For a general survey of the origins of parliaments, see Bertie Wilkinson, ed., *The Creation of Medieval Parliaments* (New York: John Wiley, 1972).

18. On the significance of the Charter, see James C. Holt, *Magna Carta* (Cambridge University Press, 1965); and his *Magna Carta and the Idea of Liberty* (New York: John Wiley, 1972). A copy of *Magna Carta* is to be found on pages 173-84 of the latter work.

19. See Austin Lane Poole, *Obligations of Society in the XII and XIII Centuries* (Oxford: Clarendon Press, 1946), pp. 12-34.

20. Bryce Lyon, *A Constitutional and Legal History of Medieval England*, 2d ed. (New York: W. W. Norton, 1980), pp. 59-82, 166-79, 274-78, 391-407.

21. Christopher Brooke, *From Alfred to Henry III, 871-1272* (New York: W. W. Norton, 1966), p. 74.

22. Frederick Pollock and Frederic William Maitland, *The History of English*

Law Before the Time of Edward I, 2 vols, 2d ed. (1898; reprint ed., Cambridge: Cambridge University Press, 1968), 1, p. 177.

23. Sidney Painter, *The Rise of the Feudal Monarchies* (Ithaca: Cornell University Press, 1951); Joseph R. Strayer, *On the Origins of the Modern State* (Princeton: Princeton University Press, 1970).

24. For a convenient introduction to European political life in the eighteenth century, see R. R. Palmer, *The Age of Democratic Revolution*, 2 vols. (Princeton: Princeton University Press, 1959, 1964), 1, pp. 27-84; see also, Paul Hazard, *European Thought in the Eighteenth Century* (New Haven: Yale University Press, 1954), p. 173.

25. John Hall Stewart, *A Documentary Survey of the French Revolution* (New York: Macmillan, 1951), p. 231.

26. August 4th decrees, Ibid., p. 107.

27. Jay A. Sigler, *American Rights Policies* (Homewood, Ill.: Dorsey Press, 1975), p. 5.

28. A. P. d'Entrèves, *Natural Law: An Introduction to Legal Philosophy* (London: Hutchinson University Library, 1951), pp. 23-26.

29. R. W. Carlyle and A. J. Carlyle, *A History of Mediaeval Political Theory in the West*, 6 vols. (Edinburgh: William Blackwood, 1903-1936), 5, pp. 441-45.

30. F. L. Ganshof, *Feudalism*, trans. Philip Grierson, 3d English ed. (New York: Harper & Row, 1964), p. 113.

31. J. N. Figgis, *Political Thought from Gerson to Grotius: 1414-1625*, reprint ed. (New York: Harper, 1960), p. 20.

32. Ibid., p. 5.

33. Hayes, *Essays on Nationalism*, especially essay 4, "Nationalism as a Religion," pp. 93-125.

34. Fustel de Coulanges, *The Ancient City*, reprint ed. (Garden City, N.Y.: Doubleday, 1956), p. 127.

35. This view of a religion's social function was articulated about the middle of the second century A.D. by a Roman writer named Celsus. See Ernest Barker, *From Alexander to Constantine* (Oxford: Clarendon Press, 1956), pp. 379-80, 431-32.

36. Naphtali Lewis and Meyer Reinhold, eds., *Roman Civilization: Selected Readings*, 2 vols. (New York: Columbia University Press, 1951, 1955), vol. 2, *The Empire*, p. 574.

37. Ibid., pp. 580-81.

38. Salo Wittmayer Baron, *A Social and Religious History of the Jews*, vol. 1, *Ancient Times*, part 1, 2d ed. (New York: Columbia University Press, 1952), pp. 244-45.

39. Ibid., pp. 218-19.

40. Tacitus, *The Annals of Imperial Rome*, trans. Michael Grant (London: Cassell & Co., 1963), 15.49, p. 354.

41. Jean Daniélou and Henri Marrou, *The Christian Centuries*, vol. 1, *The First Six Hundred Years*, trans. Vincent Cronin (New York: McGraw-Hill, 1964), p. 83.

42. Barker, *From Alexander to Constantine*, pp. 353-54.

43. A.H.M. Jones, *Constantine and the Conversion of Europe* (London: English Universities Press, 1949), pp. 85-87.

44. Christopher Dawson, *The Making of Europe*, reprint ed. (New York: Meridian Books, 1958), pp. 48-49.

45. Daniélou and Marrou, vol. 1, *The First Six Hundred Years*, pp. 90-93.

46. Edward K. Rand, *Founders of the Middle Ages*, reprint ed. (New York: Dover, 1957), pp. 14-21.

47. Brian Tierney, ed., *The Middle Ages*, 2 vols. (New York: Knopf, 1970), vol. 1 *Sources of Medieval History*, pp. 22-23.

48. Ibid., pp. 24-25.

49. Robert Ignatius Burns, *Islam Under the Crusaders* (Princeton: Princeton University Press, 1973); Joseph F. O'Callaghan, *A History of Medieval Spain* (Ithaca, N.Y.: Cornell University Press, 1975), pp. 462-66.
1975), pp. 462-66.

50. Hans Eberhard Mayer, *The Crusades*, trans. John Gillingham (New York: Oxford University Press, 1972), pp. 43-44.

51. Friedrich Heer, *The Medieval World, Europe 1100-1300*, trans. Janet Sondheimer (London: Weidenfeld and Nicolson, 1926), p. 255.

52. George Clark, *English History: A Survey* (Oxford: Clarendon Press, 1971), p. 311.

53. James Muldoon, *Popes, Lawyers, and Infidels* (Philadelphia: University of Pennsylvania Press, 1979), pp. 50-51.

54. Jeffrey B. Russell, ed., *Religious Dissent in the Middle Ages* (New York: John Wiley, 1971), pp. 10-11.

55. H. Bettenson, ed., *Documents of the Christian Church*, 2d ed. (Oxford: Oxford University Press, 1962), pp. 185-86.

56. Henry St. Lawrence Beaufort Moss, *The Birth of the Middle Ages*, 395-814, reprint ed. (London: Oxford University Press, 1963), p. 113.

57. *The Liber Augustalis or Constitution of Melfi*, trans. James Powell (Syracuse: Syracuse University Press, 1971), pp. 7-9.

58. Bettenson, *Documents of the Christian Church*, pp. 186-87. Concerning Aquinas's political ideas, see *Aquinas: Selected Political Writings*, ed. A. P. d'Entrèves, trans. J. G. Dawson (Oxford: Basil Blackwell, 1970).

59. Bettenson, *Documents of the Christian Church*, pp. 251-55.

60. For a discussion of Wycliffe's political ideas, see *The Political Theory of John Wycliffe* (Chicago: Loyola University Press, 1962).

61. Bettenson, *Documents of the Christian Church*, p. 252.

62. Both Luther and Calvin called upon the secular rulers to impose religious reform upon their subjects as a fundamental obligation of good rulers. See Roland H. Bainton, *Here I Stand: A Life of Martin Luther*, reprint ed. (New York: New American Library, 1955), p. 17; John T. McNeill, *The History and Character of Calvinism*, reprint ed. (New York: Oxford University Press, 1967), p. 127.

63. Hajo Holborn, *A History of Modern Germany*, 3 vols. (New York: Knopf, 1959), vol. 1, *The Reformation*, pp. 201-46.

64. Bettenson, *Documents of the Christian Church*, p. 301.

65. Ibid.

66. C. V. Wedgwood, *The Thirty Years War*, reprint ed. (London: Jonathan Cape, 1964), pp. 492-93.

67. Bettenson, *Documents of the Christian Church*, p. 304.

68. McNeill, *History and Character of Calvinism*, pp. 237-54; J. W. Allen, *A History of Political Thought in the Sixteenth Century* (London: Methuen, 1928), pp. 73-102, 280-342.

69. Allen, *A History of Political Thought*, pp. 292-96.

70. Bettenson, *Documents of the Christian Church*, p. 302; McNeill, *History and Character of Calvinism*, pp. 247-52.

71. W. H. Lewis, *The Splendid Century*, reprint ed., (Garden City, N.Y.: Doubleday, 1957), pp. 102-11.

72. H. G. Koenigsberger and George L. Mosse, *Europe in the Sixteenth Century* (New York: Holt, Rinehart and Winston, 1968), pp. 225-26; John B. Wolf, *Louis XIV* (New York: W. W. Norton, 1968), p. 365.

73. Pierre Janelle, *The Catholic Reformation* (Milwaukee: Bruce, 1963), p. 226.

74. Lewis, *The Splendid Century*, p. 148.

75. Palmer, *The Age of Democratic Revolution*, 1, pp. 439-65.

76. Geoffrey Bruun, *The Enlightened Despots*, 2d ed. (New York: Holt, Rinehart and Winston, 1967), p. 36.

77. Muldoon, *Popes, Lawyers, and Infidels*, pp. 10-11.

78. Hugo Grotius, *De Jure Belli ac Pacis Libri Tres*, trans. Francis W. Kelsey, et al., 2 vols. *The Classics of International Law* (Washington, D.C.: The Carnegie Endowment for International Peace, 1925), p. 14.

79. Edmund Burke, *Reflections on the Revolution in France*, reprint ed. (Indianapolis: Bobbs-Merrill, 1955).

80. J. L. Talmon, *Romanticism and Revolt: Europe 1815-1848* (New York: Harcourt, Brace and World, 1967), pp. 95-109.

4

International Protection of Groups

DURING the United Nations General Assembly debate concerning the draft Universal Declaration of Human Rights, its chief author, United States delegate Eleanor Roosevelt, argued that the Declaration ought not to include mention of the rights of minorities. She also insisted that so far as the American continents were concerned, the minorities problem did not exist.[1] The Belgian representative, Guy Lebeau, felt that the issue of minority rights was essentially one of tolerance, and he reminded the Assembly of Adolf Hitler's policy of raising the problem of the treatment of German minorities in countries adjacent to Germany as a pretext for Nazi expansionism.[2] The Soviet delegate, at another session of the General Assembly, proposed incorporation of guarantees to "national minorities . . . to use their native language and to possess their own national schools, libraries, museums and other cultural and educational institutions," while "every people and every nationality within a state shall enjoy equal rights."[3] The Soviet proposal was defeated, but in its wake have come a series of subsequent international pronouncements meant to guarantee some aspects of minority rights. In spite of the fact that the Universal Declaration of Human Rights makes no mention of minority rights, there is a rich history of the international protection of those rights prior to the passage of the Declaration, but there is no longer a trend toward the international protection of minority rights.

The problem of minority rights grew up in the wake of the breakup of the European state system following the defeat of Napoleon. The slow disintegration of the Ottoman Empire, occurring also roughly in the same period, gave rise to other important minority problems. Added to these postimperial problems were the uncertain claims of nationalism, an ill-defined ideology that was at its height in the nineteenth century and has spread more widely in the twentieth to the postimperial problems of our own age. Doubtless there were minority confrontations with majorities in past ages, but the contemporary minority rights issues with which we have familiarity are largely rooted in the nineteenth century. An examination of those roots should reveal how claims of local communities and groups became converted into international declarations and matters of concern to international politics. The situations of the Greek Cypriotes, the Walloons, or the Palestinians can best be understood by examining the manner in which these (and other) minorities were created or appeared and the attempts of the international system to deal with them.

The nineteenth century was concerned less with religious or racial groups than with linguistic and ethnic groups. Talleyrand, writing from the meetings of the Congress of Vienna to his monarch, Louis XVIII, reminded the king that the old order had vanished in France and elsewhere in Europe after Napoleon's conquests. The clergy and the nobility were no longer potent groups. Instead, to apply his much prized "principle of legitimacy," the support of the people would be needed to restore authority to the post-Napoleonic regimes. The sovereign could not rule alone, but he required "the people" to accept and believe in him.[4]

But which "people" did Talleyrand have in mind? For France, the Netherlands, and Belgium, there was no question of changing the political base of the regime, although there was considerable talk of redrawing boundary lines—and some were redrawn. Napoleon had unleashed new forces on Europe. Latent nationalism sprung up in the German and Italian states, in Poland, all over Austro-Hungary, and in the Balkans. New groups were asserting themselves. New actors were making claims for international recognition. Peoples who had long been silent made claims to nationhood or at least some sort of autonomy. The Congress of Vienna, an assemblage of victorious allies attempting to redraw the boundaries of Europe, was ill-disposed to accommodating these new forces, but to some extent it did. In the process the first modern international documents on behalf of minority rights were produced.[5] These launched the modern age of minority rights. They also helped create the riddles of minority rights by recognizing some groups while ignoring others and applying no clear-cut principles.

The game of European power politics was intense at the Congress of Vienna. One of the major boundary provisions gave Prussia two-fifths of Saxony, while the remaining three-fifths was restored to the ancient Saxon dynasty. Prussia also obtained Swedish Pommerania and the Duchy of Westphalia, thus becoming the leading power in northern Germany. Austria conceded dominance in those areas and received in exchange the Tyrol, Salzburg, Illyrian provinces on the Adriatic and further promises in Italy. This settlement avoided a risk of war between Prussia and Austria but further retarded the hopes of Italian peoples for self-government. But minority rights recognition was obtained for Belgians, Savoyards, and especially for the Poles.

Poland had been wiped off the map of Europe by a 1795 treaty. Napoleon recreated a small Polish state in 1807, called the Duchy of Warsaw. Napoleon lost the Grand Duchy of Warsaw to the armies of Tsar Alexander. The tsar's forces had overrun all of Poland, including portions claimed by Austria and Prussia. The Polish settlement and Polish national integrity were largely in his hands. For reasons of power politics, Prussia and Austria received parts of Polish territory, but a new Kingdom of Poland was formed, with a lengthy constitution guaranteeing certain rights to the Polish people. Although a majority within Poland, the Poles were treated as a minority within a greater Russia. This Polish constitution, drawn up in 1815, is the first modern document giving international status to a minority group.

The "Principles of the Constitution of the Polish Kingdom" was drafted by Prince Adam Czartoryski. The constitution itself was the product of a joint Polish-Russian team, which the Russians dominated. The "Principles" emphasized the national character of the Polish kingdom and the rights of Polish citizens. The "Principles" promised an equitable protection of the rights of Jews, a feature sacrificed in the final version of the constitution. The first article of the constitution guaranteed to "the Polish people" full independence and a separate political structure, while subsequent provisions retained Russian control over foreign policy. A considerable degree of Polish autonomy over cultural affairs was permitted, while legislative power was held by the landed Polish classes.[6] The tsar reigned over Poland as a Polish king. Thus, the powers of Europe came to accept a limited degree of group (and national) autonomy—a first step toward the recognition of minority rights, (though the Poles were a majority in their own territories). Rather than ignore the claims of the Poles, the Concert of Europe came to recognize the legitimacy of this politically weak linguistic and cultural group.

A clearer example of minority rights might have been provided if the claims of the Jewish community in Poland and Germany had been recognized. The Jews failed in both instances. During the negotiations over the German settlement, Jews actively pressed for emancipation and an extension of the limited rights available to them in some of the German states. None of the major powers was sufficiently interested. No international (or national) protection of the rights of Jews ever emerged.[7]

The German settlement at the Congress of Vienna was no triumph for Metternich, the Austrian diplomat. Metternich was bitterly opposed to nationalist and ethnic movements, but he acceded to the desire for a united Germany. The German Confederation, however weak, included all territories populated by Germans except for the Swiss and Baltic territories. Prussia and Austria were considered German, although Austria included many non-Germans. However, the seeds of later minority friction were sown by the inclusion of Slavic and Italian minorities from Trieste, the Tyrol, and elsewhere. The political structure of the German Confederation was extremely fragile, and the dominance of Austria and Prussia an obvious fact. Nonetheless, a unified Germany was created by international agreement, a Germany linked by language and culture.

Minority rights had emerged less deliberately within the Ottoman Empire. This ancient Empire was crumbling when the Congress of Vienna concluded its work, but the Ottomans had evolved a system of dealing with religious and ethnic minorities because of the policies of progressive sultans, anxious to maintain their hold on territories populated by non-Muslims. The non-Muslims in many cases, were numerical majorities but effectively status minorities.

Under the Ottoman system, Muslim religious law determined the organizational and representational basis by which the sultan's subjects were divided. Non-Muslims were allowed their own religious laws and institutions, since they were generally not members of the ruling class. Ottoman society was divided into communities according to the *millet* (nation) system, under which each individual had to belong to a *millet* representing his religious group.[8] This *millet* system was established in the fifteenth century, during the height of Ottoman power, by Sultan Mehmet II and lasted until the twentieth century, an impressive example of group rights based on religion.

The *millet* system was originally established to gain the support of Christian religious leaders in conquered areas and to thus discourage the possibility of Greek Orthodox affiliation with Rome. Autonomous self-government under recognized religious leaders became a prevalent Ottoman principle of governance. The principle was gradually extended to the Armenians, the Jews, and other non-Muslim minorities.

Actually, the Ottomans were borrowing a page from the Roman book. The Romans allowed their subjects to apply their own laws to themselves. The medieval European empires and the Middle Eastern empires also had applied a similar policy. But the Ottomans expanded upon these ancient practices to create something akin to modern minority group rights. Each *millet* "established and maintained its own institutions . . . such as education, religion, justice, and social security" including, "separate schools, hospitals and hotels, along with hospices for the poor and aged."[9] *Millet* courts and many of these other social institutions remained in operation until the twentieth century.

These Ottoman expressions of minority rights were known and were acceptable to other states. In that sense, they were international in character. Nonetheless, warfare between the Ottomans and the Europeans became more frequent, especially after the Ottoman Empire pressed to the gates of Vienna. While it is true that the Ottoman example was not supported by international treaties such as those flowing from the Congress of Vienna, its practices were still important to minority groups all over Europe and the Middle East. The Ottomans translocated peoples from Asia to the Balkans and from the Balkans to Asia Minor, and the ethnic history of the Balkans and the Near East was shaped by Ottoman policies. The Ottomans scrambled the population of their territories in a way that gave rise to new arrangements of groups.[10] All this helped lay the foundation for the minorities problems that played so large a part in the post-World War I era. The Ottoman policies could be a model of recognition of group rights (the *millet*) or could destabilize an area in such a way as to arouse minority unrest and agitation. Either way, their policies were of international interest and concern.

Ethnic minorities became a political issue only after the rise of nationalism in the nineteenth century. Religious minorities had existed since earliest times. Attempts to root out heresy often resulted in persecution of religious minorities. In Christian Europe the bitter wars between Protestants and Catholics following the Reformation eventually resulted in international understandings to stabilize the conflicts. The 1648 Treaty of Westphalia attempted to settle the conflicts in the German states. Protection of religious minorities was accomplished in a number of seventeenth- and eighteenth-century treaties between the great powers. However, ethnic claims did not arise until the following century, when the group animosity that formerly had been displayed in religious conflict took another form.

Nationalism was enflamed by the writings and speeches of prominent intellectuals.[11] In Germany the philosopher Gottfried von Herder (1744-1803) had emphasized the importance of a mother tongue in the social and cultural development of the individual. Smaller nationalities throughout Europe and the Near East, fed by the message of Herder and other cultural nationalists, became more conscious of their linguistic and cultural heritage. Intellectuals within the heterogeneous Austrian, Russian, and Ottoman Empires took up the cause of preserving their native languages and culture. Dormant nationalistic sentiments were aroused, endangering the national unity of many of the long-established states.

In eastern, central, and southern Europe, nationalists often insisted each nationality was somehow entitled to its own territory. Giuseppe Mazzini preached of an Italy uniting within the borders of all those who spoke the Italian tongue. Slavic minorities became aroused to clamor for independence from the political states in which they lived. Since many of the Slavs lived in Austrian and Turkish territories, Pan-Slavism became a major aspect of Russian foreign policy, Russia being the only independent Slavic power in the nineteenth century.

Minorities began to play a larger role in international relations. The problems posed by minorities enflamed by nationalist sentiments helped unsettle the relationship between the major states of Europe. The same forces helped accelerate the decomposition of the Ottoman Empire. Nationalism was the seedbed of modern minority rights, and minority discontent was one of the most unsettling forces in international relations. Throughout the nineteenth century the great powers attempted by treaty and other international arrangements to treat the claims of Eastern European minority groups. In the end all these international efforts failed. The shot at Sarajevo which helped launch World War I was fired by an advocate of a minority group. Small wonder that during and after World War I the treatment of minority groups became a matter of prime international concern.

The victors of World War I who met together in Paris in 1919 were keenly concerned with the treatment of minority groups. This concern was not so much due to the desire to describe minority rights as it was due to the fear of political instability created by dissident minorities. As Woodrow Wilson put it, "nothing, I venture to say, is more likely to disturb the peace of the world than the treatment which might, in certain circumstances, be meted out to minorities."[12] Humanitarianism and a concern with human rights were both present at the Paris Peace Conference, but political concerns were paramount, and minority group rights were recognized as international law for political reasons.[13]

National minorities had been overtly aroused by wartime Allied propaganda. Many of them had been submerged in the Austria-Hungarian Empire, the Ottoman Empire, and the Russian state. Many of their representatives came to Paris in the expectation that their peoples would become masters of their independent states.[14] Nationalism among the minorities was a fervent force at the Peace Conference.

The leaders of various minority groups had convened their own "Congress of Oppressed Nationalities" at Rome a year before the Paris Peace Conference. The delegates carved up central and eastern Europe according to their own notions. Their dreams had been fed by nationalist ambitions and by the speeches of American President Woodrow Wilson. Had he not preached the principle of the right of the national self-determination of peoples? Had he not said that self-determination was an essential corollary of democracy?[15] He had, and in so doing he created a rational justification for minority rights, but a justification that encouraged the expression of those rights in a claim for nationhood, or so it seemed.

The international protection of minorities through the League of Nations was a product of the Paris Peace Conference. Various minorities treaties were written creating legal obligations among the signatories on behalf of racial, linguistic, ethnic, and religious minorities. These treaties bound only the signatories. Austria, Hungary, Bulgaria, and Turkey, defeated states in World War I, were bound by minority provisions inserted in their peace treaties. New or enlarged states, including Poland, Greece, Czechoslovakia, Rumania, and Yugoslavia, concluded special minority treaties with the Allied Powers. Albania, Lithuania, Latvia, Estonia, and Iraq later made similar declarations to the Council of the League of Nations. Thus was established the postwar minority system, with the Council of the League of Nations as guarantor. Minority rights had been truly internationalized, although many of the world's minority groups were not involved in the system.

Minority rights were, in most cases, imposed upon the nation states. Defeated nations had been compelled to recognize international obligations to some of their minorities. New states—those few that had obtained Wilsonian self-governance—were similarly bound. The League minority system protected national minorities particularly; not all racial, religious, and linguistic minorities.[16] These minorities were provided the critical right to acquire and hold citizenship. National minorities were also allowed, in many instances, to choose the nation-state in which they would become members. Migration of minorities was encouraged because it was hoped that the location of minorities in states of their own choosing would dampen minority nationalism. In this way minorities that had not obtained statehood would be satisfied with the lesser prize of choice of residence.

The minority rights created were novel in their coverage. Positive minority rights were created with respect to language, education, and religious and cultural activity. Minorities were given rights to maintain their own charitable, religious, educational, and social institutions. They were to receive an "equitable share" of public subventions for educational, religious, and charitable purposes.[17] Encouragement of these positive minority rights promised to maintain minority distinctiveness, but many statesmen believed that they would, at the same time, encourage national unity.

Positive minority rights are group rights. As such, they are outside the liberal, Western tradition of individual rights. These group rights were developed in Paris in response to the severe minorities problems of the prewar era and were intended to satisfy the high hopes of liberated peoples of central and eastern Europe. Unfortunately, the questions of whether the groups had rights as legal entities was left unclear. The League system was permeated with individualistic ideas of rights, for "Wilson and his fellow-architects of the League were saturated with the individualist traditions of liberalism, and consequently found the concept of group rights alien to their thinking."[18]

Individual rights were extended to members of minority groups. These were provided in the more familiar negative form of rights available through the principle of nondiscrimination. Signatory states were bound to assure members of national minorities full protection of life and liberty and complete equality with national minorities with respect to civil and political rights.[19] Individuals, then, could assert their claims if they had been denied rights solely because of their group affiliation. The rights in question adhered to individuals, not to the groups themselves. Equal treatment, not special treatment, was the thrust of these individualized rights of minority group members.

The post-World War I minority treaties, while international, were not universal. Africa, Asia, most of the Near East, Latin America, the Pacific regions, and North America were not included. Wilson's efforts to include protections of national, religious, and racial minorities within the Covenant of the League of Nations proved unacceptable. The British, partly in response to pressures from Australia and New Zealand, insisted on dropping those references from the proposed covenant.[20]

Only a few states were compelled to accept the guarantee clauses. Poland and Czechoslovakia agreed because they received accessions of German territory, a source of German agitation in later years. Rumania, Greece, and Yugoslavia, being weak states, also agreed to protect their minorities. The great powers did not. There is even some question of whether anyone was seriously concerned with honoring the international obligation to safeguard certain minorities in the years between the two world wars.

The enforcement procedure for aggrieved minorities was most cumbersome. The minority group, through its representatives, could petition the Secretariat of the League of Nations, alleging the violation of its rights under a minority treaty. The Secretariat, in turn, would transmit the petition to the government concerned, which was supposed to send its explanation. Then the petition and the explanation were forwarded to the president of the League Council, who would invite two other Council members to join him for a preliminary examination of the question. The Committee of Three did the real work, such as it was. However, there was a strong tendency to accept the views of the government in question. As Noel Baker of the United Kingdom later observed: "Many times in the Committee of Three it was a very embarrassing and difficult quesion to say, when a government said its conduct had been irreproachable, to insist nevertheless the matter must go forward for investigation and decision by some international tribunal."[21]

The Committee of Three had no means of enforcing its decision, nor did the League Council.[22] Minorities, aware of the risks of offending their own governments, became afraid to petition the League. Persuasion and conciliation sometimes were attempted, but they rarely worked. German settlers in Poland did petition the League on November 9, 1921. The League, in a rare act of daring, did support the German petition. However, nothing substantial was done until December 1923. By then Poland had expelled most of the settlers.[23] Yet, this case was one of the League's few "successful" defenses of minority rights.

Perhaps the new states that were saddled with minority rights treaties were too weak to resist minority group pressures, particularly when the minority was supported by a kindred state just across its border. Czechoslovakia particularly suffered from its minority problems, even though it treated its minorities generously. The Sudeten German problem led to the downfall of Czechoslovakia, but those minority Germans were clearly agitated by Nazi propaganda and German expansionism.

The collapse of the international system of minority rights protection under the League of Nations came swiftly. In 1933 Germany left the League of Nations, partly for reasons allegedly based upon the treatment of German minorities elsewhere. A year later Poland announced that it would not abide by the League's minority protection policies. The dismemberment of Czechoslovakia in 1938 came in a year when only four minority petitions were received by the League of Nations.[24] In December 1939 the minorities section of the League Secretariat was disbanded. This ended a twenty-year experiment in the international protection of minority rights.

The failure of the League of Nations minority system was not a failure of the concept of minority rights. Rather, it was a misapplication of the minority rights concept. The international imposition of measures on behalf of minorities was perceived as a threat to the national sovereignty of newly created states. Under international law, states are supposed to be equal to each other in their sovereignty. The fact that some states were subject to minority rights doctrines while others were exempted was offensive to the sensitivities of leaders such as Jan Paderewski of Poland. As a Polish representative once stated, the League should "grant to minorities such satisfaction as is legitimate and compatible with the interests of the state."[25] In doing so, the minority states believed, the League would be treating them in a more equal fashion. The confinement of the minority rights system to small eastern and central European states was a defect that could hardly be justified when Germany, Belgium, and Italy failed to undertake similar obligations.

Minority rights principles were not universal in application. They were international only among those states that were new and weak. Assimilation of diverse groups was impeded, and national disintegration was indirectly encouraged. Kin states took a special interest in protecting their adjacent minorities. In 1930 the British delegates to the League "frankly adopted the view that where German minorities were concerned it was for the German government to look after their interests."[26] Later, of course, Germany pressed the rights of German minorities to the uttermost, finally using it as a pretext for subversion and war.

On the other hand, many of the minority states of central and eastern Europe did try to reduce the power and influence of internal minority groups. The majority nationality often persecuted "disloyal" minorities in the name of national security. Discriminatory and oppressive measures were adopted in many minority states.[27]

The collapse of the first system of international protection of group rights by an international organization was symptomatic of larger disorders. The League of Nations minority system failed for reasons similar to those that resulted in the subsequent failures of the League in other areas. The world order was disintegrating under the pressures of aggressive, expansionist policies. Weaker minority nations feared the powerful expansionist states and curtailed the liberties of their minorities in order to protect themselves against fifth column subversion. Also, the virulent nationalism of Nazi Germany and Fascist Italy was a central and eastern European disease as well. The League was impotent to manage these fears and tensions.

The rise of nazism in the 1930s spelled the triumph of racism. The persecution of Jews was novel in its vicious intensity. Genocide, the slaughter of a group, became virtually an official policy of the Nazi regime. Nazi racism was extended to Slavs, gypsies, and others deemed inferior races by Nazi propagandists. The brutal treatment of certain groups by the Nazis raised anew the issue of the fragility of minority rights. Moreover, the minorities who were victims of Nazi policies were not the national minorities of post-World War I days. Instead, they were members of groups that were often barely conscious of their common identity. Nazi racial ideology generated new demands for collective rights. Minorities still needed the protection of a sound international order. Although the League experiment had failed, the vulnerability of groups to persecution, genocide, and oppression had been clearly demonstrated by the theory and practices of the Fascists and the Nazis.

During World War II some demands were renewed for a new international standard of human rights, including a universal standard for the protection of minority groups. But many of the former minority states opposed returning to international guarantees of minority rights. The Czech government in exile asserted its determination to never again concede a special status to minorities.[28] Czechoslovakia, Poland, and other minority states did not wish to return to a condition that encouraged dissension by ethnically alien groups. In Latin America and North America, various resolutions were adopted maintaining that the concept of international protection of minorities was inapplicable in the Western Hemisphere.[29] Nazism had produced a general reaction—the concept of international protection of group rights.

Jewish groups, particularly, were sensitive to the need for international group protection. A 1943 resolution of the American Jewish Conference called for an international bill of rights which, in addition to ensuring individual rights, would recognize "the inalienable right of all religious, ethnic and cultural groups to maintain and foster their respective group identities on the basis of equality."[30] During World War II, Max Gottschalk, an American Jewish leader, called upon the proposed United Nations Organization to include among its human rights measures some "special guarantees for all minorities everywhere."[31] Prominent international law scholars Hersh Lauterpacht and Hans Kelsen proposed forms of international protection of minority rights for the postwar world.

Unfortunately, governmental leaders did not respond to these pleas. There was no Woodrow Wilson to encourage minority hopes. There was no official sentiment to support the reinstatement of the League system and precious little official concern with the issue.

American officials played a major role in forming the structure of the world after World War II, but most of them denied the significance of minority rights. Sumner Welles, the American undersecretary of state, declared in 1943:

> Finally, in the kind of world for which we fight, there must cease to exist any need for the use of that accursed term "Racial or Religious minority." If the peoples of the earth are fighting and dying to preserve and to secure the liberty of the individual underlaw, is it conceivable that the peoples of the United Nations can consent to the reestablishment of any system where human beings will still be regarded as belonging to such minorities?[32]

Welles articulated views held by Roosevelt and other American leaders who perceived no need for a special protection for minorities. The kind of discrimination with which they were familiar was discrimination *against* a group that sought integration into society, such as American blacks. What they could not conceive is that a group might want to separate and be apart from the rest of society and feel the need of guarantees of special treatment.

In 1945 a United Nations Conference on International Organization met in San Francisco to give final shape to the United Nations Organization. The Charter declared that the United Nations Organization would promote respect for human rights, making human rights violations a matter of concern in international law.

The United Nations Charter shows no evidence of a consideration for minority rights. The Charter did not recognize minority rights as a problem of international concern. The neglect of minority rights did not rule out future treatment of those issues, but minority rights were not high on the international agenda.

The Charter is not totally silent on the question of collective rights. The right of the self-determination of peoples is mentioned twice in the

Charter.[33] This right has always been limited by the existence of United Nations trusteeships, which obviously are not based upon self-determination. Nonetheless, the United Nations Organization has often taken stands favoring the termination of dependency relationships. Self-government of peoples has been accepted in important decisions of The Hague International Court of Justice.[34]

The right of a people to be independent of foreign domination is an ultimate group right, although it is not actually a minority right. However, if the right extends to peoples within the boundaries of a national state, then it is tantamount to a minority right. If the right of self-determination implies a right to secede, then a minority group may remove itself from minority oppression by exerting its collective right. This is what the Bengalis did when they established Bangladesh. The Ibos of East Nigeria failed to create their new state of Biafra, but their rallying cry was, essentially, "self-determination."

Secession is not actually condoned by international law. The dismemberment of a state is not a right. However, self-determination, as a principle, contains an implicit threat to the integrity of multiracial, multiethnic, and multinational states. The right seems to include peoples living under colonial domination or peoples living with well-established states such as Ukrainians in the Soviet Union and Scots in the United Kingdom. However, a recent United Nations study links the collective right of self-determination to anti-colonialism and to the enhancement of national integrity.[35]

All that self-government seems to require is that "the seceding people is located in a well-defined territorial area in which it forms a majority."[36] The territory claimed by the seceding people may create conflicts between them and other peoples who may claim competing rights to self-government. The Palestine problem in which two peoples have claimed the same territory for generations has embittered the Near East to the point of war on several occasions. Current Palestinian terrorism against Israel is a continuation of a war by one people against another. Israeli treatment of West Bank Palestinians is a further example.

There is, of course, not much likelihood that a sovereign state would peacefully consent to its own dismemberment. The right of self-determination may practically mean little more than a justification for those people who succeed in their independence movement. But international law seems to support the self-determination of people as a right, regardless of the uncertainty of the outcome of any independence movement and the ambiguity of the word "people."

The 1966 International Covenant on Civil and Political Rights does proclaim a minimal version of minority rights. The Covenant provides that:

> In those states in which ethnic, religious or linguistic minorities exist, persons belonging to such minorities shall not be denied the right in community with the other members of their group to enjoy their own culture, to profess and practice their own religion, or to use their own language.[37]

The Covenant represents a minimalist version of minority rights. Minority rights are not promoted by such a provision. Minorities are not given special economic, social, or political advantages, nor is their position made secure against majority culture, language, or religion. Certainly no kind of autonomy is envisaged by the 1966 Covenant, nor are minorities entitled to any institutional safeguards.

The 1960 Convention Against Discrimination in Education goes much further, in the education area, to protect minority values and culture. The Convention states that "it is essential to recognize the right of members of national minorities to carry on their own educational activities, including the maintenance of their own schools."[38] However, this article mentions only national minorities, not religious or linguistic groups.

While these two conventions are all that is left of a general international concern with minority rights, they express little more than a gesture, although the conventions are widely accepted. At times the United Nations General Assembly has singled out a group for special consideration. In 1974 the United Nations General Assembly resolved that "the Palestinian people have 'inalienable rights' " including a "right to self-determination without external interference" and a "right to national independence and sovereignty."[39] Of course, the legal effect of such a declaration is questionable, and the political motivations are fairly obvious, but the resolution does rest upon a group claim that violates or limits the sovereignty of a member state—Israel.

There remain some vestiges of international protection of minorities in the European Convention on Human Rights, which permits groups, as well as individuals or states, to bring complaints to the European Court of Human Rights.[40] National sovereignty has been somewhat infringed by this European Convention. The fourteen states that have accepted the compulsory jurisdiction of the European Court have had to make a few concessions to minority rights. The European Court has concerned itself with linguistic minorities in Belgium and the Roman Catholic minority in Northern Ireland among other cases.

In addition, the European Convention on Human Rights does include rights that have relevance for minorities. Rights to nationality, freedom of religion, of expression, and of association are important. However, except for the right of "association with a national minority," the European Convention strongly resembles the Universal Declaration of Human Rights in its vagueness concerning minority rights. This phrase, found in Article 14 of the Convention, falls short of the generous language proposed for minorities by the Minorities Sub-Committee of the Legal Committee of the Council of Europe Assembly.[41]

However, the general position for minority rights in international law is quite weak nowadays. While the United Nations has never pronounced the minority protection system dead, neither has it vigorously attempted to cope with the protection of minorities, except as an aspect of racism.[42] There is a United Nations subcommission ostensibly devoted to the Prevention of Discrimination and the Protection of Minorities, but little has been issued from that docile body.[43]

One international law scholar has declared that the fashion for the international protection of minorities has "become nearly obsolete" because "today the well-dressed international lawyer wears human rights."[44] But the need for international protection is no less than in the past. The Palestinians, the Kurds, and the Basques are fighting for what they perceive to be their rights. Indeed, it may be concluded fairly that "in the world of reality . . . there is scarcely a state today (even in Europe) which is free of minorities and their problems" and "it is clear that the exclusive pursuit of individual human rights, without paying heed to the collective needs of minorities, is a counter-productive policy."[45]

In 1964 at a Security Council meeting of the United Nations, the Indian representative stated that many of the world's minorities wish for governments of their own. The breakup of member states was considered a hazard of an undue emphasis upon minority rights.[46] India itself has been repeatedly endangered by separatist threats. Perhaps, "the subject of international human rights has almost from the very beginning been dominated by the politician, who has been the true midwife of virtually all innovation in this field."[47] International law may no longer be innovating minority rights because it is not prudent to do so in a period when civil wars and international disorder are more dangerous than in the nonnuclear past. The priorities of international politics no longer favor minority rights. This doesn't invalidate the concept. It does require fresh thought, new approaches, and a review of the errors of the past.[48]

Other international conventions may hold some promise as a future source of minority rights. The International Convention on the Elimination of All Forms of Racial Discrimination, adhered to by ninety-four nations, mentions "special measures taken for the sole purpose of securing adequate advancement of certain racial or ethnic groups" that are permitted within the terms of the Convention.[49] The International Covenant on Civil and Political Rights, adhered to by forty-four nations, declares that "all peoples have the right of self-determination" and goes on to assert that "by virtue of the right they freely determine their political status and freely pursue their economic, social and cultural development."[50] Most other sections of this Covenant refer to individuals, rather than to "peoples." But most promising of all is the provision of this same Covenant that specifically endorses a principle of minority rights. The following clause contains the essential elements that can lead to an eventual complete international recognition of minority rights:

> In those states in which ethnic, religious or linguistic minorities exist, persons belonging to such minorities shall not be denied the right, in community with the other members of their group, to enjoy their own culture, to profess and practice their own religion, or to use their own language.[51]

Under this Covenant a Human Rights Committee has been established with the power to scrutinize alleged rights violations. The Committee has had little to do with minority rights claims, but at least the principle of minority rights has been formally accepted by most of the nations of the world.

At least international law has learned something from the Nazi excesses. Minorities do have a basic right to physical existence. The Convention on the Prevention and Punishment of the Crime of Genocide is based upon a clear perception of minorities. The crime of genocide is defined as any act "committed with intent to destroy, in whole or in part, a national, ethnical, racial or religious group, as such."[52] These principles concerning minorities are generally "recognized by civilized nations as binding on states, even without any conventional obligation," according to the view of the International Court of Justice.[53] This Convention treats minorities as groups and recognizes a group right of existence. However, the Convention does not establish a right to specific characteristics of groups so that the destruction of cultural, linguistic, religious, or other group traditions is not prohibited.[54]

The concept of minority rights still retains some international regard. Even though the vigor of the early years of the century have waned, there is a continuing sense of the importance of respect, at least, for the claims of minorities. The latest evidence of the continuing international support for some limited version of minority rights can be found in the Helsinki Accords subscribed to, among others, by the Soviet Union and the United States in 1975. The Accords declare that:

> The participating States on whose territories national minorities exist will respect the right of persons belonging to such minorities to equality before the law, will afford them the full opportunity for the actual enjoyment of human rights and fundamental freedoms and will, in this manner, protect their legitimate interests in this sphere.[55]

This minimal statement, restricted to national minorities, may represent a realistic, contemporary, international assessment of the status of minority rights. Clearly, much progress remains to be made in the international arena. It may be necessary, as a practical matter, to "stress the essential, mutually complementing functions of minority rights and human rights,"[56] but it is unlikely that formulating a new international convention on minority rights will be an attractive task for the United Nations.

NOTES

1. UN Doc. E/CN 4/S.R., 73, p. 5.

2. Ibid., p. 6.

3. UN Doc. A/784, p. 1.

4. See Guglielmo Ferrero, *The Reconstruction of Europe*, trans. Theodore Jaeckel (New York: W. W. Norton, 1963), pp. 59;60.

5. There were isolated examples of minority rights guarantees extended by monarchs by virtue of special treaty arrangements as in Saint Louis of France's 1250 promise to the Maronite community and the 1660 Treaty of Oliva promise of Poland and Prussia on behalf of religious groups.

6. W. F. Reddaway, eds., *Cambridge History of Poland* (1950) (Cambridge: Cambridge University Press, 1951), pp. 275-76.

7. See Harold Nicolson, *The Congress of Vienna* (New York: The Viking Press, 1961), pp. 214-15, in which Nicholson recounts a snub by Castlereagh to Nathan Rothschild, a prominent English spokesman for German Jews.

8. Wayne S. Vucinich, *The Ottoman Empire* (Princeton, N.J.: D. Van Nostrand, 1965), pp. 59-60.

9. Stanford Shaw, *History of the Ottoman Empire and Modern Turkey*, vol. 1 (Cambridge: Cambridge University Press, 1976), p. 151.

10. Vucinich, *The Ottoman Empire*, pp. 56-58.

11. The meaning of the term "nationalism" is by no means settled. "Nationalism has been called a state of mind similar to religious belief involving an emotional loyalty to the idea or the fact of the national state": Carlton J. H. Hayes, *Essays on Nationalism* (New York: Macmillan, 1928), p. 94. But there are many varieties of nationalism. Sociologist Anthony D. Smith identifies two types of national claims, territorial and ethnic, which he then subdivides according to whether or not a movement represents a group that is already independent. However, Smith does not believe that language and culture are essential to nationalism. See Anthony Smith, *Theories of Nationalism* (New York: Harper & Row, 1972). On the other hand, Ernest Gellner believes that language is the most fundamental aspect of modern nationalism. People who share the same language and culture will only accept the rule of individuals or groups they recognize as of their own cultural group, which may include race and religion. See Ernest Gellner, *Thought and Change* (Chicago: University of Chicago Press, 1963).

12. Speech delivered at the League of Nations on May 31, 1919, in H.M.V. Temperley, *A History of the Peace Conference of Paris*, vol. 5 (London: His Majesty's Printing Office, 1920), p. 130.

13. Pablo de Ascarte, "Protection of Minorities and Human Rights," *Annals of the American Academy of Political and Social Science* 243 (1946), pp. 124-28.

14. See C. A. Macartney, *National States and National Minorities* (London: Oxford University Press, 1934).

15. See Ray S. Baker and William E. Dodd, eds., *The Public Papers of Woodrow Wilson Authorized Edition: War and Peace: Presidential Messages, Addresses and Public Papers*, vol. 1 (New York: Harper and Brothers, 1925), p. 462.

16. President Wilson helped identify the national beneficiaries. See Ibid., pp. 463, 543.

17. Polish Minority Treaty, Articles 7, 8, 9. Other treaties contained nearly identical provisions.

18. Inis L. Claude, Jr., *National Minorities*, (Cambridge: Harvard University Press, 1955), p. 19.

19. Polish Minority Treaty, Articles 2, 7, 8, 12.

20. Even religious rights for minorities were dropped. See David Hunter Miller, *The Drafting of the Covenant*, vol. 2 (London: G. P. Putnam, 1928), p. 105.

21. UN Doc. E/P V/5, p. 70.

22. See Joseph Roucek, *The Working of the Minorities System and the League of Nations* (Prague: Orbis Publishing Company, 1929).

23. Ibid., pp. 93-102.

24. See Jacob Robinson, *Were the Minorities Treaties a Failure?* (New York: World Jewish Congress, 1943), p. 331.

25. Statement of Polish representative before the League Council on March 6, 1929. LN Doc. C.8 M.5. 1931. 1, p. 193.

26. See Macartney, *National States and National Minorities*, p. 491.

27. See Lucy P. Mair, *The Protection of Minorities* (London: Christophers, 1928), chapters 6 through 12.

28. See Edward Benes, "The Organization of Post-War Europe," *Foreign Affairs*, 21 (1942), p. 237.

29. U.S. Department of State, *Bulletin*, August 24, 1940, pp. 132-34; February 7, 1942, p. 128.

30. See Ruth Hersham, ed., *The American Jewish Conference: Proceedings of the Third Session* (New York: American Jewish Conference, 1946), p. 241.

31. Cited in Inis L. Claude, Jr., *National Minorities*, p. 65.

32. U.S. Department of State, *Bulletin*, June 5, 1943, p. 482.

33. UN Charter, Article 1 (2); Article 55.

34. Legal Consequences for States of the Continued Presence of South Africa in Namibia (South-West Africa) notwithstanding Security Council Resoution 276, 1970 (1971), *International Court of Justice Reports 16.*

35. *The Rights to Self-Determination* (Aureliu Cristescu, Special Rapporteur) UN Doc. E/CN 4/Sub. 2/404/ Rev. 1 (1981).

36. Yoram Dinstein, "Collective Human Rights of Peoples and Minorities," *International and Comparative Law Quarterly*, 25 (1975), p. 109.

37. 1966 International Covenant of Civil and Political Rights, Article 27.

38. 1960 Convention against Discrimination in Education, Article 5 (1) (cc).

39. UN General Assembly Resolution 3236 of 1974, 24 GAOR, Supp. (No. 30), 25.

40. Article 25, Articles of the European Convention on Human Rights, Austria,

Belgium, Denmark, France, West Germany, Ireland, Iceland, Italy, Luxembourg, The Netherlands, Norway, Sweden, Switzerland, and the United Kingdom.

41. Report on the Rights of National Minorities European Consultative Assembly, 13th Sess., Doc. No. 1299 at p. 2 (1961).

42. Rudolfo Novo, "The International Protection of National Minorities and Human Rights, *Howard Law Journal* 2 (1965) pp. 274, 290.

43. John P. Humphrey, "The United Nations Sub-Commission on the Prevention of Discrimination and the Protection of Minorities," *American Journal of International Law* 62 (1968), pp. 869-88. The 34th annual session of the Sub-Commission on the Prevention of Discrimination and Protection of Minorities, a body which reports to the UN Commission on Human Rights, met in Geneva in the summer of 1982 and again failed to grapple with any important issues. The Sub-Commission has frequently been attacked for failing to stay within its authorized guidelines as laid down by the Commission. The Minorities Sub-Commission has requested authority to conduct on-site investigations of complaints (with the consent of the country concerned) but has recently dropped even this modest proposal. Perhaps the most important activity of the Sub-Commission has been the decision to help develop guidelines on the rights of indigenous populations. However, the Sub-Commission has expressed its concern to the parent Commission in several cases of apparent gross violations of minority rights and has complained of events in Israeli occupied territories, in El Salvador, in Afghanistan, and Kampuchea.

44. Josef L. Kunz, "The Present Status of the International Law for the Protection of Minorities," *American Journal of International Law* 48 (1954), p. 282.

45. Dinstein, "Collective Human Rights," p. 117.

46. Cited in Moses Moskowitz, *International Concern with Human Rights* (Dobbs Ferry, N.Y.: Oceana Press, 1968), p. 158, a book which is particularly concerned with the failure to develop a rational minority rights policy and a rational view of human rights.

47. Ibid., p. 99.

48. One of the few new views is offered in J. J. Lador-Lederer, *International Group Protection* (Leyden, The Netherlands: A. W. Sijthoff, 1968).

49. International Convention on the Elimination of All Forms of Racial Discrimination, Part I, Article I, Section 4.

50. International Covenant on Civil and Political Rights, Part I, Article I, Section 1.

51. Ibid., Part III, Article 27.

52. Convention on the Prevention and Punishment of the Crime of Genocide, G.A. Res. 260A, 3 UN GAOR, pp. 174-77, UN Doc. A/810 (1948).

53. Reservations to the Convention on the Prevention and Punishment of the Crime of Genocide, Advisory Opinion, (1951) International Court of Justice Reports, p. 15 at p. 23.

54. In the original formulation of the Ad Hoc Committee on Genocide such "cultural genocide" was covered. The proposed Draft Convention defined genocide as including "any deliberate act committed with the intent to destroy the language, religion, or culture of a national, racial, or religious group on the grounds of national or racial origin or religious belief." 7 UN EXCOR Supp. (No.

6) 6, UN DOC. E/794 (1948). Had this language been adopted, a broad-based international recognition of minority rights would have been attained.

55. Helsinki Accords, Basket One, A, Clause VII (U. K. Cmnd. 6198). A careful analysis of this language and its significance (which may be much less than implied by the text) may be found in Harold S. Russell, "The Helsinki Declaration," *American Journal of International Law* 70 (1976), pp. 242-72.

56. Patrick Thornberry, "Is There a Phoenix in the Ashes?—International Law and Minority Rights," *Texas International Law Journal* 15 (1981), p. 458.

5

Minority Rule

IN international law a minority is usually viewed as a population group with a characteristic culture and a sense of identity that is in a subordinate political, social, or economic status. Indeed, many believe that minorities are, of necessity, in a subservient, inferior, or dependent status. Numerous societies have been based upon the rule of small elites sometimes composed of members of languages, religions, races, or castes different from those of the subject populations. These numerical minorities, whether through enslavement, military domination, imperialism, or colonialism, have maintained ascendancy over long periods of time. These types of minority rule regimes are uncommon in the modern world, but linger on in South Africa and some portions of Asia. Minority rule is an important phenomenon; it is the antithesis of minority rights, for the numerical minority actually allocates rights and privileges. Minorities need not be subservient and, as recent African experience suggests, black minorities may dominate black majorities.

Minority rule persists in the modern world as a vestige of prenationalist sentiments or as a holding action for colonialist settlers and their offspring. One of the saddest, most brutal examples of minority rule resulted in warfare in the 1950s in two African ministates, Rwanda and Burundi. In both countries a minority tribe, the Tutsi, representing only about 14 percent of the population, rules over the numerically superior Hutu. The Tutsi had invaded the region (part of the former Belgian Congo) before the fifteenth century. They subjugated the Hutu, converting the majority population into virtual serfs. At the end of World War II this long-time condition was upset by modernization and intervention by the United Nations and Belgium, the Trust Administrator. Democratic institutions were introduced. Parties emerged. Eventually bloody civil war broke out. In Rwanda, at least, the Tutsi minority rule was shattered.[1] Nationalism, Western ideals, and modernization destroyed the basis of minority rule, repeating a process that had taken place in Europe a century or two before. In southern Africa minority rule clearly derives from other impulses. We shall return to these examples.

SLAVERY

The ancient world generally practiced slavery. Egyptian slaves built the pyramids. Slaves toiled in Babylonia, Persia, and all over the civilized world. Even Athens, at its height of glory, was supported by slaves who worked for its free citizenry. While ancient slavery was not accompanied by race prejudice, it was rarely benign, and in most cases, as in ancient Greece, it rested upon the power of a minority; even Athenian democracy itself rested somewhat upon minority rule, although experts disagree as to the extent and scope of Athenian slavery.[2]

Plato argued against the enslavement of Greeks. Most Athenian slaves probably were Greeks obtained through conquest and war. Plato condemns the practice—but only as it applied to Greeks.[3] Even so, Plato regards slaves as having inferior, undeveloped minds, as a different and lower order of beings.[4] Apart from the issue of enslaving other fellow Greeks, Plato accepted the conventional view of slavery prevalent in Greece and elsewhere to justify subjugation of a majority by a more potent minority.

Aristotle more consciously developed the notion of minority rule supported by slavery. Free citizens would be a minority in the city because they must be free to be active participants in politics. Essentially, "for Aristotle, citizenship is the privileged status of the ruling group, able to practice the good life and therefore learn more about it, and free to do so only because it is a leisured class."[5] Aristotle was able to justify this position with the argument that slaves are unfitted to rule themselves and are necessarily dependent. Aristotle also contended that many men were slaves by nature because they lacked the ability to reason and benefitted from subjection to a master who was better able to make reasoned judgments.[6]

In ancient Greece no slave ever held public office or sat on a council or a jury. The majority of slaves were non-Greeks. The main sources of supply were war and piracy. Captives, usually barbarians, were enslaved and sold on an open slave market. So-called Greek democracy did not discourage slavery. On the contrary, "the cities in which individual freedom reached its highest expression—most obviously Athens—were cities in which chattel slavery flourished."[7] The minority ruled and the majority were enslaved or were unrepresented.[8]

Slaves were never in a numerical majority in ancient Greece or Rome, but they were the largest fraction of the unrepresented populations.

Minority rule was based on a number of disenfranchising conditions, but slaves, together with women and noncitizens, were always without political voice. The political power of the ancient world rested largely in the hands of free, male citizens, who rarely were concerned that they formed a minority of the populaton.

Slavery continued into the nineteenth and twentieth century, when it was isolated in smaller, backward areas. Burmese ascendancy in Assam led to the enslavement of Assamese in the early nineteenth century. These slaves formed the bulk of the population in various villages throughout what is now modern Burma. Slavery persists today, it is said, in the Sudan and parts of Saudi Arabia and once flourished under the early Ottoman Empire. But the mass enslavement and subjugation of a conquered people by external invaders has virtually disappeared in the modern world. Slave states, the most arbitrary form of minority rule, were never prevalent, but they have now ceased to exist.

INEQUALITY AND ELITE RULE

All human societies have been marked by social differentiation and inequality. The division of labor among men produces a series of graded distinctions in social ranks. Even modern political democracies exhibit social stratification and social inequality. However, modern democracies, based as they are upon the formal equality of all individuals, deny the legitimacy of political inequality. This modern, democratic commitment to formal political equality is less than 150 years old. Prior to modern times all societies were based upon some form of elite rule, whether by aristocrats, kings, classes, castes, or conquerors. In a sense all premodern societies accepted political inequality and the rule of some kind of elite. In that sense minority rule has been the norm in human history, while political equality has been an exception.

Elite political minorities have been prevalent in the governance of almost all political institutions. Only utopians, radicals, and political opportunists deny this fact of political life.[9] The history of political philosophy provides many rationalizations for one or another form of minority rule. Plato justifies the rule of the intelligent; Thomas Hobbes proposes a sovereign Leviathan; John Calvin glorifies his church; Karl Marx extols the proletariat and its temporary dictatorship. John Locke describes a majority principle, but it may be a legislative majority or a majority of adult males. Thomas Jefferson argued that a majority of Americans should formulate public policy, but he didn't include slaves or women in his calculations. Few modern democrats recall the brief history of majority rule and fewer still would admit the fragility of the principle in operation.

For most societies minority rule has been virtually unquestioned. Indeed, it is doubtful whether either rulers or ruled thought much about the matter until the rise of the modern state and the later rise of capitalist democracies. The unequal distribution of political power was virtually a part of the natural order. If there was any question, it was which minority should rule; church or king, army or nobility, one dynasty or another, the Red Rose of Lancaster or the White Rose of York. Most men were mere pawns and peasants during such struggles. They were indifferent to the outcome, since they would, in any event, be relatively powerless.[10] Feudalism was probably a result of a form of militarism, but it provided a firm hierarchy of minority domination.

An elite ruling group may derive authority from military power, ownership of land, conquest, religious belief, factory ownership, or from a political party. In premodern societies it is fairly easy to locate the source of authority, but in modern societies it is frequently very difficult to discern which group, if any, dominates. Because of this dispersion of political power and authority in modern, democratic states, minority rule rarely is evident, yet many observers of democracies find that even they exhibit signs of elite dominance, of minority rule.[11]

In the past most people were classified as elite or nonelite according to their parentage. There was a Spartiate caste in Sparta, Eupatridae in Athens, and Brahmans in India. First-born sons of royalty and noblemen had a natural claim to elite status. In simpler societies accidents of birth sometimes conferred elite status.[12] Birth and parentage are important sources of social power in the modern world, especially in societies in which caste and class are significant. Monarchy, of course, usually rested upon parentage, but even after the decline of monarchial institutions, elite authority through parentage remains a potent force in the world, a force for minority dominance, if not minority rule.

Education has also provided the basis for elite political dominance. The Inca nobility preserved its elite status by means of a system of education reserved exclusively for the nobility. The Inca Empire provided noble students with information on religion, laws, customs, and the arts of governance. Poetry, music, philosophy, and astrology were in the curriculum. Military training was emphasized so as to aid in the repression of the peasantry.[13] The use of education to perpetuate elite rule, frequently coupled with a denial of education to the subservient masses, has continued to modern times.

History also discloses some remarkable examples of the emergence of new elites from an earlier condition of servitude. Perhaps the best example is provided by the Mamelukes, a warrior caste who were dominant in Egypt and sometimes elsewhere in the Middle East for over 700 years. The Mamelukes were originally non-Arab slaves used as soldiers by their Arab masters. Gradually the Mameluke soldiers became powerful enough to unseat their Arab masters. By 1250 Aybak, the first Mameluke to actually become a ruler, was able to force the mother of the last Arab sultan to marry him after she had murdered her own son. The Mamelukes were not fully defeated until the Turks bested them in the sixteenth century. Mameluke governors retained vast regional powers until Napoleon eventually defeated them during his 1798 invasion of Egypt.

Probably the most impressive example of minority rule in history is provided by the Aryans of India. Sometime around 1500 B.C. the Aryans invaded the Indus civilization of northern India. For 2,000 years they ruled in numerous kingdoms. Maintaining a cultural separatism by means of a well-developed caste system, the Aryans gradually created a whole new civilization.

Cultural assimilation eventually defeats a conquering minority. The Norman invasion of Great Britain (eleventh century) resulted in a superimposition of a Norman aristocracy on the English and the rise of a new elite, which brought with it Norman feudalism. Norman French became the language of the upper classes. However, in a few centuries Normans and English had emerged into a distinctive new culture.

In modern times elite rule is rarely based upon culture or language. Economic status, party, and social position may be more significant than family, religion, or even race. Military cliques, dictatorial parties, major corporations, and economic classes provide the pools from which modern elites are usually drawn. The decade of great conquering empires imposing their alien culture on a vastly more numerous but defeated foe has passed. Nationalism and the urge for self-government are usually too strong to permit direct rule by a occupying minority. Perhaps nazism, with its doctrine of elite Aryan dominance, was the last effort to deliberately promote direct minority rule.

Probably South Africa is the only major modern example of direct, intentional minority rule. Rhodesia has passed away. But these nations are so distinctive as to require separate and detailed consideration. Their deliberate effort to retain elite, minority power requires explanation and elaboration.

COLONIAL ELITES

Imperialism, as a phrase, has been reduced to a catchword. The vigorous pursuit of adjacent territory has been a constant feature of world history. Dominion over territory after successful conquest was a policy of Egyptians, Babylonians, Persians, Medes, Greeks, Aryans, Mongols, and countless other peoples pressing against their neighbors and sometimes conquering them and ruling over them. The empires of history were often warrior nations that were usually based upon force. Thus, "a will for broad conquest without tangible limits, for the capture of positions that were manifestly untenable—this was typical imperialism'' in the ancient world and for a period extending into the fifteenth century age of European discovery.[14] Booty and tributes were extracted from the conquered peoples, but nationalism was absent. Conquered peoples retained their religion, culture, and language (with some exceptions, as in the religious imperialism of the Arab conquests in the name of Allah and Mohammed), but for the most part old-style imperialism did not usually create a new social order with new elites drawn from the conquering peoples. Modern imperialism and colonialism had that impact. Unlike premodern imperialism, the dominant powers of recent centuries have created new elites. We live in an age of the collapse of these colonial elites. Colonialist minority rule is dead or nearly so, even though imperialism of another sort is very much alive.

Irrational expansionism was the hallmark of premodern imperialism. Roman imperialism eventually threatened the stability of the domestic political scene, but it continued inexorably and aimlessly until it collapsed.[15] Eventually, the elite corps of the soldiery, the Praetorians, determined the rise and fall of the emperors. In seventeenth- and eighteenth-century Europe, the absolute monarchs pursued a policy of personal aggrandizement intended to stamp out the feudal nobility and to centralize power in the hands of the king. The policy succeeded in Spain, France, and parts of Germany, where a centralized state was created under the military and political dominance of the crown.[16] But this kind of imperialism was not colonialist in nature. The absolute monarchs succeeded where the Romans had failed. They created viable, large-scale governing units. The product of monarchial aggrandizement was not an empire, it was a state. Some of these states themselves launched colonialist ventures. In many ways colonialism depended upon the prior existence of a state. It is not coincidental that the European colonies in the Western Hemisphere were launched at a time just after European states were being formed.

Modern imperialism has been defined as ''that consciously undertaken state activity in which force, intrigue, or even negotiation is employed to secure the long-range political or economic domination by the state of foreign territory or foreign peoples it wishes for some reason to control.''[17] Modern imperialism did not depend solely upon war and it was not purposeless. It proceeded from familiar state policies, which were intended to benefit the mother country. The ''imperialist sponsor—individual group, or class—is aware of and committed to its activities, which it invariably undertakes in the name of the state.''[18] Imperialism of this sort was principally a European activity during the past four centuries, but Asian imperialism also existed, as the defeat of the Japanese in World War II amply illustrates. In some ways the Eastern

European Communist states may be perceived as another chapter in Western imperialism, although the definition has been extended slightly to encompass the available facts.[19]

The initial European impulse toward foreign dominations was for gold, silver, and spices. The Spanish conquest and subjugation of Peru is a classic example. In 1532 Francisco Pizarro arrived on the Peruvian coast with a small band of adventurers. Pizarro encountered another empire, the Incas who held sway over large parts of South America. Pizarro met and imprisoned the Inca emperor, Atahualpa, who had refused to accept Spanish suzerainty or Christianity. The emperor's followers gathered a hugh ransom in gold and silver to procure his release, but to no avail. Atahualpa was executed and Pizarro went on to capture Cuzco, the Inca capital, and the Inca Empire disintegrated. In 1542 Pizarro founded Lima as the Spanish capital, and Lima became the center for Spanish rule in the New World. After a series of unsuccessful revolts, the defeated (majority) Indians were put to work in the gold and silver mines. Spanish landlords acquired titles to vast estates and they, too, put the Indians to work. Spanish galleons carried away the gold and silver from their colonies back to Spain. The defeated majority Indians and Creoles (those of Spanish descent born in Peru) were rendered powerless and poor, while Spanish royal power was extended into the New World.[20] Minority rule had arrived but not for the first time in the Americas. Aztecs and Incas had once ruled slave empires of Indian subjects.

The British, Dutch, and French East India companies exhibited a new and special kind of imperial development, a quasi-private national trading imperialism. Queen Elizabeth of England chartered the British East India Company in 1600. The company was composed of a group of merchants who gradually procured trade privileges that yielded large profits. The British East India Company began to intervene more and more in political affairs, especially in India. Ultimately the British government itself assumed more direct responsibilities for the administration of British affairs in India, setting up a board of control for India. This indirect, quasi-private imperialism was based upon the private pursuit of profit. In France economic activity was subservient to the state's interest in power. Louis XIV's devoted finance minister, Jean-Baptiste Colbert, pursued a conscious policy of national imperial development that was to become the model of European imperialism until the nineteenth century. Mercantilism or "Colbertism" was based on the principle that national power was based upon the national accumulation of wealth. For the Spanish imperial wealth meant New World gold and silver. For Colbert and his successor's national wealth meant a favorable balance of trade, the predominance of exports over imports. For this purpose Colbert encouraged and planned the French East India Company for the purpose of trading in the East. In Colbert's day the chief idea was to transport all French merchandise in French ships and to retain an exclusive trading relationship between the mother country and the colony. Ideally, the French East India Company was to acquire colonies. Failing that, it was to acquire trade monopolies and preferences. Minority rule would be more indirect, less obvious.

English mercantilism was similar. The English colonies in the New World were perceived to be a source of raw materials to be transported on English ships back to the mother country where, after being manufactured into finished goods, they would become English exports to the rest of the world. Thus, the American colonists were discouraged from manufacturing even rum or cloth. The discouragement of manufacturing in America, the requirements of an exclusive trading relationship between the American colonies and Great Britain, and harsh English enforcement policies help lead to the American Revolution, the first, modern successful anti-imperialist rebellion. Yet in America, the native Indians did not fit into the system.

The American colonies were an example of imperial settlement policies similar to those used by Spain in settling their lands in the New World during the sixteenth and seventeenth centuries.[21] The colonists moved into marginal lands sometimes displacing the native populations, sometimes slaughtering them. Emigrants came as a distinct minority and gradually pushed out the indigenous people who became a numerical or a virtual minority.[22] The French, Dutch, and Swedes attempted settlements in North America, but none persisted. The friction between colonist and homeland grew in time. Eventually every New World settlement erupted in rebellion. The empires of settlement created a host of problems of minority group relationships in the newly independent states, but the European states learned a lesson in imperialism. Settlement imperial policies are extremely costly to maintain and, as transportation and communications technologies improved, settlement as a means of imperialism was replaced by a newer form of imperialism resting firmly upon colonialism without settlement.

The empires of settlement were gradually abandoned as the European powers came to the realization that mercantilist policies were not benefitting their national interest. The first French colonial empire ended in 1763, while Spain and Portugal lost South America in the early 1820's. The first British empire ended in 1783, although the loss of the American colonies delivered substantial benefits to English foreign trade. The unending accumulation of gold and silver proved a foolish national policy, and the single-minded pursuit of a favorable balance of trade required a national regulation of production and distribution that only hampered the accumulation of capital in private hands. In effect, industrial production as a form of wealth depended upon free markets and laissez-faire, at least that was the gospel according to Adam Smith, the patron saint of the new age of capitalism.

Adam Smith's *Wealth of Nations* was published in 1776, a fateful year in world history. The American Revolution in the same year was, in many ways, a protocapitalist revolution. The American colonists wanted to develop their "infant industries," although the colonial system discouraged it. The artifical regulation of imports and exports led to outbursts like the Boston Tea Party and to protests over taxation without representation. But the American Revolution was also a blow against the old imperial economy, and it was supported by many members of the British Parliament partly because they were infected by the new liberal doctrines of freer trade, which became best explained and rationalized by Adam Smith and later by Richard Cobden. The English remained virtually alone in the empire business after 1815 and, for more than a century thereafter there were no important colonial rivalries. Imperialism seemed almost dead.

Suddenly, in the period between 1870 and 1900, most of the European powers became deeply involved in imperialist policies. France, Germany, Belgium, Portugal, Italy, and others expanded their colonial interests or made new colonial claims. None could match the British Empire, upon which the sun never set. Even the Americans, having spread themselves from the Atlantic to the Pacific, pursued imperialist policies. Belatedly the Japanese launched some ventures, to their great sorrow. Australia and New Zealand found a few islands to their liking. This new imperialism was one of the great events in world history.[23] New imperialism gave rise to widespread minority rule by distant colonial administrators and their indigenous agents. New imperialism created the artificial national boundaries within which new minorities were formed.

New imperialism became the subject of lively and bitter political disputes ever since. Lenin called it "the monopoly stage of capitalism," the last phase of capitalism prior to the revolution. Since Karl Marx died in 1883, long prior to the full development of imperialism, we do not know the correct Marxist view of overseas expansionism. Joseph A. Schumpeter regarded imperialism as an aberration, as an atavism, and as not a necessary feature of capitalism. Debate still rages abut the sources of the imperialist impulse, but regardless of the theoretical debate, imperialism has been discredited, and the term is now one of approbation and condemnation. No nation can openly and honorably pursue a policy of imperialism today.

Even conservative capitalist writers condemn and criticize imperialism. The criticism began to mount with the 1902 publication of J. A. Hobson's *Imperialism*.[24] Hobson vividly argued that Great Britain's absorption in maintaining her colonial possessions and obtaining new possessions was not worth the cost in terms of money, energy, and blood. Imperialism was bad business policy, and it did not provide a genuine outlet for so-called surplus population. Hobson observed that there was no true

British settlement in tropical climes. The use of national power to secure new markets by annexing fresh tracts of territory was regarded as an unsound policy for an advanced industrial country. Lenin took Hobson's argument several steps further by concluding that the new imperialism was a form of capitalist suicide, capitalism's highest, final stage.[25]

Regardless of the linkage between capitalism and imperialism, their is little doubt that "imperialism is, in a sense, synonymous with the appropriation by the Western nations of the largest part of the rest of the world."[26] This appropriation led directly to the most massive example of minority rule in world history. Never before had so many people come under the political control of so few people. The new imperialism provides the best example of minority rule. With the decay of that imperialism, minority rule has become a rarity, unless one describes certain Communist states as another form of new imperialism, or unless one accepts a Leninist view of finance capital in its penultimate phase.

The social, psychological, economic, and political sources of new imperialism are much debated and little understood. However, nationalism was clearly a major factor. European countries, many of which had themselves been recently unified, attempted to express their newfound national sentiments through expansionism. Germany, Italy, and even Belgium were latecomers to imperialism because they were newer nations. Cecil Rhodes and Henry Livingston were British heroes because they glorified the sense of British nationality. In its American version, imperialism was celebrated in theory by Josiah Strong[27] and practiced, among others, by Theodore Roosevelt. The net effect of the heightened sense of nationalism was a sense of cultural superiority, coupled quite naturally with a sense of mission. Of course, the subject majorities were denied their nationhood.

Racialist themes were also prevalent in the new imperialism. This racialism was another pretext for minority rule when the poet-laureate of imperialism, Rudyard Kipling, called upon his brethren to "take up the white man's burden" and "serve your captive's need." He justified this because "your new-caught, sullen peoples" were "half-devil and half-child."[28] Colonialism had existed in the past without regard to skin color, but the new imperialism often resulted in a few white men ruling over large numbers of dark-skinned peoples. Indeed, for many whites that was its prime function.

Another explanation for the outburst of the new imperialism was the competitive drives of the leaders of the European nations. When Prince Bernhard von Bülow, the German foreign minister, said "we do not want to put anyone in the shade, but we demand a place for ourselves in the sun," he clearly expressed the envy of the newly unified Germans for a share of the uncolonized world. The map of Africa became varicolored as the competing European powers staked their claims. In

Asia, too, the Europeans carved out their zones and spheres of influence. Europeans, armed with modern weaponry and moved by rapid transportation, were technologically far superior to native Africans and Asians. Their competitive lust for empire was irresistible.

The key element in the new imperialism was its organization. When the British government supplanted the private East India Company, it gave great attention to constructing a thin layer of top administrators through whom India was to be governed. A bureaucratic tradition was developed for the administration of overseas territories. Virtually every European imperialist power followed suit. With considerable variation, every European state established a chain of command extending from a central ministry in charge of colonies to a governor in the colony. The governor was served by one or two levels of provincial administration, which supervised the local districts in which orders were carried into practice. Administrative functions were usually divided among the ministries as in Europe: army, justice, health, education, and so on.[29]

The pattern of rule placed a handful of Europeans in charge of a huge native population, which itself was divided into many cultures, groups, and factions. All the nineteenth-century empires depended upon the cooperation of native officials or at least a locally recruited staff of subordinates. The French tended to rule more directly than the English, but in practice there were too few Europeans to rule over the natives. Consequently, native traditional chiefs, sultans, kings, and regents were placed in the colonial employ whenever possible.

Doubtless, many European powers changed their motives over time. Uplift of the native population and improvement of the economy were sometimes by-products of imperialism. In many colonies education was provided and notions of self-government were, at least, discussed and considered. But in the final view the new empires were administrative and expropriative in nature. They were based upon minority rule and suppressed, discouraged, or merely ignored the native populations for the most part.

European residence in most colonies was minimal. Only Algeria, South Africa, and Rhodesia received sizable numbers of European immigrants. Most European residence was temporary anyway, and a sense of detachment from the indigenous populations was widespread. Europeans remained detached from native society. In colonial India the English made the barriers clear in their clubs and social life. Further, the English lived on the high ground, the Hindus below.[30] Minority rule was institutionalized in the community life of the empires.[31]

By World War I many of the European colonies were on the brink of revolution. In India a great riot broke out on April 13, 1919, which resulted in the killing of over 400 Indians by British gunfire. When the incident was investigated, it was revealed that under martial law the

British General Dyer had issued his infamous "crawling order." This order required that no Indians should pass on a certain street where a white woman had been attacked. If Indians wanted to pass on that street "they must go on all fours, and pickets were placed at certain points to enforce obedience to this order."[32]

By the end of World War II imperialism was in disarray. Within a decade after the end of the war, virtually all European empires had vanished. Portugal and Spain held out the longest, but eventually Mozambique, Angola, and the Spanish Sahara gained their independence. Decolonization was often the result of warfare, as in Indonesia, Indochina, and Algeria. Violence in Malaya, Kenya, and the Belgian Congo helped speed independence. Elsewhere European powers, exhausted by their wartime struggles with each other, "voluntarily" relinquished their colonial holdings. Colonial elites, the ruling Europeans and their native agents, were replaced by nationalist leaders. A new elite had arisen, but an elite grounded in the people of the region, an "elite which rose in response to the colonial presence," not an alien minority elite.[33]

The postcolonial elites in Africa and Asia were largely educated in the West. They were sons of the native bourgeoisie who had entered into business and law. They converted the colonial administrative system into a representative political system. Independence from colonialism did not usually give rise to political democracy, but it did end alien minority rule and put in its place representative national leaders.[34] Unfortunately, the boundaries for the newly independent countries had been drawn rather arbitrarily by the European powers, giving rise to problems of national integration and minority group relations that still plague many of these former colonial states.

MINORITY RULE IN SOUTH AFRICA

The Republic of South Africa, which stands out as the world's leading contemporary example of minority rule, cannot be explained merely in terms of the heritage of colonialism and imperialism. Racial separatism is an old story in South Africa, and minority rule has been prevalent for centuries. White Afrikaners, descendents of Dutch immigrants, cling to a privileged position that effectively excludes blacks from political life and renders white descendants of the English virtually powerless.

In South Africa four million whites (or probably fewer) have political power, while 20 million blacks have no voice in national government. Slightly less than half the black population lives in black reserves, called Bantustans, while the other half lives in cities. The urbanized blacks pose a particularly great threat to white minority rule, since they live close to the areas of white population and greatly outnumber the whites. No one knows exactly how many blacks live in the crowded slums on the edge of predominately white Johannesburg. Other minorities, the Indians and the mixed breed coloured population, also are denied full political rights and are segregated in industry, education and home life from the dominant whites.

Minority white rule in South Africa is a unique phenomenon (save Rhodesia until Zimbabwe was created). There are other authoritarian regimes in the world. There are more brutal dictatorships. There are even more repressive regimes. But in no other nation is the principle of minority rule so glorified. Nowhere else is the minority so firmly in control, in spite of its cultural and ethnic position as a minority.

The first European settlement in South Africa was made in 1652 by the Dutch East India Company at Tabler Bay on the Cape of Good Hope. The early Dutch immigrants brought in their own cattle and private agriculture, leading to conflicts with the nomadic Hottentot tribes. The Dutch farmers pushed further away from Cape Town and extended their farmlands further into the countryside. Gradually, the Hottentots were converted into herdsmen and laborers for the Dutch. Slavery was also introduced; by 1701 there were 1,780 freeholders of European descent (including 200 Huguenot refugees) and 1,100 slaves.

Separatism was the policy almost from the beginning. Hottentots were not subject to Dutch law. The Bushmen (San) were driven off the newly acquired white man's grazing lands. The Bantu people were to the north and east of the original Dutch settlements. They were 600 miles away from Cape Town, separated from the whites by the barrier of the Great Fish River.

The white farmers (known as Boers) had become a distinct culture by the mid-eighteenth century. In this protracted warfare against the black Xhosa, the whites gained control over more and more territory, which they settled, having expelled the blacks.

Boer separatism was an old practice and policy. When the British replaced the Dutch at the Cape, separatism was retained as a British policy. While the British called for better treatment of the Coloured and black Africans who served the Boers as workers, servants, and slaves, they still attempted to keep the blacks and whites apart. In 1819 Lord Charles Somerset, the British governor of the Cape, entered into a treaty with the native chief, Gaika, which established the first separate black Bantustan territory.[35]

British colonial policy in South Africa was aimed at resistance to Boer expansionism, but between 1835 and 1843 a Boer migration from the Cape Colony took place. This migration of Dutch farmers, known as "the Great Trek" brought the Boers into conflicts with the Zulus. The Boers established their farms and formed their own republics of Transvaal and the Orange Free State. In doing so, native lands were taken and white farmers converted the indigenous blacks into laborers and worse.

British efforts to control the Boers failed until the South African (Boer) War of 1899-1902, which resulted in the Boers defeat. Concessions were made to appease the Boers but none proved successful. Indeed, Afrikaner nationalism grew apace until the bonds of the commonwealth itself were broken. For in spite of their defeat by the British, the Afrikaners hold most of the political power and form the core of the ruling white minority.

The triumph of Afrikaner nationalism did not arrive until after World War II. Afrikaner nationalism shattered the compromise which created the Union of South Africa as a member of the British Commonwealth and instituted the basic policies of racial segregation and separatism for which South Africa is best known.

When the National Party came to power in 1948, it took steps to institute a frankly racist policy to uphold and strengthen the minority rule of whites, but particularly of Afrikaners who compose most of the membership of the party. The party was not only anti-black, it was also anti-Asian, anti-coloured, and somewhat anti-English. The consolidation of Afrikaner rule seemed its prime goal.

The coloured group was removed from the common roll, meaning that they were stripped of their vote in the national government. Instead, they were given greater autonomy over their own affairs through a Council for Coloured Affairs, which was supposedly to help the group maintain its "ethnic identity." The same "autonomy" was given the Indian community through an essentially advisory Indian Council. Eventually, the blacks were given so-called homelands while the coloureds, having no homeland, were given a "brown parliament," the Coloured People's Representative Council, in place of the representation they formerly had (through white members) in the central parliament.

Racial segregation and separation had existed in South Africa prior to 1948, but not to the extent and scope with which it is still practiced. Daniel F. Malan included his policy of apartheid in the Afrikaner Nationalist party platform. Initially, the government applied separatist policies to the urban areas. To accomplish strict separation, a large number of Asians and coloured citizens were forced to relocate out of so-called white areas. Black Africans (called Bantus by the government) were removed beyond the borders of the cities into new townships leaving most cities to the whites.

Almost all social relations are subject to the conditions of apartheid. In particular, the blacks have been victims of this policy by being assigned to separate homelands, rather than being treated as full citizens. Each of the black (Bantu) groups was to be assigned a homeland. About 14 percent of South Africa's territory has been set aside for such homelands. The policy of separate development, used to justify the creation of the homelands, gives the cities and the major populated areas to the whites. Black Africans have some rights as citizens of their homelands, but they may be treated as virtual aliens within South Africa. Movements of black Africans are carefully monitored through an elaborate pass system. African residence is regulated, employment is controlled, and blacks do not vote. The cynicism of this policy becomes evident when it is seen in practice. Third and fourth generation urban blacks are closely identified with their so-called homelands. All Africans living outside their homelands are subject to strict curfew and pass regulations, the violation of which results in prompt arrests. Much more could be said about apartheid and "separate development," but both are clearly designed to perpetuate minority rule.[36] The policies have succeeded, but at great cost in lives and tension.[37]

The ruling white minority is well entrenched, but growing restive after the collapse of the Portuguese colonies in Angola and Mozambique. The Dutch Reformed Churches, the Nationalist party, and the military have a firm grip on the country. Every prime minister since 1948 has been an Afrikaner Nationalist. Given the demographic situation, some modification of strict race separation has taken place. South Africa is no longer a racial despotism; separate development has been questioned, although tentatively. The ruling whites have not hit upon a better formula for minority rule, but they are looking for one. Some form of pluralism or power sharing in which whites might still predominate would, possibly, be considered, although Afrikaner intellectuals are vague about the details. However, majority rule is out. No substantial body of white opinion exists to support a surrender of power to the majority. Minority rule will persist until events force a reconsideration of that most fundamental South African ruling principle. Federation of the Bantustans or confederation with them may be possible, but then only as a last resort. White rule and ethnic exclusivity are the bases for life in South Africa today. Riots and brutal repression still seem able to suppress black African discontent. Blacks seem to want majority rule but they are prevented from organizing for it in a setting that dampens all non-Afrikaner political action.[38]

CONSTITUTIONAL MINORITY RULE: ZIMBABWE/RHODESIA

Zimbabwe/Rhodesia is just north of the Republic of South Africa. A pure product of nineteenth century colonialism, Rhodesia was ruled for over eighty years by a small group of white settlers. Now, in the wake of black majoritarian drives that have triumphed elsewhere in Africa, the white elite is seeking to preserve some of its long-held privileges by means of constitutional arrangements. Minority rule has ended in Rhodesia, but the transition from minority rule to black dominance has not been easy. There is still the possibility that minority rule will persist until violently terminated, but the minority could be a black minority element of the black majority.

White rule in Rhodesia succeeded a series of various black states which themselves were the results of conquest. At the time of the white incursion into Rhodesia, a military state existed in the southwest of the territory occupied by the Ndebele, Mzilakazi, the king of this warrior group, had concluded a treaty of friendship with Britain as early as 1836. The death of King Mzilakazi in 1868 coincided with European discoveries of gold in Southern Rhodesia, whetting the British appetite for more territory. The impulsive adventurer Cecil Rhodes fulfilled the British dream of a white dominance in South Africa by launching a series of invasions which toppled all of the black kingdoms that occupied the territory now know as Zimbabwe/Rhodesia.

Rhodes and the British succeeded in the colonization of one of the last areas of Africa still under native rule. In 1870 less than one-tenth of Africa was under European rule. By 1890, with the white invasion of Rhodesia, nine-tenths of Africa was placed under white rule. Moreover, Cecil Rhodes succeeded where the Portuguese had failed. The conquest of the various black kingdoms of Zimbabwe/Rhodesia by a millionaire white imperialist closed a chapter in European history. Rhodesia was the last European white colony in Africa.

Cecil Rhodes, while a member of the parliament of the Cape Colony, organized the British South Africa Company. In 1889 he received a charter from the British government for the private settlement and colonization of the region of Zimbabwe/Rhodesia. Leander Starr Jameson, an associate of Rhodes, led a column of whites deep into the interior, eventually defeating the Ndebele and occupying their territories. Rhodes, who had been politically discredited in South Africa, turned his attention to the development of the country that bore his name.

The social and political attitudes of Cecil Rhodes helped entrench white minority rule in Rhodesia. Rhodes believed that the Anglo-Saxon race and the British Empire had a special destiny. The British government itself was reluctant to extend the Empire into the territory, but Rhode's vision prevailed. Rhodes gained and retained the support of the British governing classes for his ventures. Even the looting of the defeated Ndebele and the theft of their lands was tolerated by a British government which at the time shared Rhodes's view of white British supremacy.[39]

By the end of 1898 the major instruments of white rule were in place. There was a legislative council with a minority of elected members. The franchise was limited by property and monetary qualifications that eliminated most Africans. The literacy requirement, in particular, had this effect. A Native Affairs Department was established to be responsible for governmental relations with Africans. Legislation was passed providing for the control of Africans in urban areas. Land reserves for Africans were created. All this was accomplished "at the time when Britain had a complete control of legislation."[40]

For eighty years the white settlers entrenched and strengthened their position. In form minority rule appeared to be democratic and nonracial. The franchise was based upon criteria of education and wealth. The voters' roll was kept almost exclusively white between 1898 and 1969.[41] In 1908 only 50 native voters were enrolled. In 1928 there were 62 African and 22,000 European voters. In 1939 there were 39 African voters, and in the 1948 election 136 Africans were registered. Even by 1969, when Ian Smith and the Rhodesian Front abolished the common voters' roll, there were fewer than 560 African enrolled voters. British rule supported a form of minority rule in Rhodesia. By the time of the 1961 Rhodesian Constitution, electoral reforms allowed 5,127 Africans to vote in an electorate of 88,820. That was the best the British could do for Rhodesian democracy.[42]

Africans in British-ruled Rhodesia were not without a government. They were administered separately by a special government department. The Ministry of Internal Affairs (formerly Native Affairs) was entirely controlled by whites and responsible only to the white elected government. The Ministry made little pretense of being representative of the African majority. Minority rule was greatest in rural areas where whites were outnumbered eighty to one. Movement to industrial areas was tightly controlled by elaborate rules to restrict freedom for Africans.

The franchise was the key issue in Rhodesian history. When the break with England finally came about in 1969, the die was cast. There would be no majority rule in Rhodesia. All the efforts of the English to alter their traditional policy supporting minority rule in Rhodesia were in vain. When threatened with the prospect of a gradual transition to African majority rule, the white settlers united behind Ian Smith and the Rhodesian Front and cut their ties with Britain and the Commonwealth.

In 1953 Southern Rhodesia became a member of a new federation of Rhodesia and Nyasaland, despite the objections of Africans to a new British-created, white-dominated federal structure. Only 429 Africans were eligible to vote in the referendum which created the short-lived federation. By 1964 the federation was dissolved, and Ian Smith was prime minister of Southern Rhodesia. African majority governments were formed in former Northern Rhodesia and in Nyasaland (renamed Malawi). Ian Smith's Rhodesian Front party swept the 1965 elections. The Smith government proclaimed a unilateral declaration of independence on November 11, 1965.

Britain called the 1965 declaration an act of rebellion but refused to apply force to reestablish control. After the breakdown of negotiations in 1966, Britain requested United Nations economic sanctions against

Rhodesia. On March 2, 1970, Rhodesia became a self-proclaimed independent republic. Its Constitution provided for complete separation of the franchise along openly racial lines. Minority rule was preserved, in spite of belated British support for eventual majority rule, and independence was sought largely because of the issue.

Britain continued to refuse to recognize Rhodesian independence until 1979 when, as a result of constitutional changes engineered by a conservative British government, a form of black majority rule had been translated into one of protected white minority rights.

By 1979 the white-ruled Smith regime receded into history with the election of a black prime minister, Bishop Abel Muzorewa. Black majority rule was disputable because so many powers were reserved under the 1969 Constitution to white voters. Moreover, a protracted civil war was still under way when the 1979 elections were held. Black rebels contended that majority rule was a fraud and the Constitution a farce.

The recent constitutional history of Rhodesia merits special attention. Under pressure, both diplomatic and military, the Ian Smith regime yielded its exclusive hold on governmental power in Rhodesia. The 1975 collapse of Portuguese rule in neighboring Mozambique seemed to produce a grudging white acceptance of the inevitability of its loss of exclusive power. Constitutional provisions were created to create some sort of transition away from strict minority rule.

The 1961 Southern Rhodesian Constitution marked a first step toward encouraging the black majority, but minority rule was preserved. African representation in the legislature was guaranteed. In the 65-member legislature, 50 seats were elected from European constituencies and 15 from newly created African electoral districts. Thus, Southern Rhodesia conceded some representation to the previously unrepresented majority. The British government was committed to some form of representation for Africans. However, dissatisfaction with minority rule precipitated a violent reaction by some black leaders, while many Europeans also rejected the Constitution because they feared increased African nationalism. The white Rhodesians chose to write their own constitution in an independent, white-ruled Rhodesia.

Constitutional disputes between Britain and her rebellious colony continued from 1965 until 1979. Britain never accepted Rhodesian independence and regarded every Rhodesian self-proclaimed constitution as illegitimate. Prime Minister Harold Wilson pressed the Ian Smith regime for a better constitutional settlement that would move the country toward majority rule. In 1968 the Whaley Commission made recommendations for a system that would produce eventual parity between whites and blacks. However, the resultant 1969 Constitution of Rhodesia cleverly preserved the essence of minority rule while giving the appearance of equal black representation.

The 1969 Constitution created a two-house legislature. The lower house, the House of Assembly, has much greater authority than the Senate, which has only a suspensory veto, which can be overridden in the Assembly. The 66-member Assembly had 50 European seats, ensuring white dominance. In the weak Senate blacks had a parity of representation. The 1969 Constitution provided for an increase in African representation in the House of Assembly amounting to eventual parity, but this was dependent upon an increase in income tax paid by Africans. The 1969 Constitution also seemed to permit racially discriminatory legislation when required in the interests of "harmonious relations" or for the "security of the state."

Britain, finding strong African objections to the 1969 Constitution, continued to withhold recognition of Rhodesian independence. Upon British insistence the Smith regime made some minor concessions by constitutional amendments in 1974 and 1976. The amendments failed to satisfy the British or the radical Africans who turned to terrorist raids to unseat the Smith regime. Finally, after intervention by U.S Secretary of State Henry Kissinger and South African Prime Minister Vorster late in 1976, the Smith regime proclaimed that it would accept majority rule in two years, conditional upon the dropping of sanctions and the end of terrorism. In 1977 Ian Smith again agreed to work toward majority rule, this time after joint British and American pressure.

Finally, in 1978 the white leadership met with three internalist black nationalist groups and agreed to set up an interim government leading to black control. An agreement was signed on March 3, 1978, between Smith and three black leaders that provided the basic principles for a new constitution to be based upon majority rule. In 1979 such a constitution was prepared, although Zimbabwe/Rhodesia, as the nation was styled, was involved in open warfare, with radical blacks warring against the government.

In 1979 the new constitution was approved. In the referendum for white voters, 85 percent voted in favor of adoption, even though whites would hold only 28 seats in the new parliament, and blacks held 72 seats. Although whites were overrepresented, the 1979 Constitution put them in the majority. Elections were held in wartime Zimbabwe/Rhodesia and black Bishop Abel Muzorewa led his party to a smashing electoral victory. Yet the black rebels abstained from voting, declaring the election a fraud and a sham. Britain was still not appeased and continued to press the new government, which came into office under Prime Minister Muzorewa on June 1, 1979.

The 1979 Constitution created a facade of majority rule. Actually, the Constitution entrenched white privileges for at least 10 years. The police, the military, the judiciary and the civil service were effectively to be white controlled for that length of time.[43] Furthermore, white interests were protected by entrenched provisions in the Constitution that were placed beyond the reach of the black majority.[44] These and other features were offensive to Britain and the black rebels.

In the fall of 1979 a constitutional conference was held in London at the behest of the British government. Delegates from the Zimbabwe/Rhodesia government and from the rebel forces led by Joshua Nkomo and Robert Mugabe met under the chairmanship of Lord Carrington. The British plan for an independent constitution was on the table. In spite of the opposition of former Prime Minister Ian Smith, the new independent constitution was agreed to by Bishop Muzorewa and the representatives of the rebel Patriotic Front. The new constitution restrained the ability of the white minority to frustrate the black majority, while still protecting the property interests of the whites.[45] The army, the police, the judiciary, land, and the civil service were all opened up to Africans. However, many features of the Zimbabwe/Rhodesia Constitution were retained, so that the scope of white powers was ill-defined. Minority rule was effectively ended in Zimbabwe/Rhodesia.

In 1980 a new government with black African leadership was elected into office. Robert Mugabe became prime minister in an uneasy cabinet coalition with his political adversary, Joshua Nkomo. The enmity between the two black leaders resulted in Nkomo's 1982 expulsion from government.

Zimbabwe attained black majority rule in 1980. Unfortunately, black minority groups who did not fit in the plans of larger black tribes were placed in a subordinate position. This seems to be the significance of the expulsion of Joshua Nkomo. Nkomo had been the originator of the movement for black majority rule in the late 1940s when the nation, which was then called Rhodesia, was dominated by a white minority. In 1982 Nkomo and his party, the Zimbabwe African People's Union (ZAPU), were removed from a leadership position because of a suspected coup. Nkomo is chief of the minority Ndebele tribe based in southwestern Matabeleland Province. Nkomo went into exile in 1983, and his tribe can anticipate continued repression from Prime Minister Robert Mugabe. Sadly, the end of white minority rule set the stage for black minority rights problems.

NEW FORMS OF MINORITY RULE

In recent years new forms of minority rule have arisen. The most dramatic example is that of migrant workers in some of the Persian Gulf states. Curiously, some of the world's richest nations have imported huge numbers of foreign workers to extract oil and natural gas. In the process some of these nations have taken in a majority population of strangers.

In Qatar, with one of the world's largest fields of natural gas, only one-third of the total population of 180,000 are citizens. In the United Arab Emirates noncitizens outnumber citizens by 600,000 to 250,000. In these nations and soon in Saudi Arabia, the citizens are the minorities and the "guest worker" immigrants are the majorities. These majorities are essentially "helot classes employed to enable the citizens elite to live a life of pampered ease."[46]

These worker immigrants are divided into many ethnic and racial groups, although Palestinians seem to enjoy more positions of trust and responsibility than do Egyptians, Syrians, Baluchis, Pakistanis, and Bengalis, while Indians are usually at the bottom of the heap, employed as road sweepers and unskilled laborers. Lebanese appear to be better off than most immigrants.

The immigrant laborers do receive free medicine and, if they are government workers, free education, but most dwell in hovels and slums. To a large extent the labor of immigrant workers has modernized the countries in which they reside. Nonetheless, they are only temporary residents, to be expelled at will by the ruling minority. Their rights are limited and subject to capricious recall.

The gap between the privileges of the ruling minority and the life prospects of the majority migrants is evident. Whether these small, fortunate minority-rule states will be able to continue their rule over the majority is questionable. Unless some formula for expansion of rights is found, these fragile regions run the risk of coups and rebellions. Where citizenship is the only access to social standing, it may be impossible to deny some form of citizenship to long resident workers when they are in the majority. This latest form of minority rule is not well known but is still significant as an example.

NOTES

1. See René Lemanchard, *Rwanda and Burundi* (New York: Praeger, 1970).

2. See Ernest Barker, *Greek Political Thought* (New York: Barnes & Noble, 1960), pp. 32-38 for the view that the average citizen didn't depend upon slaves. C. G. Starr, "An Overdose of Slavery," *Journal of Economic History* 18 (1958), pp. 17-30, contends the majority were not slaves.

3. Although condemned in the *Republic*, slavery is accepted in the *Laws*. Even then the slaves of the *Laws* are essentially serfs, not personal chattels or industrial laborers. Athens did use slave labor in its mines.

4. Barker, *Greek Political Thought*, p. 375.

5. Charles Vereker, *The Development of Political Theory* (New York: Harper & Row, 1965), p. 26.

6. Aristotle, *The Politics*, Book I, chapters 4 and 5.

7. M. I. Finley, "Was Greek Civilization Based on Slave Labor?" in *Slavery in Classical Antiquity*, ed. M. I. Finley (Cambridge: W. Heffer & Sons, 1960), p. 164.

8. There is a real argument over numbers. Some put the slave population of Athens as low as 33 percent. Even so, free women were unrepresented.

9. This argument is best set forth by Ralph Dahrendorf, *Essays in The Theory of Society* (Stanford: Stanford University Press, 1968), pp. 151-78.

10. See J. R. Lander, *The Wars of the Roses* (New York: Putnam, 1966).

11. According to Joseph A. Schumpeter, *Capitalism, Socialism, and Democracy* (London: Allen and Unwin, 1943), pp. 12-13, and generally.

12. Margaret Mead, *Sex and Temperament* (New York: Mentor, 1960), describes among other things the Mundigumor of New Guinea, who gave elite status to those persons born with the umbilical cord twisted around the throat.

13. Edward Hyam and George Ordish, *The Last of the Incas* (New York: Simon and Schuster, 1963). pp, 106-8.

14. Joseph Schumpeter, "The Sociology of Imperialism," in *Social Classes/Imperialism*, (New York: Meridian Books, 1955), p. 25.

15. See H. H. Scullard, *A History of the Roman World* 3d ed. (London: Methuen, 1961); and F. W. Wallbank, *Awful Revolution: The Decline of the Roman Empire in the West*, 2d ed. (London: Methuen, 1969).

16. England is a special case, since the monarchs extended their powers in a more gradual and less militaristic fashion.

17. Raymond F. Betts, *Overseas: Phases of Imperialism* (New York: Basic Books, 1969), p. 5.

18. Ibid., p. 6.

19. It is not here intended to use imperialism in a pejorative sense, but for descriptive purposes.

20. See J. M. Lockhard, *Spanish Peru* 1532-1560 (Madison: University of Wisconsin Press, 1960).

21. See O. M. Dickerson, *The Navigation Acts and The American Revolution* (Philadelphia: University of Pennsylvania Press, 1951).

22. Emer de Vattel, the most widely read of eighteenth-century authorities on international law, helped provide a rational justification for the brutal treatment of indigenous peoples. Vattel denied the critical right of sovereignty to "wandering tribes" of hunters and gatherers. Vattel argued that European settlement in the New World was proper "and the Nations of Europe, which are too confined at home, come upon lands which the savages have no special need of and are making no present and continuous use of, they may lawfully take possession of them and make colonies of them." (Found in Philip D. Curtin, ed., *Imperialism* (New York: Harper & Row, 1971), p. 45.

23. There are a few who find little difference between the new and old imperialism. See J. Gallagher and R. Robinson, "The Imperialism of Free Trade, *The Economic History Review* 6 (1953), pp. 1-15.

24. J. A. Hobson, *Imperialism: A Study* (London: George Allen and Unwin Ltd., 1902).

25. V. I. Lenin, *Imperialism: The Highest Stage of Capitalism* (New York: International Publishers Co., 1939).

26. William L. Langer, "A Critique of Imperialism," *Foreign Affairs* 14 (1935), p. 105.

27. Josiah Strong, Our Country (New York, 1885).

28. Rudyard Kipling, "White Man's Burden," a poem first published in the

London Times on February 4, 1899. The poem was written directly after America's victory in the Spanish-American War and was, in part, an invitation to Americans to enter into imperialist policies and practices.

29. Phillip Curtin, ed., *Imperialism.* (New York: Harper & Row, 1971), p. 248.

30. Some argue that the lack of social integration was a factor in modernization. See John Plamenatz, *On Alien Rule and Self-Government* (London: Longmans, 1960).

31. Most agricultural and industrial work was conducted by non-Europeans. Plantations were sometimes used for agricultural production with Europeans involved, if at all, as overseers.

32. Great Britain, *Report of the Commission Appointed by the Government of India to Investigate the Disturbances in the Punjab*, Cmd. 681 (London: Her Majesty's Printing Office, 1920). pp. 122-23.

33. Betts, *Europe Overseas*, p. 83.

34. Fatma Mansur, *Process of Independence* (London: Rutledge 1962); and Rupert Emerson, *From Empire to Nation* (Boston: Little, Brown, 1962).

35. Hector Monteith Robertson, *South Africa, Economic and Political Aspects* (Durham, N.C.: Duke University Press, 1957), pp. 11-12.

36. United Nations Educational, Scientific, and Cultural Organization *Apartheid: Its Effects on Education, Science, Culture and Information* (Paris: 1972).

37. See T. Dunbar Moody, *The Rise of Afrikanerdem* (Berkeley, Calif.: University of California Press, 1975).

38. Lawrence Schlemmer, *Black Attitudes: Reaction and Adaptation* (Durban: University of Natal, Institute for Social Research, 1975. See Edward Feit, *African Opposition in South Africa* (Stanford, Calif.: Hoover Institution Press, 1967).

39. See Robert Blake, *A History of Rhodesia*, (New York: Alfred A. Knopf, (1978) pp. 111-22.

40. Clare Palley, *The Constitutional Law and History of Southern Rhodesia: 1888-1965* (Oxford: Clarendon Press, 1966), p. 155.

41. After a series of electoral reforms under British rule, a 1957 Electoral Act was passed which increased the number of African voters. But the same act also ensured the Africans could never exceed 20 percent of the vote. See C. Leys, *European Politics in Southern Rhodesia* (Oxford: Clarendon Press, 1959), for an account of the effects of earlier British electoral laws.

42. See Richard Hodder-Williams, "Rhodesia's Search for a Constitution—or Whatever Happened to Whaley?" *African Affairs* 69 (1970), pp. 217-35.

43. Chapter VI, Constitution of Zimbabwe/Rhodesia of 1979, including Articles 88 through 13.

44. Article 260, Constitution of Zimbabwe/Rhodesia of 1979 and Second Schedule (Specially Entrenched Provisions).

45. The effect of the changes introduced in the fall 1979 were hotly disputed. Many condemned them as insufficient for majority rights.

46. John Andrews, "Migrant Workers in the Gulf States," in *World Minorities in the Eighties* ed. Georgina Ashworth (Sunbury, U.K.: Quatermaine House, 1980), p. 90.

6

Leading National Examples of Minority Rights Arrangements

THE emergence of minority rights and of group rights generally has been most notable in certain nations that, for various reasons, have attempted to accomodate minorities in their midst. While there are many pluralistic, multi-ethnic societies, there still has not been a formal recognition of minority group rights in all such societies. Furthermore, there are many examples of the failure of minority rights arrangements to satisfy the claims of the minorities. There are few prevalent examples of states that have successfully managed to provide extensive protections for minorities while also maintaining national stability. There are also two leading failures of minority rights arrangements that must be considered first in order to obtain a rounded view of minority rights.

TWO FAILURES: LEBANON AND CYPRUS

Two tiny nations only a few hundred miles apart in the eastern Mediterranean have long attempted to provide a peaceful, constitutional framework for the political and social protection of large population groups. Cyprus and Lebanon, each in their own way, experimented briefly and unhappily with a complex, well-defined set of constitutional and legal arrangements designed to deal with the conflicting claims of major groups. Today Cyprus is under Turkish domination, and Lebanon has recently been under Israeli and Syrian occupation. Both Cyprus and Lebanon have experienced bitterness, bloodshed, and open warfare among their major groups. Paper protections have proved insufficient.

Lebanon's population is half Muslim and half Christian, but these groups are subdivided into different sects. Each of the sects was represented proportionally in the legislature. Until 1947 the Lebanese Constitution provided that Senate seats would be assigned to various religious groups as follows: five Maronites, three Sunnites, three Shiites, three Orthodox, one Catholic, one Druze, and one "minorities."[1] The provision was abrogated on November 9, 1947.

The abrogation of 1947 was also a violation of an unwritten agreement known as the National Pact, which had become a part of a far-reaching minority rights settlement. Under the terms of the agreement, the office of the president was reserved to a Maronite Christian, the prime minister would be a Sunni Muslim, the speaker or president of the Chamber, a Shiite Moslem, and the commander of the armed forces would be a Maronite. There were further understandings that would give the ministry of defense to a Druze and, perhaps, the foreign office to a member of the Greek Orthodox community. These specific allocations of public office were intended to reduce tension by providing some governmental roles for all major groups.

In 1966 parliamentary representation was expanded to 99, while maintaining a ratio of 6 Christians to every 5 Muslims. Membership in the parliament was assigned on the basis of religious groupings, so that Greek Orthodox, Greek Catholics, Protestants, Sunni Muslims, Shiite Muslims, and Druzes were all awarded seats in proportion to their populations.[2]

None of these arrangements sufficed to ward off political instability. After 1970 the additional presence of armed Palestinian resistance groups led to turmoil and eventual Israeli invasion. Civil war broke out in 1975 as the fragile Lebanese state collapsed. After widespread death and destruction, Syrian troops intervened to maintain order and to prop up the Lebanese government. In 1982 Israel invaded southern Lebanon again, but on a major scale. Lebanese independence is questionable, and, though the structure of the religious settlement still exists in the executive and legislative branches, the delicate balance of group rights has been jeopardized. Yet, in spite of all that has happened, the various government ministries are divided among the previously warring factions of Lebanon.

Cyprus is an even more tragic case of constitutional failure. Cyprus had an estimated population of 650,000 before the Turkish invasion of 1974. At that time, the population was predominantly (80 percent) Greek. Another 18 percent were ethnic Turks, with the remaining population being Armenians and Maronite Christians. Cyprus became independent in 1960 under a constitution that created entrenched guarantees for the Greek and Turkish communities.

The Cypriot Constitution of 1960 was one of the most complex attempts to satisfy competing ethnic groups ever written. The Constitution recognized the separate existence of a Greek and a Turkish community, provided for separate communal institutions, separate holidays, separate seats in the legislature, separate ballots, and numerous other devices to ensure separate group development while providing political power to both major groups.

The 1960 Constitution provided that the Cypriot president would be Greek and the vice-president a Turk.[3] The President of the House of

Representatives would be a Greek, the vice-president a Turk.[4] The clerks of the House would be two Greeks and one Turk. Greek and Turkish representation upon parliamentary committees was assigned by the Constitution, and even the votes were to have been jointly counted by a Greek and Turkish clerk.[5] Significant for group rights, the Cypriot Constitution provided for separate communal chambers with exclusive powers over religious matters, education, certain charitable organizations, and similar community matters.[6]

The civil service, the police, the armed forces, and the gendarmerie were all staffed according to ratios found in the Constitution. There were also separate systems of Greek-Cypriot and Turkish-Cypriot courts and separate law-enforcement machinery for each. The Council of Ministers was divided strictly between the Greek-Cypriots and the Turkish-Cypriots. To solidify these arrangements, the key constitutional provisions were made unamendable.

In spite of the statistical overrepresentation of the Turkish-Cypriots, the constitutional arrangements irritated both the Turkish minority and the Greek majority. The Greeks sought to strengthen the national government, which they dominated; the Turks sought to block government moves whenever they felt threatened. The result was a deadlock on many issues. Added to this growing antagonism was the outside interference by both Greece and Turkey. By 1963 open intercommunal fighting broke out. By 1964 a constitutional crisis had arisen, the first of a series of crises lasting until 1974.

In 1974 a coup was staged by members of the Greek ruling junta. Turkey invaded the island on July 20, 1974, rapidly occupying 40 percent of the northern portion of Cyprus. Over 200,000 Greek-Cypriots were made homeless and fled to the south. In 1975 a Turkish-Cypriot Federated State was proclaimed. The 1960 Constituton was a shambles.

The sad fates of Lebanon and Cyprus suggest that extensive grants of minority rights can be a source for severe instability. Perhaps this is so, but both nations were short-lived as independent entities. Both lacked a sense of nationhood and of loyalty to a single state. Both were subject to outside interference and invasion. Doubtless, their minority rights guarantees were insufficient to maintain the integrity of these young countries, but the failures of Lebanon and Cyprus do not discredit all minority rights arrangements. The flawed constitutions of Lebanon and Cyprus contributed somehow to their downfall and did not cause that downfall. However, constitution drafters had best be alert to these two examples of inadequate or excessive minority rights provisions.

THE KINGDOM OF BELGIUM

Belgium, with 9 million inhabitants and 11,700 square miles of land, is one of the most densely populated countries in all of Europe. Belgium contains three distinct linguistic groups within its small territory: a

French-speaking group, a Dutch-speaking group, and a German-speaking group. For a variety of reasons linguistic differences have become increasingly salient in Belgium, compelling some major innovations in the development of group rights.

The northern Belgian provinces of West-Vlaanderen, East-Vlaanderen, Antwerpen, and Lemberg are predominantly settled by Flemish speakers who are also mostly Protestants. Catholics tend to be concentrated in the southern Belgian provinces of Hainaut, Namur, Luxembourg, and the western portion of Liege. A German-speaking majority occupies the eastern portion of Liege. Brussels, the capital is bilingual, and the Province of Brabaut is divided between the Flemings and the Walloons (French-speaking). These linguistic and cultural differences have always been reflected in the politics of Belgium, especially in a powerful Catholic party, which has often been dominant.

The political and social life of Belgium has been much more violent and intense than most people realize. Riots and bitter political strife have marked much of Belgian history. This tension has resulted in the promulgation of several constitutional changes and many adjustments in the electoral laws in an attempt to settle differences between the Flemings and the Walloons. The composition of the legislature, the nature of the monarch, the rights of minorities, and many other fundamental issues have divided Belgium.

The origins of Belgian discontent can be traced to the artificial union of its composite parts. At the Congress of Vienna in 1815 the great powers of Europe decided to unite seventeen Belgian provinces together with Holland to form a Kingdom of the Netherlands under the Dutch king. A series of constitutional manipulations by the Dutch king forced acceptance of the 1815 Fundamental Law of the United Provinces.

A rebellion against Dutch rule broke out in 1830 and a provisional government proclaimed the existence of a state of Belgium. A Belgian Constitution of 1831 was produced by the National Congress. This remarkable document launched the troubled and complex consitutional history of Belgium.

The 1831 Constitution ignored the existence of any linguistic and cultural regions.[7] Prince Leopold of Saxe-Coburg, a Lutheran, accepted the throne as king of the Belgians in 1831. After his 1832 marriage to Princess Louise of Orleans, he agreed that all children of the marriage would be brought up in the Catholic faith. In general, Catholic dominance of the nation prevailed in the period prior to World War I.[8]

In 1861 the Flemish party demanded official use of the Flemish language. Because of its similarity to Dutch, the Flemings had been politically inactive for fear of reviving memories of Dutch rule. The Flemish-speaking population, although 55 percent of the Belgian population, had been relegated to an inferior political and cultural status.

Although Flemish could be used in Flemish judicial proceedings (1873) and in administration of Flemish provinces (1878), these statutory concessions were insufficient to remove the Flemish perceptions of French domination of Belgian life.

In 1893 a number of major constitutional amendments were made, most notably a new Article 47, which provided for nearly universal male suffrage. However, the same article also provided for double voting for heads of families paying 5 francs habitation taxes and an additional vote for those who had a university degree. This system particularly aided the Catholic party, since Catholics were usually more prosperous and better educated.

Equal voting rights for all were resisted by the Catholics, leading to a major strike just prior to World War I. The German invasion during World War I brought support for the Flemings. The German occupiers favored the Flemish language at the expense of the French. This resulted in a brief period of Flemish influence.

After the war, a system of pure and simple universal suffrage was gradually introduced. Proportional representation was also put into effect. Universal male suffrage was finally placed on a constitutional plane by the new Article 47 of the Constitution promulgated in 1921. At the same time, the Senate was reformed to make it more representative.

Belgium remained a state of two divided nations throughout the interwar period. When the German invasion of 1940 again overran Belgium, a split occurred between the king, who remained in Belgium, and a Belgian government-in-exile composed of most of the king's former ministers. Pro- and anti-Leopold forces struggled to redefine the constitutional position of the monarchy, and when, in 1950, a vote was held on the question, "Are you of the opinion that King Leopold III should resume the exercise of his constitutional powers?" the voting was polarized between Flemish (72 percent pro-Leopold) and Walloon factions. The return of the king revived the animosity between Flemings and Walloons. The time had come to recognize the differences among the linguistic groups.

In 1962 a new law was passed fixing certain linguistic boundaries by dividing Belgium into four regions: a Flemish-speaking region, a German-speaking region, the bilingual region of Brussels, and a French-speaking region. The Constitution was to be revised to express these new conceptions. Drastic revision of the Constitution was mandated, but it took many years to reach agreement on the necessary changes.

Finally, in 1970 and 1973 major changes were made in the Constitution recognizing the special rights of the cultural communities of Belgium. At the same time, the representational system was altered to provide legislative power for two language groups, Flemish and French, over their own regions.

The Constitution states that Belgium comprises four linguistic regions: the French, the Dutch, the German and the bilingual region of Brussels.[9] Three cultural communities are recognized, each having certain powers vested in it by the Constitution.[10] The Constitution also guarantees the rights and liberties of ideological and philosophical minorities.[11]

A linguistic group can make a motion to delay the passage and consideration of a proposed bill that, in the view of three-fourths of its members, is of such a nature as to have a serious effect on the relations between communities.[12] This power is in addition to the powers of linguistic groups within the parliament to legislate for their linguistic region.

One of the most important parts of the Constitution provides that "for those cases prescribed in the constitution, the elected members of each house are divided into a French-language group and a Dutch-language group."[13] A cultural council was created for the French cultural community "made up of members of the French linguistic group of both houses" of the legislature.[14] A bill passed on a majority vote within each linguistic group must also have two-thirds of both linguistic groups in order to conduct most of the parliamentary business. But each cultural council is limited in the sphere of its activities to that kind of legislation which deals with cultural matters, education, the use of languages, and similar matters.[15] There is also a cultural council for the German cultural community, although its composition is unspecified.[16] The cultural councils exercise their competence by decrees that have the force of law in the respective linguistic regions to which they apply. Unfortunately, no special provision was made for the bilingual Brussels region.

This representational arrangement of linguistic groups is a novel solution to an historic problem. The political arrangement goes beyond federalism and has been denoted a "consociation" by some scholars.[17] The linguistic and cultural cleavages of Belgium are now constitutionally permanent. Yet the significance of these cultural councils remains shrouded in doubt and ambiguity. The Brussels situation is especially ambiguous.[18]

The Cabinet must, "with the possible exception of the Prime Minister," be comprised of an equal number of French- and Dutch-speaking members. Since budget bills are also subject to the potential power of linguistic groups, it is difficult to see how any major policies can be adopted by a government without the tacit consent of the two largest language groups, the Flemings and the Walloons.

In 1971 an act was passed refining the powers and structure of the linguistic groups. The act contains elaborate provisions for bilingual areas, especially Brussels. It provides formal voting procedures and even the form of main motions. Perhaps the most important portion of the act defines more clearly the cultural matters that fall under the jurisdiction of the linguistic groups. These are, among others, protection of: the language, the arts, the national heritage, radio and television broadcasting, youth policy, education, leisure facilities, and travel.[19] Nowhere else are linguistic and cultural group rights so specifically delineated and incorporated within a constitution.

The Belgian Constitution is not noteworthy because of its treatment of women, races, or religious groups. Its claim on our attention rests upon the explicit recognition of group rights of a linguistic-ethnic-cultural nature. Belgium is still experimenting with this advanced version of group rights, but it is an experiment well worth watching. Belgium's constitutional changes "have created an exotic hybrid of a political system which is neither truly federalist nor as ferociously unitarist as before,"[20] a state for which a new political term has been coined, *l'état communautaire*, the "communitarian state." The Belgium example, in spite of its endemic political instability, is a fascinating attempt to forge a new approach to minority rights.

INDIA

India is a crazy quilt and has a constitution to match. But are there any other alternatives? India has produced the world's longest constitution, but for good reason. Its population of 700 million speaks 24 languages and over 200 dialects. There are dozens of different major religious groupings and other ethnic groupings as well. Forty million or so people belong to tribal minorities with these divided into 450 or more entities.

To make matters even more complicated, India has the additional problem of caste. At the very bottom of the caste ladder is an identifiable group, referred to constitutionally as the "scheduled castes," and referred to in earlier constitutional laws and documents as the "depressed classes." Mahatma Gandhi called them the harijans, or "children of God." They are better known as the "untouchables." The horrible fact is that India's harijan population, now at 93 million, is greater than the total population of all but seven of the world's countries.[21]

Finally, adding to all of these complications, are the twin facts that India is a federal republic and that the boundaries of her 22 states and nine union territories are drawn along linguistic lines. The configurations of India's component states have been reshaped and renamed because of the pressures of various linguistic groups. During the early years following independence in 1947, the Congress party leadership resisted linguistic divisions, fearing the disruptive effect on the admittedly fragile federation. Jawaharlal Nehru reluctantly conceded to demands for the separation of Andhra from Madras in 1953 and then approved the States Reorganization Act of 1956, which resulted in a comprehensive reorganization of state boundaries on linguistic lines. Bilingual Bombay State was divided into two unilingual states in 1960; the Punjab was divided in 1966.

What makes this type of linguistic division still more complicated is the fact that people do not necessarily arrange their places of residence to meet nationally prescribed linguistic boundaries. The States Reorganization Commission, charged with revising state political boundaries, concluded that there would be at least some linguistic minorities within even the most linguistically homogeneous state. How could it be otherwise when only fifteen languages (four added by amendments) are recognized in the Constitution's Eighth Schedule?

Reading the Indian Constitution, without knowing its history and background, leaves the impression that the document is overly concerned with the protection and preservation of group rights. It is filled with institutional arrangements on behalf of its various groupings to adjust the political balance among them and to protect the weakest of them. But it was always so in India. As a matter of fact, the present Constitution, as adopted in 1948, reflected a trend in the opposite direction.

Institutional arrangements providing safeguards for the various communal minorities of India were a part of British law for the century preceding the transfer of power in 1947. And such safeguards have been part of all Indian constitution-making, going back to the Swaraj Bill of 1895. In 1906, the then-Aga Khan, as leader of Muslim elements, succeeded in obtaining the creation of separate electorates based on religious distinctions. England pursued this approach with its approval of the 1917 Montagu-Chelmsford Report, in which the authors visualized India as

> a sisterhood of States, self-governing in all matters of purely local or provincial interest, in some cases corresponding to existing provinces, in others perhaps modified in area according to the character and economic interests of their people. Over this congeries of States would preside a central government, increasingly representative of and responsible to the people of all of them; dealing with matters, both internal and external, of common interest to the whole of India; acting as arbiter in inter-State relations, and representing the interests of all India on equal terms with the self-governing units of the British Empire.[22]

By the time of the most important of all of the preindependence constitutions, the Government of India Act of 1935, it was agreed that representation through separate electorates would be given to Muslims, Europeans, Sikhs, Indian Christians, and Anglo-Indians.

> Seats were also reserved for the Marathas in selected general constituencies in Bombay. The depressed classes were given seats to be filled by election from special constituencies in which they alone could vote, though they were also entitled to vote in the general constituencies. Special seats were also allotted to women, labour, commerce, and industry, mining and planting, and landholders.[23]

In the face of the 1946 Resolutions to divide the country and to create two constitution-making bodies, one for Hindustan and one for Pakistan, the government, under the 1935 Act, expressed opposition:

The Congress was totally opposed to the division of the country. It was, however, prepared for the maximum amount of local autonomy consistent with the maintenance of the unity of the country. Accordingly, it suggested that the future framework of the country's Constitution be based on a federal structure with a limited number of compulsory central subjects such as defense, communications and foreign affairs; the federation would consist of autonomous Provinces in which would vest the residuary subjects. The Congress also suggested that there should be a list of "optional subjects" in respect of which any Province or group of Provinces would be free to accept federal executive and legislative jurisdiction. It was proposed that on the completion of the constitution-making process a Province could elect to stand out of the Constitution altogether, or federate on the essential minimum subjects, or federate on the essential as well as the optional subjects.[24]

Group rights safeguards for soon-to-be-independent India were hotly debated during the 28 months of constitutional draftsmanship that began in the summer of 1946.[25] It is still not over. There have been changes giving still more protections to India's minorities in the course of the 42 amendments promulgated to date.

It should be pointed out, however, that certain constitutional amendments have reemphasized group rights. The best example is Article 15(4), added by the First Amendment in 1951. It must be compared with both Article 15(1) and Article 29(2). These read as follows:

15(4) Nothing in this article or in clause (2) of Article 29 shall prevent the State from making any special provision for the advancement of any socially and educationally backward classes of citizens or for the Scheduled Castes and the Scheduled Tribes.

15(1) The State shall not discriminate against any citizen on grounds only of religion, race, caste, sex, place of birth, or any of them.

29(2) No citizen shall be denied admission into any educational institution maintained by the State or receiving aid out of State funds on grounds only of religion, race, caste, language, or any of them.

It is interesting to note that during the constitutional debates, the Constituent Assembly rejected the inclusion of a provision similar to 15(4).

Article 15(4) reflects the same spirit as Article 16(4), which reads:

Nothing in this article shall prevent the State from making any provision for the reservation of appointments or posts in favor of any backward class of citizens which, in the opinion of the State, is not adequately represented in the services under the State.

Note, however, that 16(4) should be read in connection with 16(1), which provides that "There shall be equality of opportunity for all citizens in matters relating to employment or appointment to any office under the State."

The equality principle—in economic terms—is stated in Article 39(a) and (d): "that the citizens, men and women equally, have the right to an adequate means to livelihood"; and "that there is equal pay for equal work for both men and women."

However, there is also an important and basic principle of state policy set forth in Article 46:

The State shall promote with special care the educational and economic interests of the weaker sections of the people; and, in particular, the Scheduled Castes and the Scheduled Tribes, and shall protect them from social injustice and all forms of exploitation.

So, the Indian Constitution creates both principles of equal treatment and of special group preference. There is some inherent conflict between these principles but Indian jurists have managed to accommodate them.

The Harijans and the Law

To understand the legal position of India's 93 million harijans, one starts with Article 17 of the Constitution. It reads:

"untouchability" is abolished and its practice in any form is forbidden. The enforcement of any disability arising out of "Untouchability" shall be an offense punishable in accordance with law.

That would appear to take care of the problem.

Relevant also are such cases as *Moosa* v. *State of Kerala*.[26] This held that a government order requisitioning land for the construction of a colony of harijans, previously held discriminatory under Article 15(1), was now valid under Article 15(4).

There is also a law, first enacted in 1955 and then amended in 1976, giving the untouchables the legal right to enter any temple, draw water from any well or tap, or use any public restaurant.

While the origins of untouchability in India are obscure, there is reference to a caste system existing since 1500 B.C. It is not a separateness based upon religion, since untouchables are also Hindus. It has been a separateness manifested by regulations on possible occupational activities. While it is true that some harijans have become lawyers and doctors, it is also true that all of the sweepers in the city of Bombay are untouchables.

Whether the origin of untouchability was or was not based upon ethnic or racial differences more than three millennia ago is a moot question. What persists is the distinctiveness of a given group within society whose members have been forced to associate and mate with each other for this extended period of time.

Both the Constitution and the laws ending discrimination against harijans are widely disregarded.

> The defeat of Indira Gandhi and her Congress Party, which had instituted a "20-point program" pressing for distribution of land to untouchables, minimum wages for them, and abolition of bonded labor (which has some 7 million in virtual lifetime slavery), has turned back the clock. Landlords in many areas are reported to have grabbed back the land formerly distributed to the harijans, and harassment is rising.[27]

There are many reports of the shooting of poor untouchables. Also reports have surfaced that the killing of wealthy landlords by untouchables had become an almost regular feature in recent times in several backward areas in India.

There can be no better example than this of the inadequacies of constitutional safeguards in trying to solve the peculiar problems of discrimination against this ethnic or cultural group. The problems of the untouchables have resisted repeated governmental efforts to solve them, and new legislation continues to be produced to deal with the situation.

Constitutional Safeguards and Their Alternatives in India

As complicated as India's multiracial society is today, it was even more complicated in the period prior to independence. At that time, the principal group right problem was the ever-present conflict between Hindu and Muslim. This was, of course, primarily a religious problem. It was also a language problem. Mahatma Gandhi had argued for the adoption of Hindustani as the language of the ethnic subcontinent—a language which would combine both Hindi and Urdu.

But Britain's Empire of India was not to become a separate, independent state. What is now a subcontinent of more than 850 million was first broken up to create India and a Pakistan. Then Pakistan was divided once again to create a new nation of Bangladesh and to reconstitute the separate nation of Pakistan.

The first separation was based on religious differences—Pakistan was established as a Muslim nation. The second separation was based upon ethnic and cultural differences—the Bengali Muslims of East Pakistan (who speak Bengali) differing in physiognomy, culture, and language from the people of West Pakistan (who speak Urdu).

The division of British India into two separate nation-states in 1947 resulted in the greatest human migration in history. Millions of Muslims left what was to become the Republic of India to go to Pakistan; and millions of non-Muslims migrated in the opposite direction. But even after all of the migrations were over, there are today at least 10 million Hindus in Pakistan and Bangladesh, and 60 million Muslims in India. The migration lessened the severity of group conflict but made legal safeguard for the minority even more necessary.

And it remains to be seen whether the constitutional safeguards preserving group rights will preserve the unity of today's India or lead to its further division. A split, if it comes, may occur over the question of language rights. The insistence of many northern Indians on the adoption of Hindi as the nation's sole official language is bitterly opposed by the south and has led to separatist threats. The revolts of the Sikhs have become more and more ominous, raising the threat of separatism.

But whatever occurs, the Indian experience must be studied and restudied, for it is here that group rights problems are most severe and it is here where the greatest efforts have been made to solve them in a legal context.

SWITZERLAND

Switzerland is a leading example of a constitutional design intended to cope with linguistic, cultural, and religious diversity. Protestants and Catholics who once struggled against each other have found a formula for a friendly relationship. Switzerland has four major linguistic groups, but these seem to have been accommodated. In fact, the Swiss Constitution is the centerpiece of Swiss social life. Doubtless, there are deeper explanations for the stability of the Swiss federal government, but the ingenuity of its constitutional arrangements partly accounts for the success of the Swiss system.

There is an important geographic noncoincidence of language, religious, and cultural boundaries. Cultural coexistence as well as religious coexistence is reinforced by the distinctly separate location of groups that pursue their own ways of life. Only a series of maps portraying these regions can heighten our awareness of this fortuitous condition. Nonetheless, the Constitution provides a sufficient amount of unity to contain this diversity and to protect minorities in regions where other majorities prevail.

The Constitution of 1848, which is still the Swiss Constitution of today, was essentially the creation of a twenty-three-man committee of the Swiss Diet. Most were the chiefs of their cantonal governments. In spite of the fervent opposition of the small Catholic cantons, the Constitution was approved on September 12, 1848. The six and a half cantons that opposed the new Constitution included three cantons, Uri, Schwyz, and Unterwalden, the originators of the Swiss confederation.[28]

To achieve a stable federal state and in order to avoid the centralizing tendency of a single-house, popularly elected legislature, the 1848 Constitution adopted a bicameral legislature. Although the Swiss reluctantly adopted this American-style compromise, they also invented the unique system of a collegiate seven-man executive serving on a rotating leadership basis. This plural executive was intended to further weaken the tendency toward centralization and the domination of a single group or canton.

The religious settlement is one of the main bases of Swiss federalism. Article 49 of the Swiss Constitution puts the central government in the position of actively defending groups and individuals against religious oppression. The old Swiss regime made Roman Catholicism unlawful in Protestant territories and vice versa. But Article 49 declares that "freedom of conscience and belief is inviolable" and also brings delicate religious matters directly under the law of the state. Primary education, marriage, holidays, oaths, and even church jurisdiction are all defined by law under the Constitution. The territorial principle is rejected in favor of a national solution to the problem of religious tolerance.

Article 50 of the Constitution guarantees the free exercise of religion, compatible with public order and decency, and Article 49 prohibits requiring a person to join a religious body or to pay taxes to a religious group of which he or she is not a member. Yet the cantons are free to create a single state church. Most cantons have recognized the courts. Ecclesiastical courts are abolished by Article 4, so that only secular courts can manage private disputes.

The provisions of the Swiss Constitution regarding religion reveal generally anti-clerical attitudes based upon the experience of the 1848 drafters following periodic religious conflicts. The increase in anti-clerical provisions by the revisions of 1874 were based on similar attitudes. Nonetheless, the decentralized structure of the federation, combined with the diversity of the religious distribution of the population, permits a great deal of local variation in the practical implementation of religious freedom.

Equality before the law is declared by Article 4 of the federal Constitution. This formal equality is extended to the cantons by Article 60, which says "every canton is obliged to accord citizens of other confederate states the same treatment it accords to its own citizens, as regards legislation and all that concerns judicial discrimination." These provisions ensure that members of different religions, cultural, or linguistic groups will not be the victims of discrimination within a canton dominated by members of another group.

The Swiss Constitution specifically provides (Article 116) that German, French, Italian, and Romansh are national languages and makes all but Romansh official languages. The three official languages are supposed to be represented in the federal tribunal (Article 107). Freedom of languages has been given unusual prominence in Swiss constitutional practice. In reality, Switzerland is treated as though the map of the country were divided into French, German, and Italian areas. Although Swiss citizens are entitled to speak their own languages, the territorial principle is regarded as superior to the personal principle. The language sovereignty of each canton is called *Sprachenhoheit,* and this extra constitutional concept fits in with the decentralization of the Swiss Federation by giving the canton the power to choose the language of school instruction and similar sensitive questions. The federal government, for its part, attempts to maintain equitable representation of linguistic groups through legislation in support of the constitutional principle of freedom of languages.[29]

The position of Romansh speakers in Switzerland is interesting. Only .9 percent of the population—approximately 50,000 of 5.35 million speak Romansh. But in 1938 the Constitution was amended by referendum to recognize Romansh as a national language.[30] The petition was made by the executive of the Canton of Grisons, and the amendment received the support of 92 percent of the voters. This is a vivid example of Swiss public policy toward weaker language groups.[31]

The Swiss constitution also gives each canton the power to choose the state churches (called National Churches). The cantonal governments support them by granting them subsidies, special tax funds, or other privileges. In order for taxes to support state churches and still conform to Article 49 of the Constitution, provisions are made for individuals to be relieved of these taxes by publicly and formally denying that they adhere to the state religion of the canton. Separation of church and state prevails in Geneva and Basle while several Catholic cantons, on the other hand, operate under a concordat system, negotiating arrangements between civil authorities and the Pope or bishops. This enormous diversity is all consistent with the Swiss Constitution.[32]

Many of the former practices of the Catholic religion are curbed by specific constitutional provisions. Article 54, inserted in the Constitution in 1874, makes civil ceremonies the exclusive means of legal marriage. Similarly, cemeteries are placed in the care of civil authorities. No new Catholic bishoprics may be set up on Swiss territory without the consent of the federal authorities. Until 1973 the Constitution contained articles (Article 54, 1874 Amendments, in particular) which expressly banned Jesuits and the foundation or ressurection of monasteries. This anti-Catholic measure has been removed, although the provision concerning bishoprics remains.

In general, the Swiss Constitution provides that "the Cantons are sovereign insofar as their sovereignty is not limited by the federal constitution, and, as such, they exercise all rights which are not transferred to the federal power."[33] This provision is reinforced, as to language rights, by the fact that the seven man federal Council always provides some representation for each of the three language groups.[34] The Constitution also permits federal subsidies for education, which amounts to linguistic generosity to support instruction in cantonally dominant languages.[35]

But there is another larger minority in Switzerland that comprises a large segment of the work force, the "guest workers"—foreigners whose labor is a mainstay of the economy. These foreign workers have few of the rights of Swiss citizens and after completing a period of work are required to return to their native countries. This unrepresented minority is an alien population of between 10 to 20 percent of the residents. But foreigners are not welcome to remain in Switzerland. In 1982 a plan to ease immigration laws to allow foreigners to remain in the country and to have the same rights to free speech and assembly that Swiss citizens enjoy was proposed by Parliament for popular referendum. The plan was defeated by 690,339 to 580,432, reflecting a strong campaign by the National Action Movement, a Swiss group which contends that Switzerland is subject to too much foreign influence.

UNION OF SOVIET SOCIALIST REPUBLICS

Soviet Russia is one of the most interesting and important multinational nations. Not only is there extreme diversity of cultures, languages, and ethnic groups, but even religion is displayed in numerous different ways in a state that is generally indifferent, if not opposed to religion. The treatment of women, too, is distinctive and important. Even if these considerations were not enough to merit our attention, there is the further significance of the Soviet constitutional examples for large numbers of nations in the world, even those which do not consider themselves to be communist or socialist.

The dominant nationality group, the Great Russians, comprise about 53 percent of the population of the Soviet Union. This third largest nation in the world, with its population of 258 million, is populated by more than a hundred different nationalities.[36] The Ukrainians, the second largest ethnic group, number 40.7 million or 17 percent of the population. There are 9 million Byelorussians. Estonians, Latvians, and Lithuanians also are linguistic, cultural groups of the Soviet Union, and each group enjoyed an independent history between the two world wars. The Georgians, with a population just under 5 million, speak their own language and have an ancient culture and religion. Jews, Tatars, Moldavians, and Ukrainians are to be found in European Russia;

Armenians, Azerbaidzhanis, Kazakhs, Kirghis, Turkmens, Uzbeks, and Tadzhiks live in central and southern Asia. Mongols, Buryats, Yakuts, Chukchi, Evenks, and Chuvash dwell in northern and eastern Asia. Yet the Soviet Union is a unitary state, a self-avowed dictatorship, dominated by a single party. There is no doubt, in spite of all appearances, that the Soviet Union is faced with a definite nationality problem.[37] However, Soviet treatment of national minorities varies enormously, ranging from tolerance to suppression.[38]

Religion, too, is a problem for the Soviet state. The Russian Orthodox Church remains as the largest and most widespread Christian confession in the USSR with a membership of between 30 and 50 million adherents. There are, in addition, smaller groupings of schismatic communities drawn from factions split off from the Russian Orthodox Church, some of which are not legally recognized.

Being associated in Russian history with Polish imperialism, Roman Catholics were never numerous in old Russia. But in the Baltic states of Lithuania and Latvia, once independent nations, there are sizable Roman Catholic congregations. Protestantism is still rather small, with the Evangelical Christian-Baptists being the largest officially recognized group. Many of the central Asian minorities are Muslims, and much of east Asian Russia is Muslim. Armenians have their own Christian Church, with its world center in Soviet Armenia.

The Jews of Russia settled in Eastern Europe even before the birth of Christ. The tsars were openly anti-Jewish. Massive pograms instituted by royal officials in 1881, 1884, and 1903 forced many Jews to flee Russia but many remained, and some were among the leaders of the Bolshevik Revolution. No one knows how many Jews there are in the Soviet Union, but there may be between two and three million. Although many Jews have been assimalated into Soviet culture, the existence of the state of Israel stirred a widespread demand for Jewish emigration.

One of the earliest Soviet decrees, personally prepared by Lenin in 1918, provided for the separation of church and state.[39] Ever since the proclamation of the first Soviet Constitution (July 1918), the religious question has been of great concern in a state committed to a political doctrine resting upon atheist principles. The first Soviet Constitution gave a right to religious and anti-religious propaganda, but subsequent constitutions wittled away religious rights, and religious communities became subordinated to the state (officially and unofficially) as the atheists gained dominance. The Stalin Constitution of 1936 made a fundamental change, permitting "freedom of religious worship and, freedom of anti-religious propaganda,"[40] but eliminating the former freedom of religious propaganda. The new Constitution of 1977 makes some interesting and perhaps significant changes in the freedom of religion. The new provision speaks of "the right to profess any religion and perform religious rites," and it says that "incitement of hostility and hatred on religious grounds shall be prohibited."[41] These two new phrases suggest a broader amount of official protection of religion against atheistic repression. It also suggests that anti-Semitism and other forms of religious persecution might be officially discouraged. The constitutional language, at least, represents a return to original Leninist principles.

Soviet constitutions have pioneered in the expression and recognition of women's rights. They have set a model for much of the rest of the world, socialist and nonsocialist, in this regard. The 1977 Constitution continues the trend. To a considerable extent, this seems to have been a genuine ideal of the Soviet state, which has attempted in the most far-reaching ways to improve the status of women. The Constitution declares that "in the USSR, women shall have equal rights with men."[42] It goes on to guarantee equal opportunities for education and professional training, for employment, remuneration, and promotion. It permits protective legislation for women, including paid leaves for mothers and state aid to unmarried mothers. The family is placed under the protection of the state, and the constitution explicitly recognizes the need for child-care institutions, family allowances, and maternity benefits.[43]

However, of all the unresolved internal problems of the Soviet Union, the nationalities problem appears most serious. As a result, it draws the most extensive constitutional treatment of all rights issues. Indeed, the Soviet Union is at least on paper an example of a society constitutionally committed to group rights. The preamble to the 1977 Constitution speaks of the "juridical and actual equality of all nations and nationalities of the Soviet Union." The very first article speaks of a socialist state composed of the working class, the peasantry, and the intelligentsia, "of all the nations and nationalities in the country." The unity of the nation and the single-party state is a constant Soviet theme, but the many group rights provisions for nationalities and ethnic and linguistic groups suggest the need to at least superficially accommodate the very numerous groups that make up the Soviet state.

A comparison between the group rights provisions of the 1936 and the 1977 Soviet constitutions reveals a growing concern with these rights. The provisions of Article I of the 1977 Constitution mentioned above represent an added category for the nations and nationalities, a significant addition to the ideologically correct recognition of the status of workers, peasants, and intelligentsia. Article 19 of the 1977 Constitution also adds new language, as it commits the Soviet state to "developing and drawing together all the nations and nationalities of the USSR."[44] Another provision says that "the state shall show concern for protecting and multiplying society's cultural values.[45]

Some changes in old articles are especially revealing. Old Article 123, which guaranteed equality of rights, made no mention of language; the new provision does.[46] The most interesting change is the addition of a new article specifically conferring equal rights upon Soviet citizens of different nationalities and races.[47] However, the same article also speaks ambiguously of "the policy of all-around development and drawing together of all nations and nationalities of the USSR" and of "education of citizens in the spirit of Soviet patriotism and socialist internationalism." Apparently the Soviet recognition of group rights is half-hearted and perhaps a cause of deep concern to the party leaders who drafted the Constitution. Nonetheless, the same article extends "the opportunity for using the mother tongue and the languages of the other peoples of the USSR." Finally, compounding the ambiguity, the same article prohibits, on the one hand, restriction of the rights of citizens on the grounds of race and nationality, and on the other, "any advocacy of racial or national exclusivity."

The right to education in the mother tongue is retained in the current constitution from the 1936 Constitution.[48] A new duty of citizenship is created by the 1977 Constitution. Now it is the duty of every citizen "to respect the national dignity of other citizens" in order "to fortify the friendship of the nations and nationalities of the Soviet multinational state."[49] This is the first constitutional reference to the multinational character of the Soviet Union.

The state structure of the Soviet Union remains essentially unchanged. The federal system is virtually identical to the system of 1936. The Soviet regime has not followed the Yugoslav example of modifications in the structure of government to accommodate its nations and nationalities. Yet, the new provision defining the structure of the state refers to "an integral federal multi-national state formed on the basis of the free self-determination of nations."[50] This second reference to a multinational is conditioned by the language of a succeeding paragraph that speaks of "the state unity of the Soviet people" and the bringing of "all the nations and nationalities together for the joint building of communism." None of this language appears in the 1936 Constitution. There is an odd omission from the 1977 Constitution that deserves attention. Omitted as a right of a Union Republic is the maintenance of its own military.

The intentions of the drafters of the 1977 Soviet Constitution are unknown to us. The document, as with past Soviet constitutions, is intended principally as a propaganda instrument for internal and external use. But even if group rights in the Soviet Union are on an uncertain basis, there is a new and heightened sense of their importance. The 1977 Constitution recognizes, albeit tentatively, the separate needs of the various linguistic, ethnic, racial, and national entities of which the Soviet Union is composed. If in this model of a Communist centralized dictatorship the centrifugal forces of group rights can gain recognition, then group rights may, indeed, flourish almost anywhere.

There is no apparent sign of a severe nationality crisis in the Soviet Union. Although suppression of minority sentiment was obvious in the 1930s and 1940s, there has been less evidence of direct discouragement of minority group activity in recent years. Major nationalities are confined to their republics, and cultural assimilation remains a distant goal of the national regime. Research "leads to the conclusion that there is evidence of both assimilative and colonial patterns in the Soviet society."[51] Doubtless some Baltic peoples, Ukrainians, and Georgians will continue their resistance to homogenization, and Muslim groups and Asian minorities generally will try to retain their distinctive cultures, but defiance is rare and violence even rarer. Minorities do enjoy some rights and protections in the Soviet Union. Perhaps the Soviet Union can be best understood as a leading vestige of the "5,000 year old tradition of the multiethnic empire."[52]

NOTES

1. Lebanese Constitution of May 23, 1926, Article 96, as amended in 1927.
2. See Michael C. Hudson, *The Precarious Republic: Modernization in Lebanon* (New York: Random House, 1968).
3. Cypriot Constitution of 1960, Article 1.
4. Ibid., Article 72.
5. Ibid., Article 73.
6. Ibid., Article 87.
7. See Val R. Lorwin, "Linguistic Pluralism and Political Tension in Modern Belgium," *Canadian Journal of History* 5 (1970), pp. 1-73.
See also, J. J. Thomassen, *La Constitution Belge Annotée, (Brussels, 1879).*

7. See Val R. Lorwin, "Linguistic Pluralism and Political Tension in Modern Belgium," *Canadian Journal of History* 5 (1970), pp. 1-73. See also, J. J. Thomassen, *La Constitution Belge Annotée,* (Brussels, 1879).

8. Henri Pirenne, *Histoire de la Belgique*, Tome III, (Brussels, 1926). See also Vernon Mallinson, *Belgium* (New York: Praeger, 1970), pp. 176-90.
9. Constitution of Belgium, Heading I, Article 3b.
10. Ibid., Heading Ib, Article 3c.
11. Ibid., Heading II, Article 6b.
12. Ibid., Heading III, Chapter I, Article 38.
13. Ibid., Chapter I, Article 32b.
14. Ibid., Chapter I, Section III, Article 59b.
15. Ibid., Chapter I, Section III, Article 59b, Section 2.
16. Ibid., Chapter I, Section III Article 59c.
17. Arend Lijphart, "Consociational Democracy," *World Politics* 20 (January 1969), pp. 207-25.
18. It is difficult to understand the meaning of the relevant section: Constitution of Belgium (B&F), Chapter I, Section III, Article 59b, Section 4.
19. Act of July 3, 1971, (B&F, Appendix 2), Chapter II, Article 2.

20. James A. Dunn, "The Revision of the Constitution in Belgium: A Study in the Institutionalization of Ethnic Conflict," *Western Political Quarterly* 27 (1974), p. 163.

21. The seven are China, India, the USSR, the United States, Indonesia, Brazil, and Japan.

22. B. Shiva Rao, *The Framing of India's Constitution: A Study* (New Delhi: Indian Institute of Public Administration, 1967-1968), p. 5.

23. Ibid., p. 742.

24. Ibid., p. 65.

25. During the course of debate, the Sub-Committee on Minorities drafted a questionnaire in the following language:

(1) What should be the nature and scope of the safeguards for a minority in the new Constitution?

(2) What should be the political safeguards for a minority
(a) in the Centre;
(b) in the Provinces?

(3) What should be the economic safeguards for a minority
(a) in the Centre;
(b) in the Provinces?

(4) What should be the religious, educational, and cultural safeguards for a minority?

(5) What machinery should be set up to ensure that the safeguards are effective?

(6) How is it proposed that the safeguards should be eliminated, in what time, and under what circumstances?

26. *Moosa* v. *State of Kerala*, All India Report, 1960, J.E.R. 355.

27. "India's 93 Million Harijans: Country Within a Country," *Intercom* (a publication of the Population Reference Bureau) 6, No. 1 (January 1978).

28. W. E. Rappard, *La Constitution Federale de la Suisse* [Neuchatel: Editions de la Baconnière, 1948).

29. On this and on many other basic issues of Swiss laws in support of the Constitution, see *Recuiel Systematique des Lois et Ordonnances,* published by the Federal chancery of Berne. Swiss constitutional law is most accessible through Jean-François Aubert, *Traitê de Droite Constitutional Suisse* (Neuchatel: Editions de laé Baconnière, 1967).

30. Required by Article 121, 1874 Constitution.

31. See K. D. MacRae, *Switzerland: Example of Cultural Co-Existence* (Toronto: Canadian Institute of International Affairs, 1964).

32. See George Codding, *Federal Government of Switzerland* (Boston: Houghton Mifflin Co., 1961), p. 53.

33. Article 3, 1874 Constitution.

34. MacRae *Switzerland*, p. 26.

35. Article 27, 1874 Constitution.

36. Figures from *USSR '77, Sixty Soviet Years* (Moscow: Novosh Press Agency Publishing House, 1977), pp. 15-22.

37. See Richard Pipes, "Introduction: The Nationality Problem," *Handbook of Major Soviet Nationalities*, ed. Zer Katz, Rosemarie Rogers, and Frederic Harned, (New York: The Free Press, 1975).

38. See Jeremy R. Azrael, ed., *Soviet Nationality Policies and Practice* (New York: Praeger, 1978).

39. See Richard H. Marshall, ed., *Aspects of Religion in the Soviet Union* (Chicago: University of Chicago Press, 1971), pp. 437-38.

40. Article 124, 1936 Soviet Constitution.

41. Article 52, 1977 Soviet Constitution.

42. Ibid., Article 35.

43. Ibid., Article 53.

44. Ibid., Article 9.

45. Ibid., Article 27.

46. Ibid., Article 34.

47. Ibid., Article 36.

48. Ibid., Article 45.

49. Ibid., Article 64.

50. Ibid., Article 69.

51. Rockey L. Rockett, *Ethnic Nationalities in the Soviet Union* (New York: Praeger, 1981), p. 153.

52. Robert L. Belknap in *Ethnic Russia in the USSR*, ed. Edward Allworth (New York: Pergamon Press, 1980), p. 325. However, much evidence of anti-Jewish activities is available.

7

Affirmative Action Policies

AFFIRMATIVE action, the conferring of special benefits upon individuals by virtue of their membership in a group, is a policy pursued only in a few nations that have diverse racial, religious, and ethnic groups. As a compensatory extension of preferences to group members, affirmative action is a modern expansion of minority rights that has been misunderstood and sometimes bitterly attacked. But affirmative action programs (sometimes called positive discrimination) are a logical application of minority rights, especially when used on behalf of disadvantaged persons. However, such programs focus upon groups; individuals may be accidental or even "undeserving" beneficiaries. The enhancement of minority group life is the goal. The repayment of past indignities and injustice is the motive. Nevertheless, few nations have actively adopted affirmative action policies.

So-called affirmative action plans have become more and more common as remedies for American blacks who have been historically denied access to the professions and the skilled trades. While there is no single, acceptable definition that describes these programs, there are many examples of officially prescribed programs for preferential hiring and for preferential educational admissions for blacks and other minority groups.[1] There have also been examples of private, voluntary efforts to provide special opportunities for blacks and other minorities. Unfortunately for advocates of affirmative action programs, the theoretical and legal underpinnings to support these programs are insecure, and the future development of preferential hiring, admissions, and other types of group favoritism are very much in doubt, especially in the light of vigorous opposition from other groups that maintain affirmative action programs as a form of reverse discrimination.

Some Americans contend that "preferential hiring favoring women and blacks represents a new form of discrimination against white males and hence is unjust."[2] Such a criticism assumes, against the evidence, that whites excluded by programs of preferential hiring or professional school admissions are as disadvantaged as traditional victims of racial and other forms of discrimination. The term "reverse discrimination" seems to equate the social position of majority whites with minority blacks, in spite of the fact that the self-esteem of whites and their social status is in no way endangered by affirmative action compensatory programs. It seems false to assert that "whatever good is accomplished by compensating members of the group discriminated against for past wrongs is vitiated by the corresponding denial of benefits to the group paying restitution."[3] (Favoritism programs, which are designed to aid minorities, do not necessarily impair the status of groups that are unfavored,) nor is it correct to maintain that a majority individual "pays" the cost of a minority preference. (To be denied a preference extended to a minority is not an act of discrimination unless there is some right to that preference.)

Nonetheless, critics of affirmative action in America contend that "the practice of reverse discrimination undermines the foundation of the very ideal in whose name it is advocated; it destroys justice, law, equality, and citizenship itself and replaces them with power struggles and popularity contests."[4] The vehemence of such criticism stems from a failure to understand the differences between anti-discrimination policies and affirmative action programs. Anti-discrimination programs are familiar parts of the American social system. Anti-discrimination programs are aimed at elimination of the barriers that inhibit the progress of members of victimized groups. However, it is unfamiliar policy in America to go beyond the removal of negative restraints upon minority group members. To actually promote and prefer minority group members with positive rewards and incentives seems to many Americans to be outside the requirements of equal treatment. Affirmative action programs test the limits of American individualistic notions. Indeed, the primary justification for affirmative action probably rests upon the idea of collective rights, of group rights, a way of thinking still beyond the grasp of many Americans.

The American Constitution makes no specific mention of group rights. Only the American Indians are referred to as a group in the constitutional text, and Indians do enjoy a special status under the Constitution. Yet the language of the rights sections of the Constitution does not refer to groups. Only the "equal protection of the laws" clause of the Fourteenth Amendment, written primarily to assist newly freed slaves, could be regarded as a constitutional justification for affirmative action. However, whether equality of the laws justifies preferential treatment of particular groups and their members is the legal center of controversy in America. Thus far, the Supreme Court has avoided directly confronting the constitutional issue.[5] Inevitably the court will have to make the leap from individual to group rights or else invalidate affirmative action programs altogether. The few clues currently available suggest a judicial willingness to accept some forms of affirmative action but no acceptance of the rather un-American notion of group rights.

In the most famous recent example of judicial scrutiny of affirmative action programs, the *Bakke* case, Justice Lewis Franklin Powell commented briefly upon the "intractable . . . difficulties entailed in varying the level of judicial review according to a perceived preferred status of a particular racial or ethnic majority," saying that "the concepts of majority and minority necessarily reflect temporary arrangements and political judgments" and that "there is no principled basis for deciding which groups would merit heightened judicial solicitude and which would not."[6] Justice Powell's vote in the *Bakke* case was critical to its outcome. Powell's theory of equal protection of the laws is hostile to group preferences and deserves attention because of the potential barriers raised by his rationale to the further extension of affirmative action programs in America. Powell insisted that "the guarantee of equal protection cannot mean one thing when applied to one individual and something else when applied to a person of another color. If both are not accorded the same protection, then it is not equal."[7] This highly individualistic reading of the Fourteenth Amendment would deny the validity of group rights and subject affirmative action programs to the same kind of intense, strict judicial scrutiny reserved for racial and ethnic distinctions generally. If Powell is correct, affirmative action programs intended to benefit members of a minority race are "inherently suspect," just as are other measures that are tainted with the suspicion of having discriminatory effects.[8]

Special treatment for disadvantaged groups has not been a favored American policy. After the Civil War Republican leader Thaddeus Stevens promised the newly freed slaves "forty acres and a mule," but Congress did not approve of his proposition. Instead, segregationist, discriminatory Jim Crow laws were passed in the American South; these kept blacks in a subordinate position for generations.[9] Constitutional acceptance of segregationist practices was provided by American courts at least through the 1940s. Legislation on behalf of blacks was blocked in the American Congress until the Supreme Court broke the logjam with its monumental school desegregation decisions.[10] These 1954 and 1955 decisions unlocked the doors of opportunity that had been closed to American blacks. Discriminatory barriers in education, housing, voting, and public accommodations were rapidly removed by court decisions and legislation. Yet blacks still lagged behind whites in economic and social terms. The removal of most discriminatory practices was partial, at best, but even the removal of all barriers might still leave a yawning gap between most blacks and most whites.[11] Affirmative action was aimed at closing the gap, but positive rewards and preferences seemed to irritate even liberal whites and to offend Supreme Court justices. Powell was willing to accept race as one of several admissions criteria, but the University of California's preferential program was, in his view, fatally flawed by "its disregard of individual rights."[12]

One of the leading observers of American constitutional law has examined the *Bakke* case and concluded that "underlying all of the opinions on the merits is the obvious need to clarify our thinking on the concept of discrimination itself, and the emerging question of individual against group rights in our constitutional order."[13] While the *Bakke* case did decide in favor of the complainant and against a particular plan of affirmative action, it left almost every affirmative action program in place, subject to the modifications hinted at in various opinions of various justices. So long as race is considered to be one of several criteria that bear upon admissions practices of public universities and so long as no obvious quota is established exclusively for members of a single racial group, affirmative action programs may be (or perhaps may not be in future years) constitutional. The fundamental issues of the constitutional rights of groups has not yet been confronted, merely postponed.

The Supreme Court must ultimately confront the group rights issue. In tentative fashion the court did approach the issue in a 1977 decision which upheld a redistricting plan that denied Hasidic Jews representation which they had enjoyed in the congressional district in which this group had previously been concentrated.[14] The court sanctioned the creation of a safe black representational district at the expense of the Jewish group by concluding that whites as a whole had adequate representation. While the result may not have been highly logical, the Court did, at least, recognize that group interests were at stake in the dispute. As more and more affirmative action cases come to the attention of the Supreme Court, this group approach to rights may become more familiar and more acceptable. If not, affirmative action is doomed in America.

The hope for future development of affirmative action in America rests mostly upon the reasoning of Justices William Brennan, Byron White, Thurgood Marshall, and Harry Blackmun in the *Bakke* case. For these jurists the "central meaning" of the opinion is as follows: "Government may take race into account when it acts not to demean or insult any racial group, but to remedy disadvantages cast on minorities by past racial prejudice, at least when appropriate findings have been made by judicial, legislative, or administrative bodies with competence to act in this area."[15] This group would not apply a strict scrutiny standard to affirmative action programs. Instead, "[to justify] racial classifications established for ostensibly benign purposes . . . an important and articulated purpose for [their] use must be shown . . . [and] any statute that stigmatizes any group or that singles out those least well represented in the political process to bear the brunt of a benign purpose."[16] Under such a view some constitutional justification for recognition of group rights with which to uphold affirmative action programs may well be forged.

There is substantial empirical evidence in America to demonstrate that blacks and women both lag behind the majority in terms of such critical indicators of social status as income, housing, and employment. Indeed, "most minority and female-headed households have only half the income that is available to majority households."[17] Thus a Civil Rights Commission concludes that "women and minority men have not achieved equal status with majority males on a series of 21 measures of equality in the areas of education, income, employment, occupations, poverty, and housing."[18] If the equal protection of the law guaranteed by the Constitution does not require a greater inequality of social condition, then these statistics pose no constitutional problem. However, if anti-discrimination policy fails to give miorities more than mere formal equality before the law, this is insufficient as a social policy for minorities. Affirmative action may be the only way to make further progress toward equality. Congress has indicated little enthusiasm for affirmative action. The Supreme Court still has yet to flash a clear signal regarding the constitutional significance of affirmative action under the equal protection of the laws guarantee.[19]

At the national level Presidents Nixon, Ford, and Carter have led the way in developing affirmative action policies. First, by executive order monies were set aside to assure that certain portions of federal expenditures were used to benefit members of minority groups. Second, detailed regulations and procedures were established for nonfederal entities, such as school systems and private employers, which obliged them to make decisions in a race, ethnic, or sex-conscious way. President Carter pressed hard to obtain more "underrepresented minorities" in the federal civil service, and his Office of Federal Contract Compliance Programs pressured private employers to hire women and minorities.

Ronald Reagan reached the White House in 1980 standing on a Republican party platform which opposed "quotas, ratios, and numerical requirements." Not surprisingly, he took gradual steps to dismantle much of the bureaucratic machinery that supports federal efforts toward affirmative action. While there is no flat ban of affirmative action, pressure on private businesses, government contractors, and even on the employment practices of federal and state governments has been reduced. Affirmative action in employment continues but is fading.

Much of the American constitutional argument relating to affirmative action surrounds the rights of the majority, the so-called victims of reverse discrimination. The most effective argument of the critics of affirmative action has been that individuals who happen to belong to an ill-defined and unorganized majority ought not to suffer in order to benefit other individuals who, because of membership in protected groups, are incidental winners in a struggle in which individuals are mere pawns. If, as one vocal critic contends, "groups [have] become the basis for rights, and those who want to own certain rights must do so as members of an affected or protected class,"[20] then America may have entered onto a path that leads to increased group friction and unlimited group assertion of claims for preferential treatment. If blacks make such a claim, why not Polish-Americans? So the argument goes. Apparently, many Americans do not perceive that some groups are much more highly disadvantaged, more unequal than others. By raising the spectre of group conflict, the policy of affirmative action may be discredited. Still, in the past courts have managed to monitor such issues, conferring suspect category status upon blacks while denying it to the poor and apparently to women. Indians have long been regarded as enjoying a special, protected status.[21] Yet in spite of these observations, there is genuine fear that affirmative action policies may endanger the uneasy balance among groups in American society. This uneasiness largely explains the hesitancy of the Supreme Court to spell out the constitutional boundaries of affirmative action in America.

Some affirmative action programs do include other American minorities.[22] The Davis special admissions program for which Alan Bakke applied included Chicanos, Asians, and American Indians. These groups are seriously underrepresented in the professions, and many group members are disadvantaged. However, Japanese-Americans and Chinese-Americans have done relatively well in economic terms, raising an issue about the legitimacy of a group denoting Asians as beneficiaries of affirmative action. A legislature or an executive agency might rationally (and constitutionally) justify preferences for such groups on the ground that they are essentially racial and have been subjected to past discriminatory treatment as a group. This issue of the identity of groups qualified for preferences remains unresolved in America.

The federal government has applied affirmative action programs to other groups, some of which are not minorities in the usual sense. Handicapped workers, disabled veterans, women, Spanish-surnamed individuals, and Orientals also benefit from various affirmative action programs. All federal contractors and subcontractors are obliged to make special efforts to hire handicapped individuals, although no specific hiring quotas are established.[23] The Department of Labor has also established affirmative action obligations for contractors and subcontractors that require them to employ disabled veterans and veterans of the Vietnam War.[24] Since 1972 all government contractors and subcontractors have been required to make special efforts to "recruit, employ, and promote qualified members of groups formerly excluded" from employment, "even if that exclusion cannot be traced to particular discriminatory actions on the part of the employer" on the premise that the maintenance of "a benign neutrality in employment practices will tend to perpetuate the *status quo ante.*"[25] Affirmative action programs in employment currently include women, minorities, disabled veterans, and the handicapped. Some of these are self-conscious groups, but they still enjoy special treatment, if not always a specific preference.

Affirmative action in America remains an ill-defined and constitutionally questionable set of programs. State, local, and national government agencies still promulgate orders in the name of affirmative action. In a few areas, such as employment, education, and housing, virtual minority quotas can be found, although these quotas run the risk of being invalidated in a judicial test. Meanwhile, controversy rages about the legitimacy of the concept of preferential treatment of minorities. Opponents of the concept are very prominent, especially since some of them are members of more fortunate minorities. The outlook for affirmative action in America will not improve until the concepts of group rights and of group deprivation is understood and accepted by opinion leaders and by the American Supreme Court.[26]

AFFIRMATIVE ACTION IN INDIA

For many, affirmative action and preferential programs generally are offensive to the nondiscrimination principle. How can you create a preference without discriminating in favor of one group and against others? The government of India has managed to do it. Although committed to the same kind of equal treatment as is required by the American Constitution, the Indian Constitution also embraces the ideal of uplifting and aiding less fortunate groups. Indian courts have learned to live with a constitutional policy that blends anti-discimination policy with affirmative action.

The nation of India is the second most populous country in the world. Geographically it is seventh largest in the world and is located at a position on the globe that has long been an area of contact between diverse peoples and cultures. According to a linguistic survey, there are 179 languages and 544 dialects spoken in India. But linguistic groups do not generally correspond to religious groups. While Hinduism is the majority religion, there are many Muslims, Christians, Sikhs, Parsis, and other minority religious groups. In addition to these groups the Constitution of India recognizes the existence of "Anglo-Indians," "castes," "backward classes," and "scheduled tribes." Probably no other nation in the world has recognized as many minority groups as has India. The laws and the Constitution of India exemplify a highly developed sense of minority rights. Anti-discrimination policy has been a major concern of Indian governments since independence was gained in 1947.

At the Constituent Assembly of India, which met from 1948 until 1950 to frame the new Indian Constitution, the principle of religious group representation was firmly established. Communal representation apportioned seats for Muslims, Sikhs, and "general" (the overwhelming majority). A number of seats were held by elected representatives of the "scheduled castes."[27] The Constituent Assembly was guided by several committees, among which was a Joint Advisory Committee on Fundamental Rights, Minority Rights and Administration of Tribal and Excluded Areas. This Joint Committee led the way in the creation of a national anti-discrimination policy as well as in the creation of nondiscrimination and affirmative-action-type policies.

From the outset India has striven for and obtained a greater constitutional recognition of minority rights than prevailed in either the United States or the United Kingdom. The extreme diversity of its population and the consequent political problem of creating a unity out of that diversity led to a series of policies that are not merely negative in character but also positive. These policies secure for various minorities certain protections and privileges that enhance their progress toward equal rights with the majority.

The prime right of all groups in India is the right to equality. The simplest statement of this principle is enunciated in Article 14 of the Indian Constitution, which asserts that "the state shall not deny to any person equality before the law or the equal protection of the laws within the territory of India." This phraseology, though derived partly from the American Constitution and from British common law, is essentially the same wording as is found in the Universal Declaration of Human Rights.[28] The Indian courts have held that this phraseology does not require identical treatment for all groups and individuals. Instead, "what Article 14 prohibits is the unequal treatment of persons similarly situated."[29]

Article 15 expands the concept of equal protection of the laws by stating among other things that "no citizen shall, on grounds only of religion, race, caste, sex, place of birth or any of them, be subject to any disability, liability, restriction, or condition with regard to access to shops, public restaurants, hotels, and places of public entertainment."[30] This constitutional anti-discrimination provision resembles various American civil rights statutes.

The principle of protective discrimination (similar to affirmative action) is also found enunciated in the same Article of the Indian Constitution. The Constitution provides that "nothing in this Article shall prevent the state from making any special provision for women and children."[31] Special provisions "for the advancement of any socially and educationally backward classes of citizens or for the scheduled castes and scheduled tribes" is also permitted.[32] This latter provision was added by a 1951 amendment intended to reverse adverse court decisions that had banned the reservation of seats in educational institutions for backward classes. As one constitutional scholar has explained: "It is quite appropriate that the backward classes should look to the constitution for special favours to redress the wrongs done in the past by creating social disabilities."[33]

Public employment is an area of constitutional concern in India. Anti-discrimination and protective discrimination both apply as policies. Equal opportunity in public employment is guaranteed all citizens, but "provision for the reservation of appointments or posts in favour of any backward class of citizens" is permitted.[34] Hardly any other constitution has combined anti-discrimination and discrimination in public employment together to secure minority rights.

Voting in India is based upon the principle of universal adult suffrage. All citizens, male and female, are entitled to vote irrespective of religion, race, and caste. Universal suffrage is the rule in all democratic societies. Nonetheless, the Indian Constitution makes an exception to this rule by reserving seats in Parliament and the state legislatures for scheduled castes and scheduled tribes and for the Anglo-Indian community.[35] This is a measure carrying forward the principle of protective discrimination, even though that principle may run counter to the general principle of universal suffrage for individuals.[36] Still, there are no separate electorates for those communities and no separate electoral rolls. Of course, the practice of reserving seats is unknown in America and the United Kingdom.

The special position of Indian linguistic, religious, and cultural minorities is amplified by specific provisions of the Constitution. The right to conserve "a distinct language, script or culture" is guaranteed to groups and individuals alike.[37] This right includes the protection and preservation of religious views, moral beliefs, and cultural practices. The Indian judiciary has interpreted this right broadly so as to include the right to agitate for the protection of a particular language.[38] Courts have also indicated that the right to language and culture is absolute and unqualified. This right applies to minorities based upon script and culture, but race, language, and religion are probably included.

Another section of the Constitution protects the right of "all minorities, whether based on religion or language" to "establish and administer educational institutions of their choice."[39] This is a negative guarantee against state interference. Another allied provision ensures that the state will subsidize such institutions to some extent.[40] Direct state subsidies to religious institutions are unconstitutional in America, but the Indian Constitution, based upon the principle of protective discrimination, encourages state aid to religious educational institutions. Indeed, in this respect the Indian Constitution goes beyond the state neutrality toward religion usually found in most constitutions.[41]

Linguistic minorities enjoy additional protections. There is a constitutional right to official recognition of the use of a language. This right begins with a demand by a group which may result in a presidential direction that the language be officially recognized within a state. Recognized minority languages may be used in the administration, if required by the Indian president. All that's needed is that the president be satisfied "that a substantial proportion of the population of a state desire the use of any language spoken by them to be recognized by the state."[42] Again, this provision is based upon the concept of protective discrimination, since it attempts to promote the interest of the minority, not merely protect it against instances of discrimination. There are other purposes to be served by this provision. In a multilingual society, important laws, regulations, and official correspondence should be in a language familiar to the local population if they are to comply with governmental policies. The national government retains the constitutional authority to prevent the linguistic domination of one group over another in a state by virtue of this provision, so in a broader sense the provision is a check upon potential linguistic discrimination.

The protective discrimination features of linguistic policies were supplemented by constitutional amendment in 1950.[43] Now the Constitution requires state and local governments to "provide adequate facilities for instruction in the mother tongue at the primary stage of education to children belonging to linguistic minority groups." The implementation of this practice is placed in the hands of the president, who may "issue such directions . . . as he considers necessary or proper." The president is also empowered to appoint a special officer for linguistic minorities who must "investigate all matters relating to the safeguards provided for linguistic minorities."[44] No nation has gone to such great lengths on behalf of linguistic minorities save, perhaps, Yugoslavia. The potentially divisive character of linguistic rights appears not to have frightened the drafters of the Indian Constitution nor subsequent national governments. Indeed, the national government continually prevailed upon state governments to protect linguistic minorities, especially in the areas of education and public employment. One expert concludes, in a self-congratulatory manner, that for India "on the constitutional side there is nothing wanting for safeguarding the legal and reasonable rights of any linguistic minority."[45] If true, this would be a situation without parallel in the minority rights field.

The constitutional treatment of India's "backward classes" is also unique. Technically, the Constitution treats three categories of Indian peoples in a very special way. Untouchables, historic victims of caste prejudice, are included as members of the so-called scheduled castes. There also are the scheduled tribes, consisting of largely aboriginal or primitive tribes; and finally, certain other depressed and deprived classes who are deemed "backward." India had suffered for centuries under the burden of a rigidly hierarchical and elitist social structure. Democratic, modern India repudiated that legacy, aiming to elevate these special and deprived groups toward equality of condition and treatment. Essentially, Parliament retains the power to include or exclude any caste, race, or tribe from these protective categories, but these groups now hold constitutional status.[46] According to the 1971 Indian census, 80 million people, 14.5 percent of the Indian people, are members of the scheduled castes. The scheduled castes, the scheduled tribes, and other backward classes amount to more than 30 percent of the total population of India, comprising the world's largest protected minority groups.

Economic uplift is the main hope of these protected groups. The economic backwardness of the scheduled castes and scheduled tribes has been largely due to the exploitation and oppression of centuries past. The Constitution is ambiguous on this point.[47] Public employment is not guaranteed them, but their claims "shall be taken into consideration . . . in the making of appointments," says the Constitution.[48] Yet the backward classes may be entitled to the reservation of appointments or posts.[49] Since government in India is the largest employer this issue is of great significance. Government service is much sought after, but it is not clear whether or not only the backward classes are entitled to special consideration in public employment.

Education is guaranteed the scheduled castes, the scheduled tribes, and the backward classes. Free compulsory education is provided until age fourteen.[50] The Constitution permits the state to make "any special provisions for the advancement of any socially and educationally backward classes of citizens or for the Scheduled Castes and the Scheduled Tribes."[51] Special care may be taken by the state to promote "the educational and economic interests of the weaker sections of the people."[52] In recognizing these departures from strict equality of treatment, the Indian Constitution has expressed an ideal of social justice above a principle of strict equality. Thus, special quotas and special educational admissions practices, though offensive to the majority and restrictive on the majority, are justifiable and appropriate objects of governmental policies under the Constitution. Some of these protective provisions are found among the Directive Principles of State Policy and may be subconstitutional in quality.[53] Nonetheless, they declare the positive obligations of the Indian State to its minorities.

The greatest evil in Indian society is untouchability. This system of debasing human beings is a basic and unique feature of the Indian caste system. Untouchability involves innumerable practices of subtle and gross discrimination, victimizing the lowest rungs of the caste ladder. So far as the Constitution is concerned, untouchability is abolished and its practice is forbidden.[54] Moreover, the enforcement of any disability arising out of untouchability is itself made punishable. Several statutes have been passed in an effort to stamp out untouchability. Yet the practice remains in more or less disguised form, serving the purpose of repressing the lowest castes, in spite of the Constitution. Traffic in human beings—slavery—and other forms of forced labor are also prohibited.[55] This provision of the Constitution has proven easier to enforce, since slavery is almost unknown. However, forced labor in some forms still persists in parts of India.

The tribal peoples of India are given special protections. Many of them are illiterate animists with primitive cultures. India has set itself the task of elevating their status while, at the same time, preserving their way of life. Whether or not integration of these peoples into Indian society is possible, the Constitution permits Parliament to provide states with funds to promote the welfare of the tribes and to aid in their development.[56] The governor of a state may be empowered to enact special legislation to protect the scheduled tribes from exploitation by moneylenders and real estate interests. Thus, the welfare of the tribes is a constitutional concern of the national and state governments. Special plans, projects, and schemes for the benefit of the scheduled tribes are contemplated by the Constitution. Exemptions from the ordinary laws of the land may be made to assist in their uplift. The opportunity of uplift is offset by the risk of disruption of the harmony of tribal life.

Religious minorities pose even greater obstacles to national unity. Tensions between Hindus and Muslims sometimes erupt into bloody riots. Sikhs outside the Punjab have claimed linguistic and cultural discrimination. But the Muslim-Hindu cleavage is a central problem of Indian social and political life. This cleavage continues to embitter Indian society.

India has no state religion. Hinduism is not given any special place in the society. The Constitution assures "freedom of conscience and free profession, practice and propagation of religion."[57] Apparently, the state cannot aid one religion or give preference to one religion against another, although it may support religious education. India's neighbor, Pakistan, has declared itself an Islamic state. India resisted the temptation to declare itself a Hindu state.

In spite of its salience in Indian life, religion is not given the protection accorded language, culture, caste, tribal, and backward status. Special protection and anti-discrimination policy are linked for many Indian groups, but not for religious groups, aside from educational subsidies.

India has provided its various minorities with different kinds of guarantees, sometimes in opposition to the interests of the majority. Equality and special preference are somehow blended together in a unique fashion. The Indian Constitution accords more protection to minorities than any other nation and deals with minority rights in greater detail.[58] Many of these rights are transitory, intended to disappear in the 1980s or at the end of the century. Equality is still the goal, but temporary inequality to help the disadvantaged is seen as a means of moving toward equality. Negative and positive rights are found side by side in constitutional provisions. The state is forbidden to act against certain minorities, while it is empowered to extend privileges to certain minorities. There is the danger that excessive regard for minority rights may lead to the slow disintegration of the Indian nation. Thus far, Indian anti-discrimination policy has continued its slow progress without a real separatist threat. Apparently, a sound anti-discrimination policy, coupled with protective provision, can work in a multicultural society. India's chief problems stem from her widespread poverty, not her anti-discrimination policy, which seems most enlightened, especially for a poor nation.

Affirmative action in India is a controversial policy still, in spite of decades of experience in developing it. Numerous protests and political actions have been raised against affirmative action. In 1981 the reservation of 25 percent of the places in medical schools for untouchables set off riots in Gujarat State that lasted intermittently from January to April. Yet the government persists in its efforts to advance untouchables and other Indian minorities.

India's neighbor, Pakistan, also provides for affirmative action in education and religion. Its Constitution provides that "nothing . . . shall prevent any public authority from making provision for the advancement of any socially or educationally backward class of citizen."[59] Malaysia, the Philippines, and Fiji have some sort of affirmative action principle on a constitutional basis. The most recent clear example of an affirmative action policy coupled with a commitment to nondiscrimination is found in the Constitution of Papua New Guinea, which declares, in one part that "all citizens have the same rights, privileges, obligations and duties irrespective of race, tribe, place of origin, political opinion, color, creed, religion or sex," but goes on to state that this provision "does not prevent the making of laws for the special benefit, welfare, protection or advancement of females, children and young persons, members of underdeveloped or less advanced areas."[60]

Obviously, it is not impossible to blend the nondiscrimination ideal with an affirmative action policy. A few nations, most notably India, have managed to do so. Such a blend seems an appropriate solution to the problems of deprived groups. Affirmative action is a legitimate means of securing minority rights. However, the popularity of affirmative action is limited. In most nations sympathy for the plight of minorities is not great enough to provide a political base for affirmative action policies. This most advanced minority policy is difficult to implement and hard to justify politically.

NOTES

1. Some anti-discrimination programs are tagged as "affirmative action" programs even by the federal departments of health, education, and welfare. Those programs, which are intended to inhibit discrimination against minorities by compelling full efforts to secure minority candidates for employment or education, are not truly compensatory in nature, nor do they, necessarily, imply goals or quotas for minority applicants. There is great confusion in America about this subject, confusion caused by the lack of a single, commonly understood definition of affirmative action. See Thomas Sewell, *Affirmative Action Reconsidered* (Washington, D.C.: American Enterprise Institute for Public Policy Research, 1975).

2. Stated in Marlene G. Fried, "In Defense of Preferential Hiring," *The Philosophical Forum* 5 (Fall-Winter 1973-1974), p. 310.

3. Onora Nell, "How Do We Know When Opportunities Are Equal?" *The Philosophical Forum* 5 (Fall-Winter 1973-1974), p. 335.

4. Lisa M. Newton, "Reverse Discrimination as Unjustified," *Ethics* 83 (July 1973), p. 312.

5. Regents of the University of California v. Bakke 438 U.S. 265 (1978); Kaiser Aluminum and Chemical Corporation v. Weber 443 U.S. 193 (1979).

6. Regents of the University of California v. Bakke, 438 U.S. 265 (1978), at 283-84.

7. Ibid., at 280.

8. Ibid., at 279.

9. See C. Vann Woodward, *The Strange Career of Jim Crow* (New York: Oxford University Press, 1974).

10. Brown v. Board of Education, 347 U.S. 483 (1954); Brown v. Board of Education, 349 U.S. 294 (1955).

11. See Derrick A. Bell, Jr., "Racial Remediation: An Historical Perspective on Current Condition," *Notre Dame Lawyer* 52 (1976), pp. 5-29.

12. Quoted in 46 U.S.L.W. 4910, June 27, 1978.

13. Robert G. Dixon, Jr., "Bakke: A Constitutional Analysis," *California Law Review* 67 (1979), pp. 69-86.

14. United Jewish Organizations, Inc. v. Carey, 430 U.S. 144 (1977).

15. Regents of the University of California v. Bakke, 98 S. Ct. 2733 (1978) at 2766.

16. Ibid., at 2785.

17. United States Commission of Civil Rights, *Social Indicators of Equality for Minorities and Women* (Washington: Government Printing Office, 1979), p. 65.

18. Ibid., at p. 91.

19. In the 1979 decision in Kaiser Aluminum and Chemical Corporation v. Weber, 47 U.S.L.W. 4851, the court deliberately circumscribed the scope of its

inquiry by refusing to "define in detail the line of demarcation between permissible and impermissible affirmative action plans" (p. 4855). The Court also treated the case on a nonconstitutional basis, emphasizing statutory interpretation.

20. Nathan Glazer, *Affirmative Discrimination*, (New York: Basic Books, 1975), p. 75.

21. See Morton v. Mancari, 417 U.S. 535 (1974), 25 U.S.C. Secs. through 1673 (1976) provide numerous references for American Indians, especially in employment (Ibid., at Sec. 470).

22. The U.S. Department of Labor classifies as minorities Negroes, Spanish-surnamed persons, American Indians, and Orientals.

23. 41 Federal Register 16147-16155 (April 16, 1976).

24. 41 Federal Register 26386-26393 (June 25, 1976).

25. U.S. Department of Health, Education, and Welfare, *Higher Education Guidelines*, Executive Order 11246 (October 1, 1972), p. 3.

26. See Guido Calabrese, "Bakke as Pseudo-Tragedy" *Catholic Law Review* 28 (Spring 1979), which proposes a rational test to distinguish disadvantaged groups from other groups in American society. The members of disadvantaged groups (blacks, Indians, women, the handicapped) seek to obtain a generalized equal opportunity by correcting for past societal prejudice that demonstrably denied group members equal opportunity. Affirmative action need not deny individualistic rewards based upon merit. It can provide for eventual expansion of egalitarian ideals once groups are given more equal chances.

27. B. Rao Shiva, ed., *The Framing of India's Constitution*, vol. 1 (New Delhi: Indian Institute of Public Administration 1967), p. 298. Professor Shiva notes that of the total 296 seats, Indian Christians had 6; Anglo-Indians, 3; Parsis, 3; scheduled castes, 31; backward tribes, 6; Sikhs, 4; Muslims, 80; and Hindus, 163.

28. Universal Declaration of Human Rights, Article 7.

29. Kishan Singh v. State of Rajasthan, *AIR* 42 (1955) para. 3, P.S.C. 797.

30. Indian Constitution, Article 15, Clause 2.

31. Ibid., Clause 3.

32. Ibid., Clause 4.

33. Ratna G. Revankar, *The Indian Constitution—A Case Study of Backward Classes* (New Delhi: Indian Institute of Public Administration, 1952), p. 50.

34. Indian Constitution, Article 16, Clause 4.

35. Ibid., Articles 330 to 333.

36. The Constitution (Twenty-Third Amendment) Act, 1969.

37. Indian Constitution, Article 29, Clause 1.

38. Jagat Singh v. Partap Singh, *AIR* 1965 SC 183.

39. Indian Constitution, Article 30, Clause 1.

40. Ibid., Clause 2.

41. See D. K. Sen, *A Comparative Study of the Indian Constitution*, vol. 2 (New Delhi: Orient Longmans, 1967), pp. 612-16.

42. Indian Constitution, Article 347.

43. Ibid., Article 350 A.

44. Ibid., Article 350 B.

45. Krishna Kodesia, *The Problems of Linguistic States of India* (Delhi: Sterling Publishers, 1969).

46. Indian Constitution, Article 366, Clause 24. The president may specify the castes, races, or groups deemed scheduled castes within a state. Article 341.
47. The Constitution (Twenty-third Amendment) Act, 1969.
48. Indian Constitution, Article 335.
49. Ibid., Article 16, Clause 4.
50. Ibid., Article 45.
51. Ibid., Article 15.
52. Ibid., Article 46.
53. See M. V. Pylee, *Constitutional Government in India* (New Delhi: Asia Publishing Co., 1960), p. 320.
54. Indian Constitution, Article 17.
55. Ibid., Article 23.
56. Ibid., Article 275.
57. Ibid., Article 25.
58. See Myron Weiker and M. Katzenstein, *India's Preferential Policies* (Chicago: University of Chicago Press, 1981).
59. Fundamental Rights Section, Pakistan Constitution of 1973, Article 22 (4).
60. Papua New Guinea, Constitution of 1975.

8

Anti-Discrimination Policies

THE principle that minorities shall not be the victims of discriminatory treatment is now well established in the constitutions and laws of most nations, but it is no older than 120 or 130 years. The first realization of this idea is to be found in an 1856 communication of the Turkish Sultan to his European treaty partners in which he describes legislation that he has introduced mainly for the benefit of the Christian inhabitants of his empire. The Sultan's legislation called for the equal treatment of his subjects, without distinction of religion or race. The European treaty partners, Austria, France, Great Britain, Prussia, and Sardinia commended "the value of this communication."[1]

Although the 1856 Turkish legislation does not extend equality of treatment on grounds of nationality, language, culture, caste, or sex, it certainly was a forerunner of the full-fledged American anti-discrimination principle. The more famous equal protection of the laws clause of the American Fourteenth Amendment, while much more influential, was not much more extensive. This American amendment, which was ratified in 1868, formids state governments from denying to any person "the equal protection of the laws." The Fourteenth Amendment, ratified in 1870, forbids the abridgement of citizen voting rights "on account of race, color or previous condition of servitude." The United Nation's Universal Declaration of Human Rights lists "race, colour, sex, language, religion, political or other opinion, national or social origin, property, birth or other status" as impermissible grounds for unfavorable treatment.[2] Probably no nation fully supports the principle of equality of treatment to this extent, but much progress has been made in the legal elimination of discrimination in the past few decades.

The principles of equality and nondiscrimination have been deemed an "absolute precondition" to the enjoyment of minority rights.[3] Unequal treatment of minorities usually takes the form of discrimination against them. Laws to forbid unequal treatment are intended to restrain the majority—to limit their freedom to discriminate. This negative approach to protection of minorities may not actually change the internal attitudes of members of the majority, but at least it is designed to prevent the obvious manifestation of those attitudes. The guiding ideal is that "no individual should be placed at a disadvantage merely because he is a member of a particular ethnic, religious or linguistic group."[4]

Anti-discrimination policy is well-established in the constitutions and laws of most nations. Segregation and discrimination are official policy only in the Republic of South Africa. Instead, equality and nondiscrimination are proclaimed as official policy in virtually every other county of the world, even those that ignore informal discriminatory practices or those that enforce official policies indifferently. The Constitution of the Soviet Union declares that "any oppression of national minorities" is unlawful, while Switzerland and Belgium refer specifically to linguistic minority groups, but the principle of nondiscrimination is generally found in constitutional provisions emphasizing the principle of equal treatment of all citizens rather than specifically mentioning minority groups.

Statutes describe many aspects of the nondiscrimination principle. A few countries have highly developed legislation intended to remove discriminatory barriers. Probably the leading examples of such legislation are the United States and the United Kingdom and these will be examined here as possible models for future expansion of anti-discrimination legislation. The highlights of these leading national examples will be emphasized.[5] But it must be remembered that laws alone cannot terminate discriminatory practices. De facto discrimination continues outside the law. Even so, minority rights cannot be expected to grow, let alone thrive, without an official anti-discrimination policy as an essential feature. The comparison of anti-discrimination policy in two leading nations will demonstrate the limits as well as the effectiveness of laws in regulating discriminatory attitudes and behavior. The obstacles to anti-discrimination policies in these two leading nations should prove instructive warnings to others moving in the same direction.

THE AMERICAN ANTI-DISCRIMINATION POLICY

American policy is strongly aimed at removing many of the barriers of race, religion, and sex. The law has only recently taken account of linguistic differences, while culture and caste have been generally overlooked. Government policy has been concerned primarily with official discrimination, but, to a limited extent, private discrimination is also made unlawful. Both the state and federal governments have established various types of anti-discrimination policies with mixed success.

The original American Constitution of 1789 countenanced slavery.

Slaves had no genuine civil rights, although they were counted for purposes of representation. The Supreme Court of the United States rarely inquired into the question of slavery. When they did so in the infamous *Dred Scott* case of 1856, it was to overturn a political compromise that limited the extension of slavery into new territories. Chief Justice Roger Taney took the occasion to observe that "Negroes had no rights which the white man was bound to respect."[6]

The American Civil War was fought partly on the unresolved issue of black slavery. However, even though the North was free of slavery, it practiced racial segregation. American President Abraham Lincoln expressed doubts that Negroes could ever be accepted as the social equal of whites. But the Civil War terminated slavery. The victorious North imposed a new racial settlement upon the defeated South.

The key elements of American anti-discrimination policy were created in the aftermath of the Civil War. The Thirteenth, Fourteenth and Fifteenth Amendments to the Constitution expressed a new arrangement of political (perhaps social) order in America. the Thirteenth Amendment barred slavery forever. The Fourteenth Amendment extended American citizenship to native-born blacks. At the same time the amendment prohibited any state from making or enforcing any law "which shall abridge the privileges and immunities of citizens of the United States." More significantly, states could not "deprive any person of life, liberty, or property, without due process of law; nor deny to any person within its jurisdiction the equal protection of the laws." This section is America's greatest contribution to anti-discrimination policy making. The Congress of the post-Civil War years enacted sweeping anti-discrimination measures under the Fourteenth Amendment, perhaps the first such broad-gauge anti-discrimination statutes.[7] Unfortunately, the Supreme Court of the day undermined the progressive work of the Congress, delaying racial progress by decades.

The slow judicial shrinkage of the Civil War Amendments is a long story of late nineteenth century conservative jurisprudence. A series of Supreme Court decisions rendered some sections of the Thirteenth, Fourteenth, and Fifteenth Amendments meaningless. Political events made black rights less significant. Congress, the states, and the public lapsed into indifference.

Three Supreme Court decisions helped limit the scope of black rights. The Slaughterhouse cases (1874) sharply curtailed the privileges and immunities clause as a protection against state discrimination, although it seems to have been designed to vastly expand black rights against state action.[8] In 1883, the court held, in *United States* v. *Harris*, that the equal protection clause of the Fourteenth Amendment applied only to state discriminatory action.[9] Other cases denied power to Congress to directly reach individual acts of discrimination.[10]

State segregation statutes abounded in this vacuum of anti-discrimination policy. The states had the power to restrict discrimination against blacks, and a few used it. But in the American South Jim Crow was born, meaning that southern states attempted to legalize white supremacy while disenfranchising blacks.[11] The courts limited the most outrageous efforts to disenfranchise blacks, but for the most part federal and state courts acquiesced to segregationist sentiment.

By 1900 blacks were close to their pre-Civil War status, even though they were technically free. The pattern of official race segregation was approved by the Supreme Court in 1896. The decision in the case of *Plessy* v. *Ferguson* was supposedly based upon the legal equality of the white and black "races" under a system of racial segregation. Actually, the decision rested upon ill-disguised notions of black inferiority. As Justice Henry B. Brown saw it, in the majority opinion, legislation could not abolish "distinctions based upon physical difference." The separation of the races was justified because "if one race be inferior to the other socially, the Constitution of the United States cannot put them upon the same plane."[12]

Slowly, but inevitably, the Supreme Court had to retreat from its racist views of 1896, until in 1954 it disavowed them by overturning *Plessy* v. *Ferguson*. The "separate but equal" policy of racial segregation was gradually abandoned, but not without some hesitation by the Supreme Court, which steered anti-discrimination policy toward blacks in the mid-twentieth century.

When it came, the Supreme Court decision of 1954 was a thunderbolt. Few expected such a strong disavowal of segregation. None could forsee that desegregation would become as complex and convoluted as it did become. Nonetheless, the decision in *Brown* v. *Board of Education* is a milestone in anti-discrimination policy. It changed the direction of American policy and drew the attention of the world.

The Brown decision concluded that "in the field of public education the doctrine of 'separate but equal' has no place." *Plessy* was implicitly overruled after 58 years of officially approved segregation. A unanimous, united Supreme Court decreed that no matter what the assertions in defense of racial separation, "separate educational facilities are inherently unequal." This logic was swiftly extended to all public facilities.

The implementation of racial desegregation in public schools was a task assigned to the lower federal courts. Desegregation proceeded in spite of initial resistance. President Eisenhower ordered out the federal troops to support Court-ordered desegregation.[14] Defiant southern politicians retreated.

Clever segregationists fought a holding action. Some closed down all public schools, while giving grants to white children to attend private schools, but all this was to no avail.[15] The Supreme Court struck down so-called freedom of choice plans, which maintained a dual school system for blacks and whites in 1963 and 1968.[16] Finally, in 1969 the Court announced its impatience with delaying tactics by pronouncing all dual school systems terminated.[17]

This forward thrust of racial desegregation in public schools has slowed considerably in the past decade. While southern school systems are no longer segregated by law, the de facto segregation of housing patterns in other sections of the country pose important policy problems. Once school segregation laws were abolished (for the most part), was there a constitutional need to compel public school integration? The creation of a truly integrated public school system required concerted efforts by courts and legislatures alike. But the Supreme Court, now led by the more conservative chief justice, Warren Burger, no longer paved the way toward greater racial desegregation.

The ambiguity that surrounds current American anti-discrimination policy is partly due to Supreme Court cautiousness and uncertainty. The Court is not trying to turn back the clock to before *Brown*, but it no longer provides the impetus for a clearly constitutional justification for anti-discrimination policy. While the federal Congress and the state legislatures have taken up some of the policy leadership, the Court has found itself placed in the position of restraining some of the more vigorous efforts to end race discrimination. In recent years the Court has signalled displeasure with judicial activism aimed at more rapid school desegregation, and housing discrimination has been placed on the constitutional agenda.

Two unresolved problems still plague the integration effort in the public schools: the constitutionality of undeliberate racial segregation and the viability of pursuing school integration in inner cities with huge black populations. Truly integrated education may or may not be required by the equal protection clause of the Constitution. If the Supreme Court had said that equal protection meant school integration, then the desegregation of nonsouthern school districts would have proceeded, accompanied, of course, by turmoil and short-term resistance or even by white flight from integrated school districts. But the Court drew a sharp distinction between de jure, legally created, and de facto, unintentional (in a formal, legal sense only) segregation—a distinction which slowed progress toward greater school integration.

Apparently, desegregation, not integration, is the basic policy of the Supreme Court with regard to schools and racial discrimination. There exists no positive constitutional obligation to promote race-mixing in the schools, in the playgrounds, on the job, or in homes. If Congress or the state legislatures wish to create such policies, the Supreme Court seems willing to sustain them, unless they go so far as to establish racial quotas that in themselves discriminate against other groups.

It is possible to sketch the trends of the early Burger Court. In 1973 the Supreme Court did strike down a northern school district plan in which school authorities had clumped one-third of a city's school children into a single black school.[18] However, the Court in 1974 seemed to virtually close the door to integration efforts in the North, which required busing between a city and its surrounding suburbs, by holding that in the absence "of any inter-district violation" no metropolitan remedy could be ordered by a federal district court.[19] The suburbs had not violated the constitutional requirements of equal protection of the laws merely because they were mostly white and the city of Detroit was mostly black.

The Supreme Court continued to issue go-slow signals in 1976, and 1977. In 1976 the Supreme Court checked the bold integration plan of a district court judge who had ordered that students be reassigned annually in order to obtain his desired goal of no school in which a majority of the students were black.[20] District courts could not order pupil reassignment when racial segregation had been in no way due to segregation policies of school officals. In 1977 the Court disapproved a lower court order for system-wide desegregation in Dayton, Ohio, on the ground that "only if there has been a systemwide impact [of earlier de jure, official, discrimination] may there be a systemwide remedy."[21] Other decisions during the same two years disapproved various court-ordered busing schemes because of the absence of "segregative intent" on the part of school officials.

Public anti-discrimination policy outside of education also tends to be shaped by U.S. Supreme Court holdings. The general rule is that the Fourteenth Amendment prohibits "state action" only, not private discrimination. Under Warren Burger the Court has held that discrimination by a private club does not become converted into state action simply because the club holds a state liquor license.[22] Even the use of public recreational facilities by segregated, private groups is permitted because the "mere use" does not amount to state action.[23] The state may not shut down public schools to avoid desegregation, but it may close its swimming pools and recreational facilities, as long as it doesn't provide aid to private facilities.[24] The Court has not, however, tolerated state laws which forbid interracial marriage.[25]

Racial discrimination in housing has also been an area of judicial concern. Housing segregation is especially prevalent in the North. Rarely is housing segregation an official policy of federal, state, or local governments. When it has been, the Supreme Court has not hesitated to take a strong position. In 1976 the Supreme Court found that the federal Department of Housing and Urban Development and the Chicago Housing Authority had joined together to promote racial segregation in public housing in Chicago.[26] The Court has upheld both federal and state open housing legislation, even going so far as to sustain an ancient statute of 1866 that prohibits private discrimination in the sale or rental of property.[27] The Court has refused to support private, restrictive concern. Housing segregation is especially prevalent in the North. Rarely private owners from selling to members of unwanted groups. Such restrictive covenants are simply unenforceable in American courts.[28] Perhaps the Supreme Court envisages a desegregated society being achieved through the elimination of discrimination in housing. That would be a long, arduous process requiring determined effort by lawmakers and bureaucrats.

Employment discrimination has been largely managed by statutory rather than constitutional means. Congressional regulation of private employment discrimination has been upheld. Such discrimination is subject to the Act of 1866 and Title VII of the Civil Rights Act of 1964.[29] Sex discrimination, as well as race discrimination, in employment falls under Title VII. Title VII makes it unlawful for an employer "to limit, segregate, or classify his employees in any way which would deprive any individual of employment opportunities or otherwise adversely affect his status as an employee, because of such individual's race, color, religion, sex, or national origin."[30] The Supreme Court has interpreted this section in such a way as to require an alleged victim of discrimination in employment to show: (1) that he belonged to a minority; (2) that he applied for a job opening; (3) that, despite his qualifications, he was rejected; and (4) that after his rejection the job was kept open for later, similarly qualified applicants.[31] Employers may use employment tests, but these must be job-related.[32] The tests must be intended to demonstrate skills really necessary for the job for which the applicant is being considered.[33] Still unclear in the Court's decisions is the extent of the employer's opportunity to prove a lack of discriminatory intent. Whether a policy is deemed explicitly designed to screen out minority group members or women and actually violates Title VII depends upon the factual setting and the inclination of the justices.[34]

Voting discrimination has been largely eliminated in the United States as a result of a long series of Supreme Court decisions under the Fifteenth Amendment and various strong federal Civil Rights Acts passed in the 1960s. Most significant is the Voting Rights Act of 1965, which requires that, where there is past history of discrimination, state reapportionment plans be approved by the attorney general of the United States or a federal district court. This provision is intended to insure that a state apportionment plan does not "deny or abridge the right to vote on account of race or color." In 1977 the Supreme Court held that the dilution of the voting strength of a Jewish group, caused by new district lines for the purpose of strengthening the influence of black voters, did not violate the Voting Rights Act of 1965.[35] Apparently, creating districts to benefit a racial group may not be a source of complaint by a white group inadvertently disadvantaged. The case is not clearly based on a theory of racial preference, but it does reveal that black voters are no longer neglected, and the Voting Rights Act may be a vehicle for the further enhancement of black voting power if legislatures are disposed to doing so.

Race is regarded as a suspect category in American constitutional law because the Fourteenth Amendment was aimed at the elimination of official race discrimination. Such discrimination is subjected to more exacting scrutiny under the equal protection clause and is held invalid unless shown to have been necessary to an overriding governmental purpose. Neither sex nor religion have been held to be suspect categories, although sex has come close to that status. This means that sex and religious discrimination are more constitutionally tolerable than racial discrimination.

Older Supreme Court decisions upheld state protective legislation that established different and less harsh conditions of employment for women. Federal legislation expanded the concept of sex discrimination. The Civil Rights Act of 1964 prohibited employment discrimination on the basis of sex. Beginning in 1971 the Burger Court expanded the constitutional significance of sex by striking down an Idaho probate code provision which gave preference to men over women as administrators of estates. The case held that statutory sexual classifications were "subject to scrutiny under the Equal Protection clause."[36]

In 1973 the court invalidated statutory provisions that allowed male members of the military to claim their wives as dependents while requiring female members to show that their husbands were actually dependent upon them in order to qualify.[37] A Utah statute was subsequently declared unconstitutional because it set the age of majority at 21 for males and 18 for women. In 1976 an age distinction between women and men was stricken down.[38] The offending statute allowed women to purchase 3.2 beers at age 18 but forbid men from doing so until age 21. Now "classifications by gender must serve important governmental objectives and must be substantially related to achievement of those objectives."[39]

Current controversy swirls around the "benevolent" classification of women that provides them rights not available to men. Perhaps only in America would such special treatment draw resistance. The significance of these cases may be greater than they seem, since they go beyond discrimination issues into the territory of positive benefits or special treatment, a claim not often recognized in American constitutional law.

Kahn v. *Shevin* upheld a Florida statute that give widows, but not widowers, a property tax exemption.[40] A later case upheld a federal policy that gave women naval officers an opportunity to remain on active duty longer than men.[41] Men who had been twice passed over for promotion were required to be discharged from service, while women could remain on duty 13 years, often being passed over for promotion. Apparently, the justification for upholding these special benefits for women was to remedy a history of past disadvantageous conditions, a theory that could potentially be stretched to cover American minority groups as well. As if to stress this point for women, a 1977 decision sustained a statute that allowed women to calculate their retirement benefits more favorably than men. The justification was that the statute "operated directly to compensate women for past economic discrimination."[42]

In fact, recent Supreme Court holdings make it difficult to establish that a governmental action that disadvantages a minority is unconstitutional. In the absence of rather clear proof of discriminatory intent, the Court has generally refused to find an act of unconstitutional racial discrimination. The Court has made it clear that proving a discriminatory purpose is very difficult and it will not be presumed merely from the statistical impact of a governmental policy.[43]

American has never admitted that its problems with minority groups and women require special legislative and administrative treatment, at least not in the established international sense. Whatever distinctions are tolerated between the treatment of men and women is based upon an American sense of compensation for past disadvantages. This is as far as American policy is able to go. As we shall observe, quotas and preferences in favor of minorities test the limits of American jurisprudence, even when based upon a theory of compensation for historical racism.

Religious Discrimination in the United States

Religious discrimination in America is also subject to a judicial refusal to decide among competing groups. America is predominately a Protestant nation. Catholics, Jews, nonbelievers and other sects do not acquire rights by virtue of their group membership. In fact, there has been different treatment of religious groups under the First Amendment of the Constitution, but this has never been officially acknowledged by the Supreme Court. Instead, the Court has insisted on the neutrality of the government toward religious groups. This position has not been consistently applied, but the theory remains intact.

The Puritan colonists in Massachusetts Bay had an established church, as did every American colony prior to the American Revolution. Toleration extended mostly to Protestants, while Catholics, Jews, and sometimes Baptists and Methodists were actively discouraged. Because of the bitterness of religious group rivalry prior to the Revolution, prominent secularists such as Thomas Jefferson, James Madison, and

George Mason urged a clear separation of church and state. This separation has been one of America's major contributions to group relations, and even though Protestants, Catholics, and Jews still differ, religious discrimination is not as severe a problem in America as in most other nations.

The First Amendment of the American Constitution simply provides that "Congress shall make no law respecting an establishment of religion or prohibiting the free exercise thereof."

The Supreme Court interpretation of this phraseology has varied a great deal over the years, but it means, at a minimum, that there is no established religion in America, and it also means that Congress (actually, all governmental agencies) is obliged to avoid interference with religious practices. The mass suicide of religious sect members in Jamestown, Guyana, shows that religion in American has taken peculiar forms, but it also shows that the government will do little to restrain aberrant religious practices.

The Constitution has nothing to say about religious discrimination, other than the provision which states that "no religious test shall ever be required as a qualification to any office or public trust under the United States."[44] This clause made void a state law that required a declaration of belief in the existence of God as a qualification to hold office.[45]

Different religious groups have fared differently in American constitutional law. Mormons lost major constitutional tests when the court upheld legislation aimed at stamping out polygamy, a Mormon practice.[46] Mormons have been disenfranchised in the past and church property has been taken away without offending the Constitution.[47] On the other hand, since 1938 the Jehovah's Witnesses have received constitutional protection for their beliefs and practices.[48] One of these Jehovah's Witness cases resulted in the 1940 holding that First Amendment provisions regarding religion were binding on states and local governments, as well as the national government, by virtue of interpretation of the Fourteenth Amendment.[49] The propaganda efforts of the Witnesses were sustained in 1943, as was the sect's refusal to permit their children to salute the flag.[50] The Jehovah's Witness cases have gone a long way toward removing religious discrimination against the sect's members, as well as incidentally benefitting all religious groups.

Seventh Day Adventists and Jews have not done quite as well under Supreme Court interpretations of the Constitution. In 1977 the Court held that the 1964 Civil Rights Act did not require that an employer establish a four day work week for a Seventh Day Adventist or make diligent efforts to satisfy the Adventists's religious practices.[51] Jews have complained about the Sunday closing laws, which in many sections of the country result in a loss of an additional business day on the part of observant Jews. Yet, the Supreme Court has sustained Sunday closing laws, even if some state supreme courts have not.[52]

Education in religious schools is a matter of worldwide controversy. In American religious schools are constitutionally protected. The state may not force all children to attend secular schools.[53] However, the question of how much public assistance may be given to religious schools has vexed constitutional scholars for the past fifty years. Supreme Court decisions have supplied rationalizations for limited public support to religious schools. Religious instruction in public schools is clearly banned, although it is possible to have religious instruction off school grounds.[54] The public school is a secular institution in America. Prayers or devotional readings in public schools violate the First Amendment.[55] The constitutional requirement of public neutrality toward religion has the effect of protecting minority religious groups and nonbelievers, since it prevents a religious majority from using the schools to spread their beliefs or to injure other religions. Even the status of Christmas celebrations is in doubt in public schools, thus safeguarding minority group resistance to such holidays.

Many American religious groups are active politically. Catholics have been active in pressing for aid to parochial education, tax exemption for church property, and censorship of sexual materials. They have also been actively opposed to legalized abortion. Protestants, although in a clear numerical majority, have not overtly pressed for legislation that discriminates against Catholics, Jews, or other minority religions, but some have been active in such groups as the so-called moral majority. Various statutes prohibit religious discrimination in employment and educational opportunity. Nonetheless, much relatively unregulated religious discrimination is prevalent at top management levels and in private life. On the whole, however, religious discrimination in America was widespread in the nineteenth century and prevalent up to World War II, but seems to be on the wane.[56]

American Indians

Two other American groups have been historic victims of discrimination: American Indians and Spanish speakers (including Puerto Ricans and Mexican-Americans). Indians of North America differ markedly from the dominant culture. These indigenous peoples lost most of their lands, and many were slaughtered in various wars against them. In the nineteenth century they were a subject people, and some tribes were virtually liquidated as a result of the actions of state and national officials.[57]

The Constitution is virtually silent about Indians. Early Supreme Court opinions did little to assist them.[58] Now there are about 750,000 Indians living in the United States, 400,000 of them on reservations set aside by the national government. Indian life on these resevations was miserable and unhealthy until the past few years when Indian activism has led to reforms in the Federal Bureau of Indian Affairs. In 1968, Title II of the Civil Rights Act gave the reservation Indians most of the protections available to other Americans under the Constitution. For example, the First Amendment is incorporated word for word into the 1968 Act, except for the omission of the restriction on the establishment of religion, a concession to the theism of many Indian groups.[59] Other portions of the Bill of Rights were also extended, with modifications, to the reservation Indians.

Indian tribal courts remain in control of civil suits and minor criminal infractions. Major crimes are removed from the jurisdiction of tribal courts. Indian customary law may be enforced by tribal courts under certain conditions.

Off-reservation Indians are frequent objects of discrimination. Neither the Civil Rights Act of 1968 nor the Constitution are much protection for them, since "terminated Indians," as they are called, are legally non-Indians. Although nonreservation Indians have all the rights and privileges of other American citizens, they are ineligible for the educational, housing, and health-care benefits available to reservation Indians.[60] Since reservation Indians have begun to receive better treatment, many Indians would prefer to remain on the reservation, but some have been compelled to leave the reservation. In general, Indian policy has not been a notable success for the advocates of equal treatment. Indians have been and are an example of the inadequacy of American anti-discrimination policy.[61] American Indians on reservations still have only attained partial self-government.[62] Indian groups have claimed the right to preserve their cultural and religious practices against the ordinary laws of the state and nation, but with limited success.[63]

Hispano-Americans

Spanish is the native language of more than 8 million Americans. One and one half millions are Puerto Ricans; five million are Mexican-Americans. The remainder are from Cuba and parts of Central and South America. Language rights are not recognized in the American Constitution. Yet discrimination against Spanish speakers is prevalent, partly based upon their skin color and partly on their poverty. Acceptance into the majority society has been difficult for these Americans, and only recently has attention been directed to their plight.

Since 1954 the U.S. Supreme Court has recognized "the ethnological and statistical identifiability of the Mexican-American classification."[64] Yet Mexican-Americans and Puerto Ricans still receive inferior public education; they rarely receive a higher education or enter the professions. As if to remedy these problems at the root, some states began to require bilingual education in public school districts with large Spanish-speaking populations. While the Constitution does not guarantee education as a fundamental right, there appears to be a blossoming right to be instructed in a language that is appropriate to the population of a district.[65] Under President Carter the Department of Education urged public school elementary instruction in the language familiar to the school children. In addition, the agency has urged affirmative action programs in employment which give greater opportunity to Spanish speakers, or at least those with Spanish surnames. However, there is a long distance to travel before Spanish speakers can be assimilated into the majority culture. The Reagan administration has seemed to withdraw from federal activism in these areas.

Conclusion

Assimilation seems to be the main purpose of American anti-discrimination policy. This goal is not pursued consistently or vigorously. The school integration effort seems to be the centerpiece of the anti-discrimination policy, at least for black Americans. The slackened pace of school integration, especially in the urban North, has signaled a slowdown in anti-discrimination efforts on other fronts. Doubtless, as new group protests arise, a reinvigorated anti-discrimination policy will emerge. No matter what specific legal changes may take place, there is little likelihood that separate development or group autonomy will be the goal. Officially, at least, the commitment is to an integrated society in which the minorities are gathered into the majority culture.

ANTI-DISCRIMINATION POLICY IN THE UNITED KINGDOM

The sources of English anti-discrimination policy are to be found in recent legislation and in commitments made to international organizations. In attempting to understand the distribution of rights in the United Kingdom there is no equivalent of the American Bill of Rights to provide a touchstone for minority rights policies. Instead one must grope around to locate the current appropriate legislation. Magna Carta, the Bill of Rights, and the Petition of Rights are all part of the heritage of Western civilization from which our modern view of individual rights has, in many respects, been developed. But these ancient English documents do little to clarify contemporary rights policies.

Until recently issues of minority rights were relatively rare in Great Britain. True, there were religious minorities: Catholics, Jews, and Protestants other than members of the Church of England. Linguistic minorities were nearly nonexistent, in spite of a Welch and Gaelic revival movement during the nineteenth and early twentieth century.

Englishmen were not very aware of their group differences, although bias and prejudice were rampant. Anti-Semitic, anti-black and anti-Irish attitudes were and are widespread in English society. Yet the law had little to say about such things, presuming all Englishmen to be equal before the law. The myth of a homogenized, integrated, and harmonious society sustained the English in the nineteenth century, although class rivalries shook the foundations of English politics.

Religious differences split England asunder for centuries. Catholics and Protestants struggled for the throne, while Jews were denied entry into the country. Religious tolerance developed during the nineteenth century as Jews and Catholics attained political rights previously denied them. However, there still is one dominant, state-supported church, the Church of England, claiming almost 28 million members, a clear religious majority. There are about 5.4 million Roman Catholics and 450,000 Jews in England. There are fewer than 4 million Protestants of various denominations.[66] There are no figures for the Sikh, Muslim, or Hindu religions, although many of their adherents live in the United Kingdom.

The Anglican Church is part of the fabric of the country. Ever since the break with Rome in 1534, when Henry VIII assumed the title of "Supreme Head of the Church in England," the church lost its independence but gained political and social power. Twenty-six Anglican bishops have a right to sit in the House of Lords, and the Archbishop of Canterbury has the right to crown the king of England. The Anglican Church once actively persecuted Catholics, and before 1829 Catholic priests were not allowed to live within five miles of towns. Dissenters (non-Anglicans) have been allowed to teach at Oxford and Cambridge only since 1871. The sovereign and the lord chancellor must both be Anglicans, although a prime minister may be of any religion. However, the prime minister, as adviser to the king, appoints the bishops (unless the prime minister is a Catholic).

The Church of England is neither owned nor subsidized by the state. Its income comes from its own lands and capital, although some of this was acquired, in the past, by means of royal seizure of Catholic lands and properties. But the church does own 223,000 acres of land, making it the largest private landholder in the country.[67] Its holdings of stocks and bonds are formidable factors in those markets.

English law requires that state and private schools begin every day with collective worship. The Education Act does not stipulate which religion must be used as a basis of worship. Religious instruction must be according to an "agreed syllabus," which is composed by representatives of churches in the area. Parents can withdraw their child from religious instruction and morning prayers if they choose. Teachers have a right not to attend religious instruction. However, pupils have no right, other than their parents expressed desires, to withdraw from religious instruction or worship.[68] So there is some, but very little, church-state separation in England, and there is nothing to forbid the official closing of a religious school or even of a church, although neither has happened in many years. Custom, not law, would seem to be protection against such an abuse of governmental power.

After 1066 no other nation conquered the British Isles. Foreigners have come to England, but their presence did not give rise to concern about their rights. In general foreigners were tolerated. The Scots, the Irish, and the Welsh, though indigenous to the islands, were, and to some extent still are, treated as foreigners. The Irish seem to have been most oppressed and remained so until the arrival of immigrants from outside Europe.

Non-European immigration hardly existed prior to World War II, although British ships had brought African and Chinese people to their seaports for centuries. Large scale non-European immigration did not begin until West Indians were attracted into the Royal Air Force to fight during World War II. Soon West Indians settled by the thousands in the larger cities and were packed into crowded living areas. Asians came later. Pakistanis and Indians, often expelled from newly independent African states, came to see England for the first time and to settle there, since there was no place for them in their home countries of India or Pakistan. The Asian immigrants brought new religions, new languages, and new customs to a country that had complacently considered itself enlightened and progressive. Color discrimination began almost immediately.

The entry of new minorities into England aroused new forces and anxieties. No minorities policies had emerged in England simply because no minorities problems were perceived, apart from religious groups. Several hundred thousand immigrants from India, Pakistan, and the West Indies have arrived in England testing the tradition of English tolerance. The word "coloured" is usually applied to them, although the word also signifies migrants from the Middle East and native British born of nonwhite or mixed parentage. Certainly, "the expression of color consciousness has generally increased in Britain among whites and nonwhites during the past decade."[69] But the race situation is still unsettled, and there are no established traditions of formal or informal relationships among the various races. Officially sponsored segregation has not taken root, although private discrimination abounds.

Color consciousness in England cannot be separated from colonialism. The coloured population derives from parts of the Commonwealth that were formerly under direct British domination. Under the Empire the native populations were often stereotyped as backward and inferior. Now that their offspring are in England, old attitudes have resurfaced.

As a defense mechanism, interest groups have emerged for each immigrant group, and each one is concerned with protecting group members from discrimination. Immigration policy and protective anti-discrimination legislation are the main concerns of these groups.

Most of the groups are affiliated with the Campaign Against Racial Discrimination (CARD), an umbrella group established in 1965 and devoted to exposing discrimination and to obtaining anti-discrimination legislation. CARD had a hand in the enactment of the British Race Relations Act of 1965. CARD agitated for better immigration laws. However, CARD finally collapsed as an interest group.[70]

By 1967 an official government study concluded that British society discriminated against coloured immigrants and against their children.[71] The English government, responding to this kind of information, rapidly developed a race relations policy to deal with this new factor in English life. In the immigration field as well as in anti-discrimination legislation, the government was prepared to move. The evidence of racial discrimination became overwhelming.[72] Beginning in 1965 the first tentative steps were taken, even before the evidence of discrimination had been assembled. The Race Relations Act of 1965 was the first legislation in Britain to establish the illegality of discrimination based on race, color, and ethnic or national origin. The Act may be regarded as a constitutional innovation in Britain.

The first British Race Relations Act was passed by Parliament in 1965.[73] The act was a personal triumph for Fenner (now Lord) Brockway, who had presented a Race Relations Bill to Parliament on nine occasions, only to have it thrown out each time. The 1965 Act dealt with discrimination in public places and with color bar clauses in leases. The act also introduced a new criminal offense of incitement to racial hatred. This act did not cover the two main areas in which discrimination occured—housing and employment. However, the act represents a constitutional innovation for England, a recognition of minority rights, and a bold new policy aimed at discrimination.

In 1968, after discovering the inadequacies of the 1955 Act, a second Race Relations Act was passed.[74] Professor Harvey Street authored a Report on Anti-Discrimination Legislation that led directly to the 1968 Act. Street examined anti-discrimination policy in England and proposed stronger measures to deal with it.

The 1968 Act dealt with discrimination on the grounds of color, race, and ethnic or national origin, but not nationality. This broader coverage included most of the area described here as minority-based. Discrimination was made unlawful in the provision of goods, services, and facilities, including education, employment, and property transactions. Enforcement was assigned to a Race Relations Board, which had the task of sifting through claims of rights violations in order to reconcile the parties and then going to the courts if no compromise could be reached. Access to the courts was placed exclusively in the hands of the board. The board had only limited powers of independent investigation and action.

The 1968 Act also proved inadequate. Discrimination in housing and employment did not decline. The Race Relations Board proved ineffectual. The board did not enjoy the confidence of minority groups.[75] The act also omitted mention of sex discrimination. Yet another tangible justification for disatisfaction with the act was widespread industrial strikes among Asian workers, who complained about discriminatory practices, especially in the hosiery industry. Trade unions also rebuffed Indian workers.[76] Finally, reform of the 1968 Act became a political issue among minority groups, particularly black youths, the second generation of West Indian immigrants.

In 1975 the government declared its policy intentions, stating that the "overwhelming majority of the coloured population is here to stay" and that meant that there had to be a determined effort "to ensure fair and equal treatment for all our people, regardless of their race, colour, or national origins."[77] A better law would be drafted that would be more comprehensive in scope and which permitted easier access to the courts. A better machinery for uncovering discriminatory practices would be developed. A strategy for dealing with the root causes of disadvantage would be devised.[78]

Unfortunately, the new act could not live up to these noble aims. Moreover, the immigration laws remained based upon racialist assumptions. The immigration laws gave black and Asian immigrants an inferior status, making their residence in England dependent upon their acceptable behavior. The immigration laws seem to assume that blacks and Asians were a potential threat to the community.[79] The immigration law remains as a restraint upon whatever positive benefits are created by the anti-discrimination policies of the 1976 Race Relations Act.

The current Race Relations Act went into effect on November 22, 1976.[80] The act deals with three kinds of discrimination: (1) direct discrimination that involves less favorable treatment on grounds of color, race, nationality, and ethnic or national origins; (2) indirect racial discrimination "in which a requirement or condition" is applied "such that the proportion of persons of the same racial group as that other who can comply with it is considerably smaller than the proportion of persons not of that racial group who can comply with it;"[81] and, (3) victimization of those who give evidence or information in connection with the act. This third category is intended to protect those who witness acts of discrimination.

Interestingly, the term "racial group" is defined in the act to mean "a group of persons defined by reference to colour, race, nationality or ethnic or national origins.'' Furthermore, the act states that ''references to a person's racial group refer to any racial group into which he falls.'' The act is based upon a group rights approach, and comparisons of treatment accorded members of groups is the underlying basis of the statute. Minority rights are placed firmly in a group context by this statute.

The law is also directed against segregation. ''Segregating a person from other persons on racial grounds'' is a violation of the act.[83] Thus, the act prohibits separate treatment of individuals on ''racial'' grounds (defining race in the broad fashion indicated above). Segregated rest rooms would be in violation of the act. Segregation is permitted whenever its purpose is to afford ''persons of a particular racial group access to facilities or services to meet the special needs of persons of that group in regard to their education, training or welfare, or any ancillary benefits.''[84] This kind of positive segregation is excepted because it bestows benefits upon the group.

The status of some groups under the act is uncertain. Jews seem not to be covered by the act. Jewish quotas for admission to private schools are a common practice in England, yet they have not been held to violate the act because the act does not cover religious discrimination.[85] Gypsies are another group that suffers as victims of discrimination in England. A 1967 case held that gypsies were not a race within the meaning of the 1965 statute.[86] The Race Relations Board did tend to treat gypsies as a race, but since the board has been replaced by a Commission for Racial Equality, the exact status of gypsies is unclear.

Genuine language discrimination is not covered by the statute. Unless the real grounds are racial, discrimination by reason of language is not a concern of English rights policy. In certain circumstances language discrimination might amount to indirect discrimination under the Race Relations Act, as when an employer's language requirement is inappropriate to the employment activity.

Discrimination in employment is the chief target of the Race Relations Act. The recruitment of employees, their pay, training, treatment, and dismissal all fall within the ambit of the act. Employment policies and practices of all businesses are open to the scrutiny of the Commission for Racial Equality. This commission has full powers to obtain company records and subpoena witnesses. The act is aimed at the elimination of discriminatory practices rather than punishment of offenders. The only criminal penalties for discrimination are for knowingly and recklessly misinforming an employment agency that a particular job is not covered by the provisions of the act.[87]

Unlike many other employment discrimination laws, the English law embraces trade unions as well as employers. This means that union officials cannot refuse entry to a worker, expel him, or deny him benefits on racial grounds. However, shop stewards are not included in the act. Unions are not held accountable for what shop stewards do.

Public employment seems to be covered by the act. Crown employees, those working for public agencies, are generally (but not at the highest levels) covered. The armed services are included, with some exception, as are police and employees in public education. Qualifying boards or professions are also subject to the act.

Excluded from the employment sections of the act are various categories of workers who may eventually be included. The Act does not apply to household workers in private homes, although they may be covered by certain other legislation. Genuine occupational qualifications based upon race are permitted, so employers have a limited right to discriminate in certain kinds of jobs, but only at the hiring stage. These special jobs are: actors portraying members of a particular race; artists and photographic models; ethnic restaurants; and community social workers, when identification with the client group is necessary.[88] Also, under the Immigration Act, immigration authorities may impose conditions restricting labor and the length of stay of most immigrants.[89] Visitors to the United Kingdom are usually forbidden to take work and may be deported if they do so without permission. Even work permits are usually limited to no more than one year.

Quotas in employment are no longer permitted by the Race Relations Act. Under the 1968 Act employers could set quotas, and refuse jobs to black or white workers if they had already filled their quota as part of an effort to maintain racial balance on the job. Thus, quotas in employment are regarded as a form of discrimination, whatever their purpose.

The Race Relations Act is also directed against discrimination in education. Discrimination is forbidden in either the public or the private sector of education. A distinction is made between public and private education, with university education placed in the private sector. Public sector complaints must go through the appropriate education minister. Investigations of anti-discrimination activity in education are conducted by the Commission for Racial Equality in both the private and public sectors. Discrimination is proscribed in terms of admission and refusal of admission, in the provision of benefits and facilities, and in expulsion of students. Even if admission to an educational institution is by means of a test, indirect discrimination charges may be upheld if the test discloses racial bias. However, it is not unlawful discrimination for religious schools to refuse to admit students of another religion.[90]

Section 20 of the Race Relations Act of 1976 makes it unlawful to discriminate in the provision of goods, facilities, or services. This means that the act covers discrimination in public facilities such as hotels, clubs, boarding houses, restaurants, barber shops, cinemas, parks, banks, and any other retail business. Wholesale businesses and manufacturers fall under Section 20, as do all services and professions. To the extent they provide services, government agencies and the police are covered. Some minor exceptions exist for private housing uses. Most of the reported complaints of violations of Section 20 are about acts of discrimination in pubs and dance halls, but enforcement against owners of these establishments seems to have been firm and consistent. Apparently, private clubs are allowed to discriminate if they are not generally open to the public and are a "private, select, group."[91]

Housing discrimination is also unlawful. Tenants, licensees, and purchasers are protected against discriminatory practices. Property owners are liable for their own acts and the acts of their employees and agents. Real estate agents must conform to the law, but these have been the biggest culprits. Another area of abuse covered by the 1976 Act is the refusal to sell or let property to individuals by reason of color or because of the pressure of neighbors who wished to prevent the entry of minorities into the community. Exceptions are made for landlords of small premises, especially if a landlord or near relative who resides on the premises.

Enforcement of the Race Relations Act is placed in the hands of the individual and of the Commission for Racial Equality. Individuals who have been discriminated against can take their case to an industrial tribunal (employment cases) or the local courts. Remedies for racial discrimination include compensation for damages and, in employment cases, a recommendation for remedial action.

The Commission for Racial Equality has the general task of promoting equality of opportunity and good race relations.[92] Pursuant to this obligation, the commission may hold hearings, institute investigations, make reports, and issue codes of practice in employment. The commission is also empowered, in appropriate cases, to issue a nondiscrimination notice requiring the recipient to cease doing improper acts and to alter his or her practices to conform to the law. Injunctions may be sought against persistent violators.

Section 69 of the Race Relations Act makes an incitement to racial hatred an offense. The offense is committed by the publication or distribution of threatening, abusive, or insulting written matter or by the use of such words in a public place. The act applies to the abuse of whites as well as to the abuse of minorities. Under this section the largest task of the prosecution is proving the likelihood of racial hatred. If a violent outbreak occurs directly after a speech, the offense is proven. Section 5 of the Theatres Act of 1968 also makes it an offense for anyone to present a public performance of a play that uses abusive or insulting words with the deliberate intention of stirring up racial hatred. Whether these acts can dampen racial tensions is doubtful.

There has been public pressure for tougher immigration laws that are aimed at coloured immigrants. The social and economic difficulties of black minorities in the United Kingdom continue and may have worsened during recent years. The severe economic setbacks suffered by the United Kingdom seem to have increased racial tensions in spite of the race relations law that is directed toward reducing them. However, in spite of prevalent attitudes, the Race Relations Act has had some impact, resulting in fundamental changes in the perception of minority rights. The best evidence of these changes may be found in the resolution of cases brought under the act in recent years.[93]

AMERICA AND THE UNITED KINGDOM: PIONEERS IN ANTIDISCRIMINATION POLICY

Many lessons are to be learned from a careful review of the experiences in the United States and the United Kingdom. Both countries have vigorously pursued the elimination of private and public discrimination against most minority groups. Both have developed sharp legislative tools and administrative techniques for detecting and correcting improper discriminatory acts. The United States and the United Kingdom both utilize courts as means of implementing anti-discrimination policy, although America has involved its courts much more heavily in policy formulation. On the other hand the United Kingdom's Race Relations Board has been more active than its U.S. counterparts.

It would be possible to contrast women's rights or the rights of linguistic minorities in the two nations. Such a study would reveal widespread social differences between these nations, which might partly account for the different treatment of these kinds of group claims. But we should remember that the two nations are vastly different in composition. Britain has been a relatively homogeneous society for centuries, while America has been composed of vastly different population groups since its independence. Moreover, immigration policies in the two countries have, until recently, been quite different, with the United States at first encouraging more and more different peoples to settle there.

Yet before overpraising the United States and the United Kingdom for their vigorous official policies, we must observe that there still is widespread public and private discrimination in both nations. American blacks still lag behind whites in income, education, jobs, housing, and virtually every other area. Similarly, Asians and African residents in the United Kingdom still suffer severe handicaps.[94] Mere official recognition and protection of minority group members is insufficient to eliminate discrimination. Anti-discrimination legislation cannot by itself change long-held attitudes and practices. Only persistent pressures by public officials and constant vigilance in support of official policies can combat discrimination. Any nation considering the experiences of the United Kingdom and the United States should be most attentive to the slow pace of progress in anti-discrimination policy.

Governmental action is only a first step on a long road toward a more just treatment of minorities.

NOTES

1. *British and Foreign State Papers*, 1855-1856, vol. 46 (London: William Ridgway, 1865), pp. 8-18. It is Article IX of the Treaty of Paris of March 30, 1856, in which mention is made of the Sultan's activities in protecting Christians.

2. Universal Declaration of Human Rights, adopted December 10, 1948, Art. 2, G. A. Rep. 217A, UN Doc. A/810 at p. 71 (1948).

3. Study on the Rights of Persons Belonging to Ethnic, Religious and Linguistic Minorities (Francisco Capotorti, Special Rapporteur) UN Doc. E/CN 4/Sub. 2/384/ Rev. 1 (1979), p. 54.

4. Ibid., p. 55. This view of discrimination is also embodied in the International Convention on the Elimination of All Forms of Racial Discrimination, which defines "racial discrimination" to include "any distinction, exclusion, restriction or preference based on race, color, descent or national or ethnic origin which has the purpose or effect of nullifying or impairing the recognition, enjoyment or exercise on an equal footing, of human rights and fundamental freedoms in the political, economic, social, cultural or any other field of public life." International Convention on the Elimination of All Forms of Racial Discrimination, Art. 1, UN Doc. A/6014 (1965).

5. For a UN survey of national anti-discrimination legislation, see *Racial Discrimination*, Study by Hernan Santa Cruz, Special Rapporteur for the Sub-Commission on Prevention of Discrimination and Protection of Minorities, E/CN 4/Sub. 2/370/ Rev. 1 (1976), pp. 52-68. In spite of the title, most forms of discrimination are included, not only racial discrimination. However, the findings of this report are sparse and rudimentary.

6. Dred Scott v. Sanford, 60 U.S. 393 (1856).

7. See United States Commission on Human Rights, *A Report to the President: Freedom to be Free* 1863-1963 (Washington, D.C.: U.S. Government Printing Office, 1966), pp. 5-50.

8. 16 Wall, 36 (1874).

9. 106 U.S. 629 (1883).

10. Civil Rights Cases, 109 U.S. 3 (1883).

11. C. Vann Woodward, *The Strange Career of Jim Crow* (New York: Oxford University Press, 1968); Louis R. Harlin, *Separate But Unequal* (New York: Atheneum, 1968).

12. 163 U.S. 537 (1896).

13. 347 U.S. 483 (1954).

14. Cooper v. Aaron, 358 U.S. 1 (1958).

15. Griffin v. Canty School Board of Prince Edward County, 377 U.S. 218 (1958).

16. Goss v. Board of Education, 373 U.S. 683 (1963); Green v. County School Board, 391 U.S. 430 (1968).

17. Alexander v. Holmes County Board of Education, 396 U.S. 19 (1969).

18. Keyes v. School District No. 1, Denver, Colorado, 413 U.S. 189 (1973).

19. Milliken v. Bradley, 418 U.S. 717 (1974).
20. Pasadena City Board of Education v. Spangler, 427 U.S. 424 (1976).
21. Dayton Board of Education v. Bronxman, 433 U.S. 406 (1977).
22. Moose Lodge v. Irvis, 407 U.S. 163 (1972).
23. Gilmore v. City of Montgomery, 417 U.S. 556 (1974).
24. Palmer v. Thompson, 403 U.S. 217 (1971).
25. McLaughlin v. Florida, 379 U.S. 184 (1964); Loving v. Virginia, 388 U.S. 1 (1967).
26. Hills v. Gautreaux, 425 U.S. 284 (1976).
27. Jones v. Alfred H. Mayer Co., 392 U.S. 409 (1968).
28. Shelley v. Kraemer, 334 U.S. 1 (1948); Barrows v. Jackson, 346 U.S. 249 (1953).
29. 41 U.S.C. sec. 1981 and 1982.
30. 42 U.S.C. sec. 2000, Title VII, Civil Rights Act of 1964 sec. 703 (a) (2).
31. McDonnell Douglas Corp. v. Green, 411 U.S. 792 (1973).
32. Griggs v. Duke Power Co., 401 U.S. 424 (1971).
33. McDonald v. Sante Fe Trail Transportation Co., 427 U.S. 272 (1976).
34. See Albemarle Paper Co. v. Moody, 422 U.S. 405 (1975); and Furnco Construction Corp. v. Waters, 438 U.S. 567 (1978).
35. United Jewish Organizations of Williamsburg, Inc., v. Carey, 430 U.S. 114 (1977).
36. Reed v. Reed, 404 U.S. 71 (1971).
37. Frontiero v. Richardson, 411 U.S. 577 (1973).
38. Stanton v. Stanton, 421 U.S. 7 (1975).
39. Craig v. Boren, 429 U.S. 190 (1976).
40. 416 U.S. 351 (1974).
41. Schlesinger v. Ballard, 419 U.S. 498 (1975).
42. Califano v. Webster, 430 U.S. 313.
43. See Washington v. Davis, 426 U.S. 229 (1976), in which the Court refused to find racial discrimination by the District of Columbia police force in spite of an employment examination that had the effect of eliminating a disproportionate number of black applicants. Similarly, in Jefferson v. Hackney, 406 U.S. 535 (1972), the Court upheld a state law providing welfare benefits that seemed to disadvantage blacks and Mexican-Americans. See also Village of Arlington Heights v. Metropolitan Housing Development Corp., 429 U.S. 252 (1977).
44. U.S. Constitution, Article VI.
45. Torasco v. Watkins, 367 U.S. 488 (1961).
46. Reynolds v. United States, 98 U.S. 145 (1978).
47. David v. Beason, 133 U.S. 33 (1889); Mormon Church v. United States, 136 U.S. 1 (1890).
48. Lovell v. City of Griffen, 303 U.S. 444 (1938); Schneider v. Town of Irvington, 303 U.S. 296 (1940).
49. Cantwell v. Connecticut, 310 U.S. 296 (1940).
50. Martin v. Struthers, 319 U.S. 141 (1943); West Virginia State Board of Education v. Barrette, 319 U.S. 569 (1943).
51. Trans World Airlines v. Hardison, 432 U.S. 63 (1977); but see Sherbert v. Verner, 374 U.S. 398 (1963).

52. Sunday Closing Law Cases, 366 U.S. 420 (1961).

53. Pierce v. Society of Sisters, 268 U.S. 510 (1925).

54. Zorach v. Clauson, 343 U.S. 306 (1952).

55. Engel v. Vitale, 370 U.S. 421 (1952).

56. See Jerold S. Auerbach, *Unequal Justice* (New York: Oxford University Press, 1976), for a description of discrimination in the legal profession.

57. See A. M. Gibson, *The Kickapoos* (Norman, Oklahoma: University of Oklahoma Press, 1963).

58. See Worcester v. Georgia, 31 U.S. 515 (1832).

59. Civil Rights Act of 1968, Section 202 (1).

60. See Leo J. Sclar, "Participation by Off-Reservation Indians in Programs of the Bureau of Indian Affairs and the Indian Health Service," *Montana Law Review* 33 (1972), pp. 205-23.

61. See Angie Debo, *A History of the Indians of the United States* (Norman, Oklahoma: The University of Oklahoma Press, 1970).

62. See S. Bobo Dean, "The Consent of the Governed—A New Concept in Indian Affairs," *North Dakota Law Review* 48 (1972), pp. 553-60.

63. They are entitled to preference in hiring by the Bureau of Indian Affairs, 25 U.S.C. sec. 472. Upheld in Morton v. Mancari, 417 U.S. 535 (1974).

64. Hernandez v. Texas, 347 U.S. 475 (1954).

65. San Antonio Independent School District v. Rodriquez, 411 U.S. 1 (1973); See Lau v. Nichols, 414 U.S. 563 (1973), which upholds HEW guidelines under the Civil Rights Act of 1964 requiring school districts to provide special assistance to non-English speaking Chinese students. The Department of Health, Education, and Welfare could prohibit a linguistic restriction "even though no purposeful design is present." The Court did not, though, reach the conclusion that the Constitution required nondiscriminatory language instruction.

66. From David Butler and Anne Sloman, *British Political Facts*, 1900-1975 (New York: St. Martin's Press, 1975). Religious statistics are notoriously unreliable, and the census does not collect such information. The churches themselves are the sources of data.

67. See Anthony Sampson, *Anatomy of Britain Today* (New York: Harper & Row, 1965), p. 179.

68. National Commission on Civil Liberty, *Civil Liberty* 3d edition (Hammondsworth, England: Penguin Books, 1978), p. 431.

69. Sheila Allen, *New Minorities, Old Conflicts* (New York: Random House, 1971), p. 170.

70. See Benjamin V. Heineman, Jr., *The Politics of The Powerless* (London: Oxford University Press, 1972).

71. Political and Economic Planning, *Racial Discrimination* (London: P.E.P., (1967).

72. See E.J.B. Rose and Associates, *Colour and Citizenship* (London: Oxford University Press, 1969).

73. 1 Statutes 926 (1965).

74. 40 Statutes 103 (1968).

75. White Paper, *Racial Discrimination*, 1975 (Cmnd. 6234), par. 33.

76. *Manchester Guardian*, "Unequal Brothers," May 25, 1973, p. 17.

77. White Paper, *Racial Discrimination*, note 77, par. 4.

78. Ibid., par. 26.

79. See I. A. Macdonald, *The New Immigration Law* (London: Butterworths, 1971).

80. Race Relations Act 1976, 1976 C. 74.

81. Ibid., sec. 1 (b).

82. Ibid., sec. 3 (1).

83. Ibid., sec. 1 (2).

84. Ibid., sec. 35. See also secs. 37 and 38.

85. Religious discrimination in education may fall under the Education Act of 1944, sec. 30.

86. Mills v. Cooper, 2 Q B. 459; 2 All E.R. 100 (1967).

87. Race Relations Act of 1976, sec. 29 (5).

88. Ibid., sec. 5.

89. Immigration Act of 1971, sec. 3 (1).

90. See Report of Race Relations Board for 1974, par. 27, 28 and 29.

91. Chater v. Race Relations Board, A.C. 868, 1 All E.R. 512 (1973).

92. Race Relations Act of 1976, sec. 43 (1) (6).

93. "Racial Discrimination at Work," *Department of Employment Gazette* (Great Britain) 89 (October 1981), pp. 431-32.

94. The British Nationality Act of 1981 deals with this most sensitive matter in a manner which makes British citizenship more difficult to acquire and makes residence by commonwealth citizens a more limited right.

9

The Future of Minority Rights

THE most recent serious study of minority rights prior to this book is now more than two decades old. In the intervening years numerous new nations have been born and many vestiges of empire have disappeared. The relationship of majorities to minorities has been virtually transformed, and thinking about the rights of minorities has changed. In 1960 it could be concluded that "the surest protection for minorities are not those written into constitutions."[1] But since 1960 over 130 new constitutions have been written, and many of them do consciously recognize some rights for minorities. Although many minorities are protected by treaties, by political custom, by national laws, and by judicial interpretation, it can be said that recognition of minority rights claims in constitutions is a growing and significant trend that shows a reversal of the "tendency of classical democracy to affirm the individual but to deny the group."[2] Yet this trend toward greater official recognition of minority rights has a very long way to go to reach the level of legitimacy accorded individual rights in democratic states. In nondemocratic states, where individualism is less significant, barriers to minority rights recognition are not as high, although oppression of minorities is not unusual. In both democratic and nondemocratic states, minority rights prospects have improved considerably. But what are the future prospects for minority rights?.

Many observers will disagree with these final observations about minority rights. Some contend that minority rights are unmodern, based on outmoded romantic nationalism. Others hold that national unity and stability may be threatened by insistence upon the claims of particular minorities.[3] Some nations assert that they simply cannot bear the cost created by the serious implementation of cultural claims of minorities. Assimilation, some say, is thwarted by undue insistence on minority rights. But the assumption of this book is that the minority rights movements of the past two decades are mostly genuine and cannot be ignored. While Welsh and Scottish nationalism may wane in the United Kingdom, Basques, Armenians, Bengalis, Northern Ireland Catholics, Palestinians, Kurds, Nagas, and others are groups to contend with in future years. Minority rights problems are likely to increase in the years to come.[4]

In his popular book, *The Third Wave*, Alvin Toffler predicts the breakup of nations, with a transfer of power to subnational regions and groups. Toffler sees this process as part of a larger demassification of public and private life. He asserts that "the nation-state has become, for many purposes, a dangerous anachronism" and forsees a restructuring of the United Nations and other international representational organs in favor of religions, ethnic groups, and regions as the mass society of the industrial era disintegrates under the impact of the forces of change to a post industrial, postimperialistic world. Such a grand reconstruction of the world may be far off, but it is conceivable that the rumblings of discontent from various minorities may, indeed, presage major changes in the political structures of nations. Minority rights issues may be a significant aspect of future politics as nations come to grips with the aspirations of constituent groups and peoples. There are many indications that long-silent minorities are becoming vocal. Claims long dormant are being asserted in ways that call for answers, not merely token responses or outright repression.

DEMOCRACY AND MINORITY RIGHTS

John Stuart Mill believed that representative democracy was virtually impossible in plural societies: "Free institutions are next to impossible in a country made up of different nationalities. Among a people without fellow-feeling, especially if they read and speak different languages, the united public opinion, necessary to the working of representative government, cannot exist."[5] In spite of this verdict, the two of the three oldest operative written constitutions are to be found in multicultural societies, the United States (1789), and Belgium (1831). Clearly, representative democracy is more difficult in multicultural societies, but by no means impossible.

The existence of strong minority groups is not a menace to democracy, although many social scientists seem to believe that it is. Some scholars contend that "the resolution of intense but conflicting preferences in the plural society [is not] manageable in a democratic framework.[6] Under this view strong ethnic or similar groups are inherently at war with other groups. This makes compromise and coalition unfeasible.[7] Less extreme critics of plural democracy concede that Western, industrial societies can support plural democracies but assert that non-Western plural societies are too weak to sustain the strains of group struggles.

The accommodation of group struggles within a democratic polity is possible under certain conditions. While authoritarian measures have often been employed in underdeveloped societies as a means of accelerating development, this means of suppressing group struggle is not inevitable. Lebanon and Cyprus have fallen as examples of pluralist democracies, but many others remain, even in the underdeveloped world. While in general most new regimes have repressed minority groups in the interest of national integration and economic development, a few have withstood the tide of authoritarian politics. Trinidad, Malaysia, Thailand, Barbados, Ghana, and Papua New Guinea are possible examples. If most of the Third World has opted for authoritarianism, this does not mean that democratic pluralism does not work.[8]

There are also socialist examples of pluralism based upon the model of the Soviet Union. Czechoslovakia, Hungary, Bulgaria, and Rumania give formally recognized minority group rights. Yugoslavia has evolved its own version of minority rights under state socialism. Whether or not Communist party power considerations or Marxist ideology permit full enjoyment of minority rights is an interesting and highly disputed issue, but certainly there are examples of generous treatment of some minority groups under communism. This treatment suggests that group rights are not incompatible with Communist practices.

Proponents of Western-style democracy contend that democratic regimes provide more individual liberties and represent a wider degree of different interests.[9] Seemingly, minority rights should fare better under Western style democracy, although the case is not yet proven.[10] One scholar has insisted that one type of democracy, which he dubs "consociational democracy," is the best hope for the recognition and development of minority group rights and interests.[11] Consociational democracy includes "all possible segmental cleavages in a plural society."[12] In spite of the breakdown of democracy in many non-Western regimes, there is no reason for despair about the appropriateness of democracy in pluralist societies. Instead, what is required is "consociational engineering," although "the prospects for consociational democracy become less and less favorable as the degree of pluralism increases" or as "the numerical balance among the segments becomes more uneven or severely fragmented."[13]

This prescription for a special form of democracy for plural societies includes a presumption that minority rights can be effectively secured in pluralist societies by novel political engineering. Consociational democracy would have certain essential features ensuring minority rights. First, there would be a grand coalition of the political leaders of all significant segments of the plural society. There would also have to be a mutual veto or concurrent majority rule to serve as a protection of essential minority interests. In addition, proportionality would be the principal standard for political representation, service appointments, and in the allocation of public funds. Internal affairs of each segment would be left to relevant minorities to a substantial extent.[14] Majority rule would not and could not always prevail. The two-party parliamentary democracy would not apply to pluralist societies. Obviously, political engineering for consociational democracy would have to be tailored to each individual national situation.

This ideal of consociational democracy may be little more than a social scientist's dream. The cases selected to support this scheme are carefully chosen and subject to different interpretations. Religious and ideological conflicts may have yielded to consociational measures in a few nations in Western Europe, but deeper divisions in other portions of the globe may be more difficult to bridge. Divisions along racial, cultural, linguistic, or ethnic lines may be too intense for democratic engineering. There are severe limitations upon the prospects for democracy in deeply divided societies.[15]

INSTITUTIONAL ARRANGEMENTS AND MINORITY RIGHTS

Clearly, the root causes of minority tensions lie deeper than the formal legal or constitutional arrangements by which peoples govern themselves. The relative size of the minorities compared to the majorities is a critical factor in determining the degree of cooperation or animosity among group members. The degree of industrialization, the amount of resources available, and the proximity of neighboring states that support the minorities are all important elements in group relations. Obviously, religious, ethno-linguistic, tribal, caste, and nationality differences are frequently very divisive factors. Faced with these powerful geopolitical, attitudinal, and historical forces, no set of institutional arrangements could provide an ideal means of resolving group differences. However, certain arrangements can be made to dampen group frictions and conflicts. Which arrangements are best suited to minority group satisfaction cannot be stated with confidence. Many attempts have been made to provide institutional devices to satisfy minority group complaints. None has worked in every case. Some seem tainted by failure. Others have had limited success.

Formal equality before the law is a favored technique for the protection of minority groups. Bills of rights enumerate civil and political rights available to all citizens without regard to their group affiliation. Presumably, the legal system and the courts must be impartial in applying these rights and in asserting the principle of nondiscrimination. This technique is the most common method of providing assurances to minorities that the state is protecting their interests. Of course, the actual enforcement of the principle of nondiscrimination varies greatly from nation to nation. All too often these paper policies of nondiscrimination are disregarded in practice. It may be little comfort to minority group members to be aware that the constitution protects them if their daily lives are essentially unaffected. The actual degree of implementation of the legal principle of nondiscrimination cannot be demonstrated for any nation, although it is probable that the principle is honored more often in Western Europe than elsewhere, although the United States has had the most litigation seeking to apply the principle.

Some nations have passed anti-discrimination statutes that are intended to change the behavior of the perpetrators of discrimination through criminal or civil sanctions. Under such statutes victims of discrimination may seek injunctions against their antagonists or even secure damages. Sometimes conciliation machinery is established for parties to negotiate and settle their grievances. In some nations government agencies are empowered to bring actions on behalf of victims of discrimination. At least, the government agency may conduct an investigation into allegations of discrimination. Increasingly popular are laws that make incitement to discriminate a crime. Merely stirring up hostility to a minority group might constitute an offense. Clearly, such statutes restrain free speech and press somewhat, but proponents claim that minority group protection may require such restraint.

More drastic legal protections for minorities are also available. Certain rights can be placed in a constitution in such a way as to be very difficult to take away. These unamendable or entrenched constitutional provisions may be used to safeguard minority representation, voting, language, culture, religion, or other political or cultural rights deemed essential. This rarely applied technique was used in the Southern Rhodesia Constitution to safeguard minority whites, but it may be available to minority groups fearful of the good intentions of the majority. Effectively, an entrenched right may not be taken away without the assent of the minority group itself. Perhaps this drastic technique deserves closer attention as a means of alleviating long-standing group tensions. The American, French, and West German Constitutions have made unamendable any alteration in the boundaries of regional governments (states, Länder, departments) without the consent of those states. These are entrenched provisions, although they are not minority rights provisions. Yet their very existence as unamendable sections suggests that high priority matters can be given extreme protection where warranted.

Other constitutional protections could fall short of full entrenchment yet help satisfy minority group feelings. Belgium provides for special areas of minority group legislation and communal representation that seem to be virtually entrenched on matters of community concern. The elaborate American Supreme Court interpretations of equal protection of the laws seem to elevate that section of the Constitution to a special plateau. While not entrenched, the equal rights provision of the Fourteenth Amendment to the American Constitution enjoys a special status that places it beyond the reach of popular majorities for all practical purposes.

Judicial action on behalf of minorities is an important institutional safeguard of minority rights. Nowhere is the judiciary assigned the specific task of protecting minorities, but this has been their role in many nations. India and the United States have had active judicial interventon on behalf of minorities. Minority access to courts is sometimes made available by statutes but could be enhanced by additional state support, especially by government suits on behalf of minorities. On the whole, litigation in the courts may be one of the best practical means of safeguarding minority rights. The gains of American blacks and other minorities have been spearheaded by victories in the courts. Other nations have begun to pursue the same tactics, but America is still far in the lead in this important respect. The European Court of Human Rights within the European community has begun to play an important role in promoting minority linguistic rights and other minority rights as well.

Regionalism and federalism have been attempted in many nations, often with an impulse to protect minority rights. Federalism, in which some degree of power is genuinely held by the local (state) government in a way that limits central government power, is attractive to minorities when they are heavily concentrated in a particular part of a nation. Retaining some sovereignty in a smaller geographic area seems to provide some autonomy for minorities. Switzerland is a successful example of this idea. Canada is a questionable case in view of the continuing discontent of many French Canadians in Quebec. Yugoslavia and Czechoslovakia are still adjusting their federal arrangements in order to adjust to minority groups in these highly diverse nations.

Regionalism, unlike federalism, accepts a unitary system of central government authority. However, when unitary states delegate or devolve their powers to particular regions, many of the benefits available under federalism appear. Regions are not independent in legislative, administrative, or financial terms. All these matters are within the effective control of the central government. Nonetheless, a devolved region can enjoy considerable cultural autonomy if the national government agrees. Several experiments in devolution were tried in Northern Ireland with a view to helping the minority Catholics there. They met with limited success. Now Northern Ireland is under direct rule in the wake of the failures of devolution. Italy and Belgium are more hopeful cases, although Belgium is the only surviving example of devolution for the sake of minority rights. A much more questionable case is that of the South African homelands, in which the central government has created semiautonomous regions for particular black groups. All are dependent upon subventions by South Africa. The real purpose of these homelands seems to be the preservation of minority white rule rather than the protection of black rights.

Minority groups can be protected by special voting arrangements. Separate electoral rolls open only to minorities were provided in Rhodesia, Fiji, and British East African territories prior to independence. The 1960 Cyprus Constitution (now inoperative) provided for 35 Greek Cypriot seats and 15 Turkish Cypriot seats in the legislature. Today, New Zealand (4 Maori seats) and India (15 percent seat reservation for scheduled tribes and castes) retain such a system, while Fiji has another version of this system. The Indian separate roll system is slated to expire in 1985 according to the Constitution.

Electoral systems, especially proportional representation, has also been attempted as a minority safeguard. Mauritius has a proportional representation (PR) system which is designed to accurately reflect the complex population mix of that island. PR has been adopted in Holland and Belgium partly for reasons of minority protection. However, proportional representation failed in Northern Ireland and was abandoned in 1973. Lebanon devised an intricate system of proportional representation in 1943 as part of the National Pact that patched together some major group differences in that nation. Communal seats were allocated on a 6 Christian to 5 non-Christian ratio, based upon the 1932 census. In spite of PR the uneasy relationship among Lebanese groups continued, and the collapse of the nation and its informal partition in 1982 were not deterred by the fact that the formal electoral system had attempted to represent Maronites, Sunni Muslims, Greek Orthodox, and Druze communities.

The Lebanese National Pact of 1943 also exemplified another failure for the policy of protecting minorities. This was the concept of power-sharing in the executive. From 1943 until 1975 all Lebanese communities had to be equitably represented in government. Cabinet posts were allocated on a religious group basis. The president was supposed to be a Maronite Christian, the prime minister a Sunni Muslim, the chairman of Parliament a Shiite. For a variety of reasons, some peculiar to the politics of the region, the system eventually failed, and only armed force, first Syrian then Israeli, could restore some leadership to Lebanon, but without power-sharing. Power-sharing was also attempted as a solution in Northern Ireland in 1974, but the majority Protestants withheld support and the system collapsed. Only Switzerland provides a successful example of executive power-sharing on behalf of minority groups. Power-sharing has been operative in Switzerland since 1874 by virtue of law and custom. The Swiss 7-man executive usually consists of 4 or 5 German-speakers, 1 or 2 French-speakers, and 1 Italian speaker.

Probably peculiar historical factors account for the success of Swiss power-sharing, although Belgium and Malaysia too have arrived at stable coalition governments that seem to be informal versions of power-sharing.

One institutional feature that holds promise for the advancement of minority group members is special employment opportunities within the civil service. Quotas or preferences in the name of affirmative action are designed to provide indirect proportional representation, but they also encourage public service by minority group members. Even without quotas, minority access to the civil service helps guarantee fair treatment of minorities at the hands of government bureaucrats. Fears of minority exclusion from the civil service led to imposed minority quota requirements in Lebanon, Belgium, and Cyprus. Malaysia has elaborate statutes requiring government administrators to be trained in minority concerns. In any event, effective minority participation in the civil service seems preferable to the more paternalistic approaches found in India, the United States, and Canada, in which special administrators are assigned the task of protecting the well-being and welfare of minority indigenous peoples. The Canadian and American bureaus of Indian affairs minister to the needs of reservation Indians with mixed results and increasing complaints from the supposedly benefitted minorities.

No one of these institutional devices has proven to be universally applicable to minority problems. Evidently each minority problem has different dimensions in each nation. But the experimentaton continues. Even the failures of particular arrangements do not establish the invalidity of an institutional approach—only its inappropriateness in a specific application.

THE NEGLECT OF MINORITY AND GROUP RIGHTS

Western political theory has been essentially individualist since the period of the American and French revolutions. There was a cross-fertilization of ideas in France, Holland, America, and Western Europe generally, which was exemplified in statements and lists of basic rights. From 1778 until 1850 European states drew up lists of civil and political rights that were the foundation of modern thinking about human rights. However, these lists gave little or no attention to the rights of minorities. They were essentially pronouncements that were aimed at the restraint of governmental power on behalf of individuals. They were reflections of liberal political theory, a theory that ignored other claims of rights, especially those of groups that did not stand to gain much from a bill of rights and were likely to suffer from a simple application of majority rule. For these groups, these minorities, liberal government under majority rule was insufficient to assure equality of treatment or to prevent discrimination. Now, in the light of the experience of the past century, many writers are beginning to perceive that minority rights are a problem that must be addressed, even if that requires an adjustment in traditional liberal values and sentiments.

Jacques Ellul is among the few major political theorists to recognize the need for a fresh approach to the subject of civil and political rights. "What is needed," says Ellul, "is groups capable of extreme diversification of the entire society's fundamental tendencies, capable of escaping our unitary structure and of presenting themselves not as negations of the state—which could be absurd—but as something else, not under the state's tutelage but equally important, as solid and valuable as the state."[16] For Ellul such groups would serve as poles of opposition to the state but would be autonomous parts of the society. Ellul admits that these groups could weaken the power of the state, but he welcomes that as a means of escaping the "political illusion," the powerful state which holds us all, democrats and authoritarians, enthralled. Ellul, while not especially a champion of minority rights, fully recognizes that our vaunted individual freedoms in the democratic West are insufficient to guarantee protection against an all-powerful state. He suggests that the concept of individual liberty needs to be supplemented by group rights (which would include minority rights) if societies are to thrive and grow.

Liberal theory has both misunderstood and ignored group rights. For many statesmen, including most delegations to the United Nations, group rights are somehow akin to South African apartheid or, even worse, an invitation to divisive political forces that will undermine established governments. People remember Hitler's exploitation of the minorities issue prior to and during World War II. Hitler made adroit use of the German minority issue to annex the Sudetenland in Czechoslovakia and to attack Poland. Later he set up puppet minority regimes in Bohemia and Moravia. But the minority issue is more acute now than ever before, and we must remember that unresolved minority rights claims helped lead to World Wars I and II. Since World War II the map of the world has drastically changed, giving rise to new minorities issues in the wake of receding colonialism. We have large groups of refugees, displaced persons, and victimized groups in compounds, tents, slums, and ghettos all over the world.[17] For these people individual rights mean little. Their suffering can be reduced by according to their groups some protections and some rights.

A leading scholar defines human rights as "a set of institutional arrangements for securing legally binding guarantees beneficial to the individual as claims against government and private individuals . . . and socio-economic claims upon government and other organizations."[18] This is an admirable thumbnail description of the dominant view, taking into account the extensions of liberal, individualist theory into the social and economic spheres. According to this perspective "human rights may be arrayed across a continuum with third world concepts falling between liberal and socialist views."[19] A balanced view of human rights, which includes group collectivist rights, can accommodate capitalism and socialism. If rights attach only to individuals, most of the world's people do not and cannot enjoy their rights.[20]

In spite of the weaknesses of liberal, individualist theory, there have been many efforts to revive and renew the roots of liberalism. The latest and most acclaimed liberal theorist is John Rawls, who has updated Locke and Mill to construct a theory of individualist social contract based upon a fundamental notion of justice as fairness to individuals.[21] Rawls assumes that all mankind is divided into societies. Society, he says, "is a more or less self-sufficient association of persons who in their relations to one another recognize certain rules of conduct as binding and who for the most part act in accordance with them."[22] No mention is made of subgroups within society. Racial, linguistic, national, or religious groupings are not mentioned seriously. For Rawls, as for most liberal theorists, there are only individuals, societies, and nations (or states), with the principle of majority rule prevailing. Rawls believes that there is an overriding principle of equal liberty, "which requires that all citizens are to have an equal right to take part in, and to determine the outcome of, the constitutional process that establishes the laws with which they are to comply."[23] So Rawls is opposed to any form of elite or minority rule, while remaining silent concerning the position of discreet minorities that confront a popular majority. The individual in his capacity as a member of a racial, ethnic, national, linguistic or religious group is not considered. The notion of shared rights is for Rawls, as for his liberal predecessors, virtually unthinkable. One man, one vote seems the acme of liberal political theory.

Professor Vernon Van Dyke has sharply questioned this single-minded view of rights. In a direct challenge to John Rawls, he marshals evidence to show that groups have been accorded certain rights even in liberal societies.[24] Van Dyke reminds us of the rights accorded linguistic groups in Belgium, Switzerland, and India. He recalls the rights of religious groups in Lebanon, Cyprus, and the United States. Indigenous people have been accorded special treatment in Peru, Brazil, the United States, India, and many other parts of the world. Race has high salience and is even a "suspect category" in American constitutional law. So Rawls has missed all of this. His theories fail to account for reality. Van Dyke has his own proposals to make, but these will be explored later. Suffice it to say that Rawls is empirically incorrect, and that "groups in fact do have status and rights at an intermediate level between the individual and the state, and it is imperative for a theory of justice to take this fact into account."[25]

In the United States the recently developed practice of affirmative action has called into question the very underpinnings of liberal, individualist theory. To accord opportunities to individuals because of their membership in a group is to treat them as more than merely equal persons. Blacks, in particular, have been given special benefits and protections unavailable to whites. The justification for this exception to equality before the law is hard to find in liberal theory. Nonetheless, it may be just to bestow special treatment on black or other minorities. The limits of the equal protection clause of the American Constitution are being tested by affirmative action policies.[26] Yet they persist as more thinking Americans realize that blacks as a group have been in a position of perpetual subordination, even if individual blacks have ascended the social and economic ladder. It must be concluded that "blacks are what might be called a specially disadvantaged group . . . but they are not the only group entitled to protection."[27] Unfortunately, the U.S. Supreme Court, still encumbered as it is by individualist conceptions of rights, has been unable to come to grips with this issue. But logic and history suggest that group rights will eventually gain consitutional status even in individualist America.

Liberal theory is not altogether lacking in concern for minority rights. John Stuart Mill was very attentive to the issue. Mill, after all, favored a scheme of proportional representation that provided a voice for minority sentiment in the legislature. For Mill democracy was not governance by a simple majority principle, for "in any really equal democracy every or any section would be represented . . . [and a] minority would be as fully represented as the majority, for to do otherwise would be to establish a government of inequality and privilege."[28] Furthermore, Mill was aware that differences of language, religion, race, and nationality were salient political factors. But Mill believed that all members of one nationality should be joined under one government. He concluded that "free institutions are next to impossible in a country made up of different nationalities."[29] Mill was familiar with the minorities problems of Eastern Europe and of the Near East, but he saw little hope of joining several peoples together peaceably under a single free government. Federalism could help, but there seemed little likelihood that any institutional arrangement could keep different religions and races joined together, or so Mill believed. Yet Mill has been wrong; minority rights do exist. Pluralistic and democratic societies have come into being in the past century. Mill's theories do not account for what has really happened. He was sympathetic to the notion of minority rights but did not understand that differences of race, religion, language, and nationality are more important than differences of class or opinion. Minority rights for Mill excluded the kinds of groups we now recognize as significant in modern societies.

THE COMMUNIST VIEW OF MINORITY RIGHTS

Karl Marx did not believe that the "nationalities problem" was a genuine factor in political life. According to Marx, "unhistorical" nationalities "whose political vitality had long been extinguished . . . had tried to profit from the universal confusion of 1848."[30] Nationality movements (which were the problem) were anachronistic and counter to the trend toward industrialization and eventual dictatorship of the proletariat or a classless society. Engels echoed this view, calling for the absorption into one great state of "all those tiny, shrivelled, weak little nations" who could only benefit from historical progress by amalgamation which might require "iron unscrupulousness."[31] Clearly, minority rights for nationalities were unthinkable, as were religious or linguistic minority rights. Race was never considered.

After the Communist Revolution in Russia, issues unforseen by Marx came to the fore. Lenin was faced with certain practical necessities in guiding the course of the Russian Revolution. The Russian government was imperial at the time of Revolution. The Russian people were themselves a minority in greater Russia, and the tsarist regime had kept many other non-Russian peoples in subjugation. Consequently, Lenin's first impulse was to adopt the slogan "complete equality and right to self-determination for all nations oppressed by the Great Russians." But such a position encouraged the early disintegration of Russia and was not adhered to in the long run. Instead, Lenin and later Soviet rulers have dampened the issue of self-determination and retained a facade of rights for nationalities or other groups.

Lenin favored centralism and a unitary state but made concessions to group feeling. Lenin stressed the right of self-determination of nations, but not of peoples or autonomous groups. By self-determination he meant "state independence and the formation of a national state."[32] This did not require federalism in multiethnic states. In fact, he at first worked against the federal system as a means of dealing with Russian governance. He preferred large state formations but recognized that self-determination implied a right to secede from a large state.[33] Later the Soviet Constitution included the right of secession, but the right has been withdrawn, leaving less theoretical justification for minority rights in the Russian Communist system.

For over sixty years Soviet leaders have sought to integrate their society, but they admit that "the obliteration of national distinctions and especially of language distinctions, is a considerably longer process than the obliteration of class distinctions."[34] When he was first secretary of the Communist party, Nikita Khruschev insisted that national differences would persist even after the worldwide victories of communism.[35]

Russification, the identification of the Soviet Union with the Russian people, is not the policy of the Communist leadership. Even though Premier Stalin glorified the Russian people and appealed to Russian pride, the unification of all Soviet peoples remains the official goal, not the withering away of non-Russians. Indeed, appeals based upon Russian nationalism have frequently irritated other groups, so that this approach has been played down in Soviet life since the death of Stalin. Indeed, some nationalities have attained considerable recognition since 1953. For example, the Ukrainians have been formalized as the "second-ranking nation."[36] Defining the place of the Russian people of the Soviet Union is an awkward task, and it has almost always been avoided, since it is evident that they enjoy many attributes of majority position even though they remain a numerical minority in the Soviet multi-ethnic state.

The Soviet Constitution proclaims the equal rights of all citizens, regardless of race or nation, in all fields of economic, state, cultural, and sociopolitical life. However, "any establishment of direct or indirect privileges for citizens on the basis of race or nationality" is unlawful as part of "an implacable struggle against all manifestations of nationalism and chauvinism, against all tendencies towards national narrow-mindedness and exclusiveness" waged "against customs and habits impeding the development of communism."[37]

In practice, local cultural customs and languages are often honored in the Soviet Union. The government recognizes over 110 nationalities and nations, 35 of which have political representation in federal or autonomous republics. There are also 8 autonomous regions and one national district. This seems to be the operative effect of self-determination. Some limited degree of linguistic, cultural, and racial autonomy is permitted, always subject to the needs and will of the Soviet Communist party. Furthermore, there is some evidence of economic, social, and political progress for many groups within the Soviet Union, at least as compared to tsarist policies.[38]

Soviet policy toward minorities is tactical, not uniform, since it does not rest upon minority rights concepts. The Baltic peoples have been treated differently from most other Soviet peoples. Curiously, the Baltic republics of Estonia, Latvia, and Lithuania have been treated in a favored fashion, as their economic development has been actively pushed by the Soviet leadership. They seem to be showplaces of economic well-being. Education is principally conducted in the native tongue, and national subjects, such as history, language, and literature are taught in state schools. Russian is gradually displacing native languages, but the major integrationist policy appears to be the in-migration of labor from other areas of the Soviet Union.[39] On the other hand, Soviet Ukrainian policies are less predictable and often suppressive.[40] Soviet treatment of Jews and certain Asian groups has been sometimes harsh and repressive.[41]

Plainly, nationalist dissidence is discouraged in the Soviet Union. Minority rights do not exist as a matter of official ideology. Yet, some recognition of minority feeling is provided by the very structure of the state. No student of Soviet affairs could fail to note the overwhelming importance of the Communist party, and in this regard, minority groups are at a real disadvantage. The party is and has been dominated by Great Russians. Party chairmen may arise from different ethnic groups, such as Stalin from Georgia, but the direction of party politics has been clear, and only a handful of ethnics has reached party eminence. There is doubt whether even ethnic leaders of the Communist party retain any significant concern with minority group aspirations.[42]

To some extent the same holds true for Yugoslavia, which is on the other extreme of communist systems. The Yugoslavian Constitution is a model of group rights, departing from the Soviet example, that serves as an archetype for most communist states. Yugoslav federalism is much more concerned with minority rights than is the Soviet, but this may be due to the peculiar history of Yugoslavia. Only time will tell whether minority rights in Yugoslavia can survive a test—if it comes to a test—with universalist communist principles. Communist states may, as a matter of expediency, bestow formidable rights upon given minorities, but they are subject to the tides of party affairs. Communist ideology seems to require centralization and integration. Classes mean more than peoples, and an eventual classless society will, presumably, gradually overcome differences of race, language, culture, and ethnicity. Ethnic diversity is a stubborn, unwelcome fact in many Communist nations, but "nationality problems are critically important in the evaluation of domestic Soviet reality today." The same goes for all Communist multi-ethnic states. The concept of minority rights finds little support in the writings of Marx, Engels, Lenin, Stalin, Mao, or other sources of ideological truths. Marx once wrote "these dying nationalities, the Bohemians, Larinthians, Dalmatians, etc. should be delighted" by the prospect of being "absorbed by their stronger neighbors."[43] There is small comfort in these words for the advocates of minority rights.

MINORITY RIGHTS AND SEPARATISM

There is historical weight to the charge that minority rights is a guise for separationist sentiment. Certainly, many champions of minority rights were striving for independence, not mere protection within a greater nation. German philosopher Gottfried Von Herder (1744-1803) helped kindle the spirit of smaller minorities in central and Eastern

Europe when he emphasized the importance of language and culture of distinctive groups. Language and nationality were linked to independence movements in the nineteenth century as the ideology of self-determination of peoples spread throughout Europe. By the end of the nineteenth century German and Italian nationalists directed their political energies into an effort to join all Italian- or German-speaking peoples into a single nation. Their aim was to convert knots of minority groups into a majority in a new nation. Independence movements among the Slavic peoples helped hasten the decay of multinational states such as the Austro-Hungarian Empire, the Ottoman Empire, and the empire of the Russian tsar. For many minority groups separatism seemed the only vehicle for self-expression. Today, with separatist movements in Canada, France, Spain, Iran, Iraq, Turkey, Pakistan, and Afghanistan, among others, there is reason to regard minority rights assertions as a variant of separatism. And this continuing process sometimes leads to bloody warfare, as in Bangladesh and Biafra. But this has come about largely as a result of an earlier failure.

As we have seen, minority rights claims helped precipitate both World Wars I and II. In the nineteenth century minority problems had caused the Russo-Turkish Wars and the Balkan Wars, as well as the Boer War. One of the objects of President Wilson's Fourteen Points, which helped form the basis for the peace after World War I, was the freeing of some of the minorities from the rule of the Austro-Hungary Empire and the Ottoman Empire, but the Wilsonian formula did not resolve the frictions among minority groups. Instead, it gave rise to new minority problems, as the new states carved out of the defeated central powers were formed of combined minorities (Czechoslovakia, Yugoslavia) or were composed of dominant majorities with small minority groups (Hungary, Austria, Poland). Minority separatist sentiment in Czechoslovakia provided a pretext for Hitler's demands at Munich. Minority separatism has, for many, discredited the concept of minority rights.

The first significant meaning of minority rights in world affairs was derived from the minorities treaties signed by the newly established or enlarged states and the Allied and Associated Powers who won the war. The vanquished states of Austria, Bulgaria, Hungary, and Turkey were compelled to make similar guarantees to their minorities. The minorities treaties that followed from the Treaty of Versailles established a system of international protection of minorities that was intended to safeguard the racial, religious, and linguistic minorities of Austria, Poland, the Serb-Croat-Slovene state, Czechoslovakia, Bulgaria, Romania, Hungary, Greece, the Free City of Danzig, the Aaland Islands, Albania, Estonia, Lithuania, Latvia, Turkey, Memel, and Iraq. Minorities in these nations were guaranteed equality of treatment and special protection as a matter of international law.[44] Eventually, this scheme failed.

The minorities treaties were designed to dampen separatist sentiment by meeting legitimate and lawful minority group demands as much as possible. Thus, the council of the League of Nations assumed the power to intervene in the event of any infraction. The way was also open to exercise the judicial function of the Permanent Court of International Justice, which had compulsory jurisdiction in matters relating to the protection of minorities. Moreover, a minorities committee was set up with the council of the League to deal with each properly received petition, and the right of petition was granted to minorities in 1920.[45] Unfortunately, there was no guarantee that the League of Nations would discipline a state which violated its minority rights undertaking.

The concept of minority rights briefly blossomed under the minorities treaties systems. But the procedural difficulties of investigation and negotiation of minority rights proved inadequate. Most minority complaints were shelved, partly due to the distrust among the minorities, the governments that encouraged and supported them in their claims, and the accused governments.[46] The Permanent Court of International Justice limited itself to a few interesting advisory opinions.[47]

The minorities treaties did not satisfy either the minorities or the signatory states.[48] Minority rights was somewhat discredited by the sad experience of the collapse of the minorities treaties protective system. The treaties did not prevent the maltreatment of European Jews nor the annexations of the Nazis and the Soviets.

The collapse of the minorities treaties system has had another side effect; it has encouraged minority separatist movements. If minority groups cannot look to their own nations, nor to the United Nations, the World Court, and regional international organizations for protection, they may feel compelled to turn to separatist politics. In the absence of a strong international system for the protection of minority-rights, resort to separatist politics may have become more prevalent. Palestinians, Québecois, Basques, Kurds, and other important minority groups cannot expect much international protection of their minority group rights. If they assert statehood or autonomy, they may gain some support and some stature. Of course, the United Nations has promulgated various international covenants that create a limited version of minority rights, but nothing as far-reaching as the old, discredited minorities treaties arrangements.

Minority rights blended with nationalism is an explosive mixture, and nationalism is enhanced by the realization that ministates composed of small populations enjoy political representation in the United Nations. Minority groups may attempt to achieve some degree of autonomy or protection with national boundaries, or they may opt for a separate line of development. But Greek and Turkish Cypriots have not been able to bargain with each other, nor have the various minorities of the Lebanon.

Where bargaining fails and international concern is slight, a resort to separatism is likely. Separatist leaders like René Levésque in Québec can appeal to the minority sense of frustration. If minority frustrations are high enough, violence is likely, as among the Palestinians, the Kurds, and especially the Afghans.

As the title of one book suggests there may be *A Case for the Balkanization of Practically Everyone*.[49] The Basques, the Bretons, the Scots, the Lapps, the Catalans, the Welsh, and even the Gypsies may make a plausible case for separatism. There are small nationalist parties and movements all over the world that have advanced some sort of claim to separation from a larger state. In the United States black leader Malcolm X once asked for an American state (Montana) as a separate homeland for blacks. The seriousness of these claims varies considerably. Basque nationalists are willing to martyr themselves for their cause, but Welsh nationalists are far less militant.

Insofar as separatist politics form a hidden agenda behind the term "minority rights," there is a false and misleading quality to minority rights claims. In the wake of the 1980 Québec Referendum, many French Canadians seem to want better treatment within Canada, although the separatist movement aimed at much more than a better deal for French speakers. The intertwining of separatist nationalism with minority rights confuses many sensitive political problems. The status of the West-Bank Palestinians can be treated as a minority rights problem or as a separatist problem. To treat them as both is to invite misunderstanding and bitterness.

For the sake of clarity and good logic, minority rights must not be confused with separatism. A minority group should be willing to choose a course of action that is either consonant with continued (but altered) minority status or to elect a line of separate development or complete autonomy. Tactically, it may not be expedient for minority group leaders to reveal their plans, but they should at least understand that those plans may risk a political or military showdown for group members. Furthermore, group members should consider the consequences of separatism and independence. Bangladesh has achieved separation, but with great cost. Perhaps minority rights are preferable to separatism. If so, a distinction between minority rights and separatism must be maintained.

The basic question for advocates of minority rights is whether minority rights claims are always a legitimate part of human rights. If minority rights are merely a rallying cry for rebellion, then the fears of many opponents of minority rights claims are well-founded. As it is, the pressure, particularly in newer nations, is toward assimilation, not the recognition of separate languages, cultures, religions, races, and ethnic groups. Interest in minority rights is not dormant in new nations, but there is a fear that singling out minorities for special treatment may threaten national unity or stability. The danger of separatism seems more threatening than the human values inherent in minority rights claims. It seems that only more stable and secure societies can actively promote minority rights.

In the modern age, group differences can be readily politicized. Many traditionally subordinate groups have recently entered into direct political action. Whether such activity inevitably leads to separatism or other anti-regime activity can be challenged. The best route toward accommodation may be some recognition of genuine minority rights as a means of group accommodation rather than suppression of group differences in the name of assimilation.[50]

MINORITY RIGHTS AS AN ASPECT OF PLURALISM

Minorities are a fact of political life. As indicated by the list in the next section most nations have substantial numbers of people who belong to minority groups. Assimilation, suppression, or silent toleration are available to governments in dealing with their minorities. However, there is another choice that is more positive—the recognition of legitimate minority rights. Since most nations are pluralistic in that they are composed of numerous racial, ethnic, linguistic, and religious groups, they are able to choose between positive acceptance of group differences or some negative approach ranging from silent toleration to outright genocide. Clearly, the more humane path is to accept minority rights as an aspect of pluralism, rather than to repress pluralism. Pluralism may result in separatist movements, but it can also produce support for a regime that accepts group differences. Seen in this light, minority rights in a pluralistic society are counter-separatist in effect, since they provide a rationale for loyalty to the regime.

Theories of pluralism are largely products of the twentieth century, the age of minority rights. This is no coincidence. Even though divergent groups have lived within common borders long before the modern period, the problem of justifying the relationships among groups has been relatively unimportant. In the past most minorities have been subjugated by others, sometimes a colonial minority. Historians have not explained the absence of a tradition of minority rights, but certainly the expectations of these groups have been raised by modern communications and by the spread of the ideals of human rights through the activities of the United Nations, the European Community, and other regional organizations.

The theory of plural society begins with the writing of J. S. Furnivall, an economist and colonial administrator who defined a plural society as "comprising two or more elements or social orders which live side by side, yet without mingling, in one political unit."[51] Furnivall noted that in a tropical Dutch colony the rulers and the ruled lived apart from each other. This resulted in a lack of consensus on public ends. In a plural society public expenditures tend to benefit one group at the expense of others.

Furnivall applied his description mostly to colonial societies, although he noted similar patterns in Canada and South Africa. His concentration upon colonialist structures seems out of place today, but he began to draw the attention of social scientists to the special problems of divided societies. The rigid divisions of colonial societies were often necessary to maintain colonial dominance, but Furnivall pointed out that colonial rule played a positive role as well, by providing external pressure to hold together an ethnically divided society.[52]

Although colonialism has receded, pluralism remains. Separate communities still go their separate ways in many places, and conflictual behavior is chronic. This is particularly true in postcolonial societies, many of which exhibit the tendencies observed earlier by Furnivall.[53] Yet most social scientists have shown that multicultural societies are not as rigidly separated as Furnivall claimed.[54]

M. G. Smith, a sociologist, added to Furnivall's definitions by distinguishing between a diverse society composed of many groups and a plural society, which, he felt, relied upon forceful regulation to keep order. Thus South Africa is a plural society while the United States is not. This definition of pluralism, which states that "the monopoly of power by one cultural section is the essential precondition for the maintenance of the total society in its current form," is unduly restrictive in that it covers only a few societies and also because it disregards the interests of groups that lack force to support their claims.[55] Smith's usage is consistent with Furnivall but not useful in describing minority rights.

Fortunately, the concept of the plural society is not exclusive to sociologists or anthropologists. Political science and political theory have suggested a more generous view of the plural society, one which accords more closely with recent experience, but they too have failed to provide a better basis for minority rights.

A number of modern political theorists have attempted to provide a perspective on the state and government that includes numerous competing private groups beyond the reach of public authority. G.D.H. Cole and Harold Laski were prominent pluralist thinkers, but Sir Ernest Barker presents the clearest statement of pluralist political thought. Barker conceived of society as constituted of a large number of voluntary associations separate and distinct from the state. Society tends to be led by the private activity of voluntary groups. Society is "the whole sum of voluntary bodies or associations" in an open political order.[56] Unlike Furnivall and Smith, Barker does not assume that a pluralistic society will be a conflict society utilizing a repressive state to maintain order.

On the contrary, the state will merely mediate among groups, respecting their autonomy, because a free society confines the role of the state.

The notion of voluntary group membership is not particularly appropriate to minorities. After all, race, language, culture, sex, and ethnicity are not usually matters of choice, although religion may be. The activities of minorities are really not like the interest groups of pluralist David Truman, even though minority groups may sometimes organize themselves for interest group activities.[57] The activities of interest groups are only one variety of life in a pluralistic society and not the variety most significant for minority groups. There is a difference between joining the AFL-CIO and being a Jehovah's Witness, and this difference accords more rights to the religious group member than to the unionist. The group theory of politics developed by political scientists Arthur Bentley, Robert Dahl, and David Truman over several decades does not provide a satisfactory justification for minority rights.[58]

Yet, an awareness is dawning among social scientists that pluralistic societies are here to stay and cultural differentiation by race, religion, language, and ethnicity is inevitable in many nations, new and old. We must close the gap between theories which accept group conflict and the realities of modern nationhood that require groups to live together peacefully or else resort to destructive conflict. To do so, we must recognize that "the principle of equality must be envisaged in terms of collectivities as well as individuals."[59] There is no simple way to do this, no single institutional device to provide fair treatment for minorities, and while there are "diverse means by which this may be achieved; recognition of the problem is the prerequisite to its solution."[60] Now we must forge a theory in which groups should be considered to have rights, not just morally justifiable claims, but legal rights as well.[61]

A PROVISIONAL THEORY OF MINORITY RIGHTS

The evidence for the support of some budding concept of collective minority group rights is in hand. Linguistic groups have special rights by virtue of constitutional and legislative provisions in Belgium, India, Switzerland, and several other nations. Religious rights have been accorded to distinctive groups in Lebanon and Cyprus (but with little success), and more effectively in the United States, Mexico, and elsewhere.[62] Racial group rights are recognized in India (as caste or tribe), Fiji, New Zealand, Panama, and some other nations.[63] Ethnicity is recognized as a group factor for rights in Czechoslovakia, Malaysia, Singapore, and Yugoslavia.[64] Indeed, some international recognition of the concept of group rights is provided by the International Covenant on Civil and Political Rights:

> In those states in which ethnic, religious or linguistic minorities exist, persons belonging to such minorities shall not be denied the right in community with the

other members of their group, to enjoy their own culture, to profess and practice their own religion or to use their own language.[65]

So group rights are springing up in the modern world, in spite of the unhappy experience with the post-World War I minorities treaties. Let me suggest the general character of these rights so as to sketch out a preliminary theory of minority rights:

1. Minority rights are group rights. They may be claimed by an individual, but they are asserted as a result of membership in a group that seeks a measure of differential treatment distinct from the majority of the population. Equal treatment is not the basis of the rights.
2. Minority rights may include individual rights, as int the well-recognized principle of nondiscrimination to be found in most of the world's constitutions and in the basic United Nations documents. This means that a member of a minority group should be able to claim that he or she, as an individual, has been denied rights available to others in the same nation. Equal treatment under the law is an individual right, although it may be claimed by a minority group member.
3. Multicultural societies must, at least, consider whether they have significant groups that are effectively treated as minorities and should develop some principled basis for the recognition of the legitimacy of minority group status. This is a complex issue in which salient issues of group identity (language, color, ethnicity, religion, or race) may be different in different societies. Trivial or frivolous distinctions (left-handedness, red-headedness, fatness, tallness) are not to be considered. Physical disabilities, age, imprisonment, or other status conditions that may be entitled to some sort of special treatment do not confer minority group status because they are acquired conditions that do not meet the historical sense of minority status.
4. Minority rights include the idea that individuals should be free to remain in the minority group or, if able, to leave it voluntarily. Individuals may abandon their religion, or marry members of another race, or surrender their linguistic rights.
5. Minority rights should not be compulsory or a pretext for discrimination. Apartheid in South Africa and segregation elsewhere are clearly departures from minority right concepts because they deny free choice to minority group members.
6. A failure of multicultural societies to recognize the existence of a substantial minority is a denial of minority rights. A leading example is the treatment of the Kurds in Iraq and Turkey and of many other peoples who are often not even counted in official census figures. Here is a place for international action, since the United Nations can reasonably be expected to be informed of the size of minority populations.
7. Under conditions of extreme deprivation, minority rights justify special treatment and advantages for groups victimized by persistent prejudice.

8. Minority rights include rights to political representation and to social and economic justice.
9. Minority rights do not include the right to revolution and secession except upon the same basis as do individual rights. Only the direct and substantial threat to life, limb, and the integrity of family life would ordinarily justify group resistance to constituted authority.

This sketch does not emphasize collisions between individual and group rights. A few critics have suggested that individual and group rights must collide. Certainly this is true in the area of affirmative action, where individual rights have been set aside in favor of group rights. But otherwise there seems no reason to believe that group rights cannot coexist with individual rights.

A provisional theory of minority rights does not create a mandate for vast change. It merely ratifies and explains changes that have taken place in the absence of theory. Theoretical problems, such as the means for legitimatizing a group's assertion of minority status, must await the passage of time and the gaining of experience. Instead, what is suggested in this section is an inductive approach to minority rights derived from the enlightened practice of leading nations. No one can legislate minority rights for other multicultural nations, but the slow accumulation of examples of minority rights is not enough. The outlines of a theory should speed further recognition of group rights by providing a rationale and a platform for those rights.

THE PAST AND THE FUTURE OF MINORITY RIGHTS

In 1980 a new state was born in the New Hebrides in the South Pacific. The termination of the rule of the French and of the British over their condominium ended an ill-fated experiment in joint colonial rule. But the people of the islands are no longer the same as the Polynesian tribesmen who first met the Europeans at the close of the nineteenth century. They are an admixture of French, British, Asian, and other peoples divided by culture, language, race, and religion into patterns so diverse that political democracy may not be able to survive the strains. Indeed, there is a possibility that one or another group will impose its will on the rest with little attention to minority rights. Whether that possibility becomes an actuality depends upon whether a sensitivity develops to minority rights, first among the departing colonialists and then among those who remain. Colonialism left many such problems among its formerly subservient peoples.

Many nations have failed to give due attention to minority rights and paid a price in blood. In Nigeria, a nation of 250 antagonistic tribes was held together by artificial boundaries of colonial creation. A civil war left the defeated Ibos with little to show for their struggle with the Yorubas of the west and the Hausa-Fulani of the north. Nigeria became independent in 1969, but an uneasy coalition between the Hausa-Fulanis and the Ibos collapsed in 1967. Ethnic hostilities mounted; civil war, mass exodus, secession, and the loss of 2 million Ibo lives led to the creation of the current Nigerian Federation. Now, in the wake of this bitter history, there is some awareness and concern in Nigeria for the rights and interests of the Ibos and of other neglected groups. These peoples must learn to live together or else fight again. Minority rights concepts may hold a formula for peace and order for this complex and potentially rich African state.

Fighting continues in Chad, Angola, and northern Ethiopia (Eritrea). Warfare occurs sporadically throughout Africa, Asia, and the Near East, and it is often fought for the cause of a group, be it religious, racial, ethnic, or linguistic. Terrorism is the tactic preferred by Palestinians in their protracted struggle against Israel. These military and guerrilla struggles seem endless so long as their termination depends upon the complete capitulation of one group or so long as the losing side fears the vengeance of the winner. Again, a recognition of minority rights may help reconcile some of these warring forces.

In the developed Western nations, some saner thinking about minority rights may also help resolve long-standing tensions. The status of Northern Ireland and the relationships among Catholics and Protestants there requires some close attention to a fair balance of majority and minority rights. In the United States black rights are growing, but attention must now be given to Hispanics who form a large and significant minority. The newly independent states of the West Indies and many of the nations of Latin America have yet to grapple with a recognition of their composite, multigroup nature. In some Latin American states, large European immigrant groups have yet to be integrated into their new countries, while the native Indians, a minority large enough to constitute a numerical majority in a few places, have few political rights, educational facilities, or economic opportunities.

Assimilation is not an answer for most nations. The homogeneity of Sweden or Denmark is the product of many centuries of painful struggle. Most of the world is less fortunate and less patient. The forging of new nationhood can take place only over a long period of time and only when nations live in relative isolation from one another. But in our age of television, radio, jet planes, and other means of rapid communication and transportation, no corner of the world is so remote that it can slowly work out its own identity. The pressures of our technological age may not permit the slow formation of nationhood known to the European states. Indeed, the Soviet Union and the United States, the most powerful of the world's nations, have not yet been able to assimilate or "melt" their vast and differing population groups. Assimilation does not work rapidly enough to permit many of the newer nations to resolve their own internal differences and to proceed with national development.

There are other answers to group antagonisms. The most dramatic, genocide, is condemned as a horrible crime by international law. Less drastic, but an expedient used several times in the twentieth century, is the technique of population transfer. Forced evacuation or involuntary transfer is nothing new in history. Jews were expelled from England in 1290 and from France in 1182, 1306, and 1394. The Russian tsars used mass expulsions when they launched their nation-building policies prior to World War I. In 1913 Turkey and Bulgaria agreed to exchange border populations, a peaceful exchange less violent than the subsequent expulsion of Greeks from Asia Minor and the massacre of Armenians. After World War I, defeated Germans from West Prussia were compelled to choose to migrate to either Germany or Austria or to become Polish citizens. Resettlement was an avowed policy of the Nazis, but this meant the gathering-in of scattered German groups and the movement of "inferior" groups to make room for Germans. Stalin also conducted vast deportations of suspect nationalities during World War II. This movement of millions of Russian citizens is partly described by Alexander Solzhenitsyn:

> The military units gallantly surrounded the awls, or settlements, and, within 24 hours: with the speed of a parachute attack, those who had rested there for centuries past found themselves removed to railroad stations, loaded by the trainload, Central Asia, and the Russian North.[66]

Population transfer has been a little-noticed solution used in our century to deal with minority problems. The victors of World War II also used expulsion against the vanquished Germans. According to official West German statistics, one million Germans were expelled from the eastern areas of Germany (East Prussia, eastern Pomerania, eastern Brandenberg, Silesia) and millions more from Czechoslovakia, Poland, Russia, and other nations of Europe. Most of these people were long-time civilian residents of their home areas. This was one result of the Yalta and Potsdam conferences among the British, Soviets, and Americans. Other examples of modern expulsions or population transfers do not match the scale of the German movement, unless one includes the population movements incident to the partition of India, involving 14 million people.[67]

The international community has concentrated its concern upon the evils of racism and racial discrimination. South African apartheid has been the special target of concern of human rights advocates. Racism and racial discrimination are now becoming problems in Great Britain,

Canada, and New Zealand, long regarded as models of fairness and tolerance among advanced nations. Yet in Toronto, Liverpool, Cardiff (Wales), Manchester, and other areas of racial mingling, conflict and discrimination have become evident. It is the black man's blackness, his group attribute, which is held against him. Seen in the light of the treatment provided by this study, racism and racial discrimination are but the other side of minority rights.

Certain groups have historically been the special victims of discrimination. The Jews, the gypsies, and the untouchables of India have all been singled out for discriminatory treatment because of religion, culture, or caste, which have tended to be confused with race. These minorities have been subjected to violence and oppression for centuries. Only in the current century has their condition improved somewhat. But each of these groups has fared differently in modern times, depending upon local attitudes and conditions. In the absence of a general theory of minority rights, these groups depend upon the shifting attitudes of the majorities in the countries where they reside. The same holds true for many other minorities, and one of the chief tasks of a rational minority rights theory is to explain that minority group status is a subjective and an objective condition—that is to say, a minority is worthy of protection because it feels that it has been suppressed, harassed, and persecuted and because there is objective evidence to support these feelings. Jews, gypsies, and untouchables have deserved protection. So, too have other historic minorities.

Minority rights imply more than nondiscrimination. It is insufficient to say that the government does not make distinctions based upon race, religion, language, or ethnicity. Minority rights begin with nondiscrimination, but they must extend to protective activities and promotional activities. This is the path of future development. Minorities such as American blacks and Indians are no longer the victims of governmental discrimination. Now they seek protections and advancement within American life, causing some concern among even liberal-minded members of the majority. But a full-blown minority rights ideal includes affirmative action programs and similar devices to advantage minorities. This is a hard lesson, but it seems to be part of the future course of minority rights development.

Minority rights are fast becoming a universal claim. Even nations exhibiting little cultural diversity now use and employ foreign work forces. These groups of "guest-workers" (a German term) may well deserve protection, too, even though they are not citizens. Much of Western European prosperity has been built upon the labor of Turks, Italians, Greeks, and southern Europeans. If this labor exploitation continues, a consciousness of minority rights is sure to swell among these groups. Sweden, a nation of 8 million people, has virtually no black or Southern European citizens. Yet in 1978 there were large numbers of Yugoslav, Greek, and Turkish aliens. It is perhaps significant that Sweden permits long-time aliens to vote in local elections and broadcasts radio and television programs in the languages of alien migrant workers. Ironically, Sweden was the last Scandinavian nation to allow Jews and gypsies to enter.

Minority rights may come at a high cost in countries with very large minority groups. Belgium, one of the pioneers in modern minority rights arrangements, suffers from chronic political instability; language problems have troubled the small nation since its founding in 1830. About half the population speak French and the other half Dutch. The Walloons (French-speakers) have tended to dominate the Flemings until recent years. The Flemings have demanded equal rights in language and politics so as to catch up with the effective majority, the Walloons. Ten years ago the government agreed to set up a unique system of nearly autonomous regions based upon language, but bickering still continues over the precise terms of the linguistic settlement. While the linguistic issue still sorely taxes Belgian political life, the fact is that Walloons no longer dominate Belgium as they once did. Minority rights for the Flemings, though divisive, have proven to be a source of great advancement for them. Belgium persists, but it is a Belgium in which a minority is entering into coequal status with a former majority.

But for most minority groups, equality is not the only goal. Protection and advancement of opportunity is just as important. Differential treatment is the aim of many minority groups wishing to preserve their basic characteristics that distinguish them from the majority. Black men do not wish to be white. Jews do not wish to be Protestants. Serbs do not want to be Croats. French Canadians do not want to lose their French heritage. Minority protection seeks to enhance the desire for nonassimilation. Certainly, there are minority group members who, as individuals, will want to merge into the majority, but the group itself has a collective interest in its own preservation, and the politics of the future may well be less concerned with assimilation than was the politics of the past.

Whatever happens to the development of minority rights, there is no reason to expect a repetition of the failures of the minorities treaties. The complicated procedures of the post-World War I agreements coupled with their arbitrary and imposed character led to ineffective recognition and enforcement of minority rights under the League of Nations. The problem today is no longer a European problem but embraces all nations of the world, particularly the many newly independent nations. The United Nations and its organs have begun the touchy task of identifying and defining certain aspects of minority rights. Meanwhile, out of the experience of many nations a practical embodiment of minority rights policies can be discerned. There has been progress in the development of minority rights, much of it of recent vintage. Newer constitutions reveal minority rights concepts, as do national legislation and judicial decisions.[68] There is no way of predicting just how far minority rights development will go in the direction of protecting and advancing minority groups, but there seems to be no turning back.[69] After the horrors of genocide and mass expulsions, there is a widespread feeling that lies ahead is the reconciliation between minority rights and majority power which begins with a recognition of the complementarity of minority rights and individual rights. These two classes of rights are both needed in a humane and just society.

NOTES

1. J. A. LaPonce, *The Protection of Minorities* (Berkeley: University of California Press, 1960), p. 43.

2. Ibid, p. 44.

3. See generally Final Report of the Intergovernmental Conference on Institutional Administrative and Financial Aspects of Cultural Policies (Venice, August 24-September 2, 1970), ch. 1, UNESCO, SHC/MD/13 (1970).

4. See Anthony H. Birch, "Minority Nationalist Movements and Theories of Political Integration," *World Politics* (April 1978), pp. 325-40, for some highly suggestive explanations for this resurgence of minority group activism. The vulnerability of technologically advanced societies to minority terrorism is one of the more disturbing factors.

5. John Stuart Mill, *Consideration on Representative Government* (New York: Liberal Arts Press, 1958), p. 230.

6. Alvin Rabushka and Kenneth Shepsle, *Politics in Plural Societies* (Columbus, Ohio: Charles G. Merrill Publishing Company, 1972), p. 217. These authors have difficulty in fitting Canada, Belgium, and the Netherlands into their indictment of democracy in plural societies. Switzerland is explained away on the grounds that "language is not the salient issue" while "most salient issues in Swiss politics are local issues." (p. 210).

7. Alvin Rabushka and Kenneth Shepsle, "Political Entrepreneurship and Patterns of Democratic Instability in Plural Societies," *Race* 12, no. 4 (April 1971) pp. 462-70.

8. Eric A. Nordlinger, *Conflict Resolution in Divided Societies* (Cambridge: Harvard University, 1977). Rabushka and Shepsle define away their unfavorable cases by distinguishing between "plural" and "pluralistic" societies. The "plural" society practices politics along almost exclusively ethnic lines. This is the source of democratic instability. However, in healthy "pluralistic" democracies, coalitions vary from issue to issue and are not based on permanent ethnic divisions. But these authors eschew any theoretical explanation for their distinction. See Rabushka and Shepsle, *Politics in Plural Societies*, p. 21, fn. 43.

9. See Arnold Rivkin, *Nation-Building in Africa: Problems and Prospects* (New

Brunswick, N.J.: Rutgers University Press, 1969). R. William Liddle, *Ethnicity, Party, and National Integration* (New Haven, Conn.: Yale University Press, 1970), suggests that in Indonesia authoritarianism was not effective in nation-building under Dr. Sukarno.

10. See Robert A. Dahl, *Polyarchy: Participation and Opposition* (New Haven, Conn.: Yale University Press, 1971), pp. 17-32. Dahl, a prominent democratic theorist, shows that there are few democracies in severely divided societies.

11. Arend Lijphart, *Democracy in Plural Societies: A Comparative Exploration* (New Haven, Conn.: Yale University Press, 1977).

12. Ibid., p. 5.

13. Ibid., p. 236.

14. Ibid., p. 25.

15. See Brian Barry, "Political Accommodation, and Consociational Democracy," *British Journal of Political Science* 5 (October 1975), pp. 502-5.

16. Jacques Ellul, *The Political Illusion* (New York: Alfred H. Knopf, 1907), p. 222.

17. There are 1.5 million Palestinian refugees; 200,000 Bengalis from Burma living in Bangladesh; 500,000 Zairians who fled to Angola; 100,000 Tutis who escaped from Rwanda; 1 million people who have been uprooted in the Ogaden; and Cubans, Tibetans, Cambodians, and ethnic Chinese who have been displaced or killed. In addition, Greek Cypriots have been made homeless, as have uncounted peoples in Vietnam, Laos, Cambodia, Afghanistan, and Lebanon.

18. Richard Pierre Claude, "The Western Tradition of Human Rights in Comparative Perspective," *Comparative Judicial Review* 14 (1977), p. 8.

19. Ibid., p. 59.

20. This dilemma of liberal theory is examined with little success, in Richard G. Flathman, *The Practice of Rights* (Cambridge: Cambridge University Press, 1975), pp. 184-89.

21. John Rawls, *A Theory of Justice* (Cambridge, Mass.: Harvard University Press, 1971).

22. Ibid., p. 4.

23. Ibid., p. 221.

24. Vernon Van Dyke, "Justice as Fairness: For Groups?" *American Political Science Review* 69 (1975), pp. 607-14.

25. Ibid., p. 614.

26. See Regents of the University of California v. Bakke, 98 S. Ct. 2733 (1978), in which Justice Powell denies that one group can be accorded greater protection than others, but notes that "the white 'majority' itself is composed of various minority groups, most of which can lay claim to a history of prior discrimination." Apparently, Powell fears that "there is no principled basis for deciding which groups would merit heightened judicial solicitude and which would not."

27. See Owen M. Fiss, "Groups and the Equal Protection Clause," *Philosophy and Public Affairs* 5 (1976), pp. 107-77, for a thoughtful proposal of recognizing group rights under the U.S. Constitution. The quote is at page 155.

28. John Stuart Mill, *Considerations on Representative Government* (New York: The Liberal Arts Press, Inc., 1958), pp. 103-4.

29. Ibid., p. 230.

30. Karl Marx, "Restoration of Order—Dret and Chamber," in *New York Tribune*, April 24, 1852. Quoted from Eleanor Maax, ed., *Germany: Revolution and Counter-Revolution* (New York: International Publishing, 1969), pp. 85-86.

31. In *Neue Rheinische Zeiting*, January 13 and February 15, and 16, 1849. Quoted in J. Borys, *The Russian Communist Party and theSovietization of Ukraine* (Stockholm, 1960), p. 13. Ferdinand Lassalle, a non-Marxist socialist, held in same view of nationalities. pp. 13-14.

32. V.I. Lenin, "The Right of Nations to Self-Determination," in *Selected Works*, vol. 1 (Moscow: Progress Publishers, 1967), p. 605.

33. Quoted in J. Borys, *The Russian Communist Party*, p. 33.

34. See Jan F. Triska, ed., *Soviet Communism: Program and Rules* (San Francisco: Chandler Publishing Co., 1962), p. 107.

35. *Documents of the 22nd Congress of the CPSU*, vol. 2 (New York: Crosscurrents Press, 1961), p. 118.

36. See Vernon V. Aspaturian, *The Soviet Union on the World Communist System* (Stanford, Calif.: Hoover Institution, 1966), p. 46.

37. M. G. Kirichenko, "National Equality in the Soviet Union," in *The Multinational Society*, ed. William F. Mackey and Albert Vendoodt (Rawley, Mass.: Newbery House Publishers, 1975), pp. 200-20.

38. An official view is N. P. Farberov, "Self-determination in the Soviet Union," in Ibid., pp. 173-85.

39. See Thomas Remeikis, "Modernization and National Identity in the Baltic Republics," in *Nationalism and Human Rights*, ed. Ihor Kamenetsky (Littleton, Colo.: Association for the study of Nationalities, 1977), pp. 115-38.

40. See Yaroslav Bilinsky, "Politics, Purge and Dissent in the Ukraine since the Fall of Shelest," in Ibid., pp. 168-88.

41. See Zri Gitelman, "Modernization, Human Rights, and Jewish Nationalism in the USSR," in Ibid., pp. 217-27.

42. Zbigniew Brzezinski, "Political Implications of Soviet Nationality Problems," in *Soviet Nationality Problems*, ed. Edward Allworth (New York: Columbia University Press, 1972), p. 72.

43. Quoted in Borys, *The Russian Communist Party*, pp. 11-14. It was estimated that the ethnic minorities of Europe were reduced from 50 million to 20 million, but "the new frontiers of Europe reduced the number of minority peoples and at the same time accentuated the difficult problem of their protection." See Edmund C. Mower, *International Government* (Boston: D.C. Heath and Co., 1931), p. 455.

44. Protection of Linguistic, Racial or Religious Minorities by the League of Nations, Series of League of Nations Publications, I.B. Minorities, 1931 I.B.I. (C. 8. M.5. 1931; I), pp. 47-58.

45. See P. de Axcarate, *League of Nations and National Minorities: An Experiment* (Washington, D.C.: Carnegie Endowment for International Peace, 1945), pp. 123-30.

46. Ibid., pp. 117-18.

47. Two important opinions were: Advisory Opinion of 21 February 1925 on the Exchange of Greek and Turkish Populations (P.C.I.J., Series B. No. 10) and

theAdvisory Opinion of 31 July 1930 on the Greco-Bulgarian Community (P.C.I.J., Series B., No. 17).

48. This is the assessment of Inis L. Claude, Jr., *National Minorities, An International Problem* (Cambridge, Mass.: Harvard University Press, 1955), pp. 35-36. This view is shared by most scholars, although the explanations for failure are different.

49. Michael Zwerin, *A Case for the Balkanization of Practically Everyone* (London: Wildwood House, 1976).

50. For an interesting argument directed against such accommodation, see Joseph Rothschild, *Ethnopolitics* (New York: Columbia University Press, 1981).

51. J. S. Furnivall, *Netherlands India* (Cambridge: The University Press, 1939).

52. J. S. Furnivall, *Colonial Policy and Practice* (London: Cambridge University Press, 1948).

53. See Stephen Morris, "Indians in East Africa: A Study in Plural Society" *British Journal of Sociology* 7 (1956), pp. 194-211.

54. See Ramesh Deosasan, "Some Issues in Multi-Culturalism: Trinidad and Tobago in the Post Colonial Era," *Ethnic Groups* 13 (1981), pp. 199-25.

55. M. G. Smith, *The Plural Society in the British West Indies* (Berkeley, Calif.: University of California Press, 1965), p. 86.

56. Sir Earnest Barker, *Principles of Social and Political Theory* (New York: Oxford University Press, 1961), p. 3.

57. David B. Truman, *The Governmental Process* (New York: Alfred A. Knopf, (1951).

58. See criticisms of G. David Garson, *Group Theories of Politics* (Beverly Hills, Calif.: Sage Publications, 1978).

59. Crawford Young, *The Politics of Cultural Pluralism* (Madison: University of Wisconsin Press, 1976), p. 525.

60. Ibid., p. 526.

61. Here, I share the general view of Vernon Van Dyke, as expressed in "The Individual, the State, and Ethnic Communities in Political Theory," *World Politics* 29 (1977), pp. 343-69. However, I do not follow his view of the right of self-determination.

62. See Wisconsin v. Yoder, 406 U.S. 218 (1971).

63. Constitution of India, Ant. 338.

64. Constitution of Czechoslovakia, Art. 2; Art. 3; Constitution of Malaysia, Art. 8; Constitution of Singapore, Art. 89; Constitution of Yugoslavia, Art. 171 and elsewhere.

65. International Covenant on Civil and Political Rights, Article 27.

66. Alexander I. Solzhenitsyn, *The Gulag Archipelago* (New York: Harper & Row, 1974), p. 84.

67. David Loshak, *Pakistan Crisis* (New York: McGraw Hill, 1971), p. 6.

68. See Arend Lijphart, *Democracy in Plural Societies* for a new theory of consociational democracy to account for minority group interests.

69. But see Abdul Said, ed., *Ethnicity in an International Context* (New Brunswick, N.J.: Transaction Books, 1978), which suggests that there may be a growing "politics of disassociation," a view rejected here.

Capsule Survey of Minority Groups

THE following nation-by-nation listings are neither exhaustive nor definitive. They are a collation of information derived from UN materials, standard reference works, and scholarly writings. As such, they are a rather personal product that is intended as a guide to further research and as an indicator of the scope of minority rights issues.

This listing attempts to avoid questionable cases, but some matters present unavoidable choices. Some groups are listed as nationality groups; others might categorize these as ethnic groups and vice-versa. Caucasians are regarded as a race, although some would dispute this. Other categorizations can be disputed as well. While the inclusion of certain groups and exclusion of others has been personal, it is not arbitrary. Of course, minority status is not always based upon numbers and is sometimes (as with Flemings in Belgium or Bantus in South Africa) based upon inferior social and political position. Women are not listed as a minority, but they, too, may be regarded as a virtual minority in most nations. Many linguistic minorities were not emphasized unless their language preference appeared to be a significant feature of minority status. The act of listing a group is not intended to justify any claim but merely to note the presence of a significant group.

KEY

E = Ethnic
I = Indigenous People
X = Racial
L = Language
N = Nationality
R = Religion
T = Tribal

AFGHANISTAN
Tajiks (E)
Uzbeks (E)
Hazara (E)
Turkmen (E)
Other tribal divisions (T)

ALBANIA
Greeks (E)

ALGERIA
Berbers (L)

ANGOLA
Various Bantu groups (X)

ARGENTINA
Jews (R)
Indians (I)

AUSTRALIA
Aborigines (I)
Various nationality groups (N)

AUSTRIA
Slovenes (E)
Croats (E)
Hungarians (N)

BAHAMAS
Caucasians (X)
Haitians (N)

BAHRAIN
Indians (N)
Pakistans (N)
Iranians (N)

BANGLADESH
Hindus (R)
Indigenous tribes (I)

BARBADOS
Caucasians (X)

BELGIUM
Flemings (L,E)
Germans (N)

BELIZE
Mestizo (X)
Amerindians (I)
East Indians (E)

BENIN
Tribal groupings including Fon, Yoriba, Adia, Bariba, Peul (T)
Somba (L)
Muslims (R)

BHUTAN
Hindus (R)
Nepalese (N,E)
Lepchas (I)
Santal (E)

BOLIVIA
Indians (I)

BOTSWANA
Bushmen (I)
Hottentots (T)
Europeans (N,E)

BRAZIL
Jews (R)
Indians (I)

BULGARIA
Turks (E)
Gypsies (E)
Macedonians (E)
Armenians (E)

BURMA
Karens (E)
Shans (E)
Kachins (E)
Chinese (E)

Hindis (R)
Pakistanis (N,E)

BURUNDI

Pygmies (I)
Hutu (T)
Tutsi (T)

CAMBODIA

Chinese (E)
Chams (E,R)

CAMEROONS

Tribal groups, almost 200 (T)
Sudanese (N,E)
Foulbe (E,R)

CAPE VERDE

Europeans (N)

CENTRAL AFRICAN REPUBLIC

Baya (E)
Mandjia (E)
M'Baka (E)
Muslims (R)

CHAD

Sarra (L,T)
Massa (L,T)
Mandang (L,T)
Bantu (T,E)

CHINA (PEOPLE'S REPUBLIC)

Chuang (E)
Vigur (E)
Tibetans (E,N)
Miao (E)
Manchu (E)
Mongol (E,N)
Korean (E)

CHINA, NATIONALIST (TAIWAN)

Aborigines (I)

COLOMBIA

Amerindians (I)
Africans (X)

CONGO

Bantu tribes (T)
Pygmies (I)
Europeans (N)

COSTA RICA

Mestizos (X)
Jamaicans (E)

CYPRUS

Turks (N,E,)
Armenians (R,E)
Maronites (R,E)
Greeks (in places of Turkish occupation) (N,E)

CZECHOSLOVAKIA

Slovaks (E)
Hungarians (E,N)
Poles (E,N)
Germans (E,N)
Ukranians (E,N)
Gypsies (E)

DJIBOUTI

Afars (E,T)
Arabs (E)
Italians '(E,N)
Greeks (E,N)
Sudanese (E,N)

DOMINICA

Carib Indians (I)

DOMINICAN REPUBLIC

Blacks (X)

ECUADOR

Indians (I)
Africans (X)

EQUATORIAL GUINEA

Fangs (E)

Fernandinos (E)
Bubis (T)

ETHIOPIA

Gallas (L,E)
Falashas (E,R)
Eritreans (N)
Sidamas (E)
Somalis (N,E)
Yemenites (N,E)
Europeans (N)

FINLAND

Lapps (I)

FRANCE

Bretons (L)
Alsatians (L,E)

THE GAMBIA

Fula (E,T)
Wolof (E,T)
Jola (E,T)
Serahuli (E,T)

GHANA

Akan (E,T)
Ashanti (E,T)
Guans (E,T)
Ga and Ewe peoples (L)

GREECE

Turks (N,E)
Albanians (N,E)
Bulgarians (N,E)

GRENADA

Carib Indians (I)

GUATAMALA

Indians (I)

GUINEA

Various tribes (T)

GUYANA

Indians (I)

HONDURAS

Indians (I)
Caucasians (X)
Negroes (X)
Caribs (I)

HUNGARY

Germans (E)
Slovaks (E)
Romanians (N,E)
Gypsies (E)
Serbs (E)
Croats (E)

INDIA

Muslims (R)
Sikhs (R)
Jains (R)
Parsis (R)
Christians (R)
Assamese (L,E)
Bengali (L,E)
Marathi (L)
Tamil (L,E)
Telegu (L,E)
Sikkimese (N,E)
Goans (N,E)

INDONESIA

Papuans (L,E)
Mollucans (L,E)
Bataks (I,E)
Minahasans (I,E)
Amborese (I,E)
Chinese (E)
Tribal groups (T)
Hindus (R)

IRAN

Azerbjanis (E)
Kurds (E)
Arabs (E)

Turkomans (E)
Baluchis (E)
Quashqais (E)

IRAQ

Kurds (E)
Christians (R)

IRELAND

Protestants (R)

ISRAEL

Arabs (E,L,R)
Greek Catholics (R)
Yemenite Jews (E)

IVORY COAST

Akan (E,T)
Krou (E,T)
Senoufo (E, T)
Lagoon People (E,T)

JAMAICA

Chinese (E)
East Indian (E)
Syrians (E)

JAPAN

Koreans (N,E)
Ainu (I)

JORDAN

Palestinians (E,N)

KENYA

Luo (E,T)
Kamba (E,T)
Kisii (E,T)
Meru (E,T)
Indians (N,E)

KIRIBATI

Polynesians (E)
Banabans (E)

KUWAIT

Palestinians (E,N)
Iraquis (N)
Iranians (N)
Syrians (N)
Lebanese (N)

LAOS

Various tribal groups (T)

LEBANON

Christians (R)
Druzes (R,E)
Armenians (E)
Palestinians (E,N)
Syrians (N)

LESOTHO

Nguni (T)

MADAGASCAR

Betsileo (E,T)
Betsimisaraka (E,T)
Sakalara (E,T)
Tsimihety (E,T)

MALAWI

Nyanha (E,T)
Yao (E,T)
Maravi (E,T)
Tumbuka (E,T)
Lonwe (E,T)

MALAYASIA

Chinese (E,N)
Indians (E,N)
Pakistanis (E,N)
East Malaysians (Sabah and Sarawak) (E.I.N)

MALI

Peul (Falani) (E,T)
Voltaic (E,T)
Songhai (E,T)
Tuareg (E,T)

MAURITANIA

Tukulor (T)
Sarakole (T)
Tulani (T)

MAURITIUS

Creoles (E,X)
French (E,N)
Chinese (E,N)

MEXICO

Indians (I)

MONGOLIA

Oirat Mongols (E)
Buryat Mongols (E)
Kazakhs (E)
Chinese (E)
Khotan Turks (E)

MOROCCO

Jews (R)
Christians (R)

MOZAMBIQUE

Portuguese (N)

NEPAL

Gurings (T)
Magars (T)
Tamangs (T)
Newars (T)
Bhotias (T)
Rais (T)
Sherpas (T)
Tharus (T)

THE NETHERLANDS

Molluccans (E,N)

NEW ZEALAND

Maoris (I)
Tongans (E,N)
Samoans (E,N)

NICARAGUA

Indians (I)
Negroes (X)

NIGER

Djerma-Songhai (T,E)
Fulanis (T)
Tuaregs (T)
Toubous (T)

NIGERIA

Ibos (T)
Hausa (T)
Fulani (T)
Edo (T)
Ibiblo (T)
Tir (T)
Ijaw (T(
Kanuri (T)

NORWAY

Lapps (I)

OMAN

Iranians (N)
Pakistanis (N)
Indians (N)

PAKISTAN

Sindh (E,L)
Pathan (E)
Baluchi (E,L)
Various tribes (I)

PANAMA

Antilleans (E,N)
Indians (I)

PAPUA NEW GUINEA

Papuans (I)
Chinese (E,N)
Australians (N)
Polynesians (E)

PARAGUAY

Indians (I)

PERU

Indians (I)

PHILLIPINES

Chinese (N)
Spanish (N)
Americans (N)
Various tribes (I,T)

POLAND

Ukrainians (E)
Byelorussians (E)

QATAR

Pakistanis (N)
Iranians (N)

RUMANIA

Hungarians (E,N)
Germans (E,N)
Ukrainians (E,N)
Turks (E,N)
Serbo-Croats (E)

RWANDA

Tutsi (T)
Pygmies (I,T)

SENEGAL

Peul (Falani) (T)
Serere (T)
Tukulor (T)
Diola (T)
Mangingo (T)
French (N)

SIERRA LEONE

Limba (T)
Loko (T)
Kono (T)
Sherbo (T)
Val (T)
Gallina (T)
Susu (T)
Kissi (T)
Mandingo (T)
Peul (Fulani) (T)
Creoles (E)

SINGAPORE

Malays (E,N)
Indians (E,N)
Pakistanis (E,N)

SOMALIA

Bantus (X)
Arabs (E)

SOUTH AFRICA

Bantus (X)
Coloured (X)
Asiatic (X)
Xhosa (X)
Jews (R)
Whites (X)
Cape Malays (X)

SPAIN

Catalans (L)
Galicians (L)
Basques (L,N)

SRI LANKA

Tamil (E,L)
Moor (X)
Hindus (R)
Muslims (R)

SUDAN

Negroes (X)
Nuba (X)
Ethiopians (N)
Beja (T)

SURINAME

East Indians (E)
Creoles (X)

Javanese (E)
Chinese (E,N)
Amerindians (I)

SWAZILAND

Zulu (T)
Europeans (E)

SWITZERLAND

Germans (L)
French (L)
Italians (L)

SYRIA

Kurds (E)
Armenians (E,R)
Turks (N)

TANZANIA

Bantu tribes (T)
Europeans (N)
Asians (N)

THAILAND

Chinese (N,E)
Malays (E,N)
Khmers (E)
Karens (E,T)
Indians (N)
Vietnamese (N)
Kampucheans (N)

TOGO

Adja-Watyi (T)
Kabrai-Lesso (T)
Mina (T)
Kabye (T)

TRINIDAD AND TOBAGO

East Indians (E)
Caucasians (X)
Chinese (E,N)

TUNISIA

Berbers (T)
Europeans (N)

TURKEY

Kurds (E)
Armenians (E,R)
Greeks (N)
Jews (R)
Arabs (E)

UGANDA

Banyoro (T)
Banyanrole (T)
Batoro (T)
Heso (T)
Lango (T)
Achole (T)
Karamojong (T)
Zairians (N)
Sudanese (N)

UNION OF SOVIET SOCIALIST REPUBLICS

Ukrainians (E)
Uzbeks (E)
Byelorussians (E)
Poles (E)
Lithuanians (E)
Letts (E)
Estonians (E)
Mordvinians (L)
Karelians (L,E)
Tatars (E)
Chivash (E)
Bashkirs (E)
Moldavians (E)
Gaganz (E)
Germans (E)
Jews (R)
Gypsies (E)
Georgians (E)
Azerbaidzhanis (E)
Armenians (E,R)
Uzbeks (E)
Kazakhs (E)
Turkmenians (E)
Tadzhirs (E)
Koreans (E,N)

UNITED KINGDOM OF GREAT BRITAIN AND NORTHERN IRELAND

Scottish (E)
Welsh (E)
Irish (N)
Irish Catholics (R) Northern Irelan

UNITED STATES

Blacks (X)
Indians (X)
Hispanics (E)
Mexicans (N)
Japanese (E)
Chinese (E)
Filipinos (E,N)

UPPER VOLTA

Bobo (E)
Gorma (E,T)
Fulani (T)

URUGUAY

Mestizos (X)
Mulattos (X)
Jews (R)

VENEZUELA

Negroes (X)
Indians (I)

VIETNAM

Khmer (E,T)
Montagnards (E,T)
Tays (T)
Muong (T)
Nung (T)

YUGOSLAVIA

Croats (E)
Slovenes (E)
Macedonians (E)
Albanians (N,E)
Bosnian Muslims (R)
Montenegrins (E)
Hungarians (E,N)

ZAIRE

Bantu tribes (T)

ZAMBIA

Bantu tribes (T)

ZIMBABWE

Caucasians (X)
Asians (E)

An Annotated Bibliography of Minority Rights

Baudoin, Jean-Louis, and Claude Masse. *"Étude Comparative et Evolutive des Droits Linguistiques en Belgique et en Suisse."* Etude E 15. Etudes Realisées pour le Compte de la Commission d'Enquete sur la Situation de la langue Française et sur les Droits Linguistiques au Québec, 1973. (In French).

Bay, Christian. *The Structure of Freedom*. Stanford: Stanford University Press, 1970. A basic explanation of pluralist democracy.

Bennett, G. I. "The I.L.O. Convention on Indigenous and Tribal Populations—The Resolution of a Problem of Vires." *British Yearbook of International Law* 46 (1972/1973), p. 382. This potentially useful article describes briefly the activities and discussion leading to, and conclusions reached, in the International Labor Organization's Convention on Indigenous and Tribal Populations. The convention was undertaken with a view to giving practical help and technical assistance to states in which the disadvantaged economic and social conditions of such groups impedes their integration into society and prevents their participation in and enjoyment of the rights enjoyed by other citizens.

Berinson, Zvi. "Freedom of Religion and Conscience in the State of Israel." *Israel Yearbook of Human Rights* 3 (1973), p. 223. Discussion of the limitations on religious practice imposed by government authority in Israel. Israel's Declaration of Independence, which includes a guarantee of religious freedom, is not of constitutional force, but is merely a pronouncement of the new state's ideals and goals.

In practice, complete religious freedom can be impinged upon by acts of the Knesset, so long as the legislation operates in promotion of the public welfare, safety and morals. Singled out for special consideration are marriage and divorce matters, which are completely under the control of religious authorities, as is the strict control placed upon the raising and butchering of swine.

Bertsch, Gary K. "Ethnicity and Politics in Socialist Yugoslavia." *Annals of the American Academy of Political and Social Science* 433 (1977), p. 88. Yugoslavia is a true kaleidoscope of ethnic groups, and such a situation brings about special problems. The political pressures brought about by such ethnic diversity and the responses to those pressures as reflected in the nation's Constitution and legislation are detailed in this article.

Beteille, Andre. *Social Inequality*. Middlesex, England: Penguin Books, 1972. A collection of essays on social class and stratification. Race, caste, and other forms of social distinctions are described by leading scholars.

Bingaman, Anne. *A Commentary on the Effect of the Equal Rights Amendment on State Laws and Institutions*. Sacramento, Calif.: California Commission on the Status of Women, 1975. Analysis of the impact ratification of the Equal Rights Amendment would have on California's educational institutions, family and labor laws, and marital property provisions. The author concludes that many state laws would have to be modified or repealed in order to eliminate discrimination against women.

Blaustein, Albert P. and Gisbert H. Flanz. *Constitutions of the Countries of the World.* 15 volumes with supplementary Volume, two historical volumes. Dobbs Ferry, N. Y.: Oceana Publications, 1971-.

Blaustein, Albert P., and Eric B. Blaustein. *Constitutions of Dependencies and Special Sovereignties.* 6 volumes. Dobbs Ferry, N. Y.: Oceana Publications, 1975-.

Boguszak, Jiri. "The Problem of Constitutional Regulation of Personal and Political Rights." *Bulletin of Czechoslovak Law* 25, no. 8, p. 46 (1967). The Czechoslovakian Constitution's human rights provisions are examined and criticized in this essay. Enactment of further human rights guarantees as constitutional provisions is advocated. The author places much hope in the newly created constitutional court and cites the Yugoslav example as a model of a workable socialist constitution.

Brown, Barbara A., Thomas I. Emerson, Gail Falk, and Ann Freedman. "The Equal Rights Amendment: A Constitutional Basis for Equal Rights for Women." *Yale Law Journal* 80 (1971), p. 871. An excellent in-depth look at sex discrimination in the United States worked around the context of the proposed Equal Rights Amendment. This article outlines past and present limits on women's rights and explains the potential effect of the Amendment's ratification on legislation and practice. The legislative history of the ERA is included as an appendix.

Bruegel, J. W. "A Neglected Field: the Protection of Minorities." *Revue des Droits de l'Homme* 4 (1971), p. 413. This essay surveys and reviews twentieth-century efforts in the international community to protect European linguistic and ethnic minorities. The impact of such documents as the League of Nations Minorities Protocols, the 1945 Potsdam Agreement, the United Nations Universal Declaration of Human Rights, and the European Convention on Human Rights are assessed. National constitutions and their provisions are not mentioned, but it is suggested that interest expressed by the international community in protecting the rights of minorities will influence states toward proper treatment of minority group members.

Bucci, P. Vincent. *Chiese e Stato: Church-State Relations in Italy within the Contemporary Constitutional Framework*. The Hague: Nijhoff, 1969. Case studies of church-state conflicts in postwar Italy, with emphasis on issues of religious freedom and clerical jurisdiction over marriage and divorce. The place of the Lateran Treaty in Italian constitutional law and history is examined.

Buergenthal, Thomas. "Implementing the United Nations Racial Convention." *Texas International Law Journal* 12 (1977), p. 87. This study focuses on the Elimination of Racial Discrimination that was established under the Convention to supervise its implementation.

Claude, Inis L. *National Minorities* Cambridge, Mass.: Harvard University Press, 1955. A classic treatment of a component of minority rights.

Claude, Richard P. "The Threshold Problem for Human Rights Research." *Human Rights Journal* 6 (1977), p. 169. Compilation and analysis of source materials for scholarly research into human rights concerns. Claude emphasizes that the prospective researcher must take care to assure that his sources are both accurate and reliable and notes that many self-serving documents on human rights are issued by governments and government agencies. A country-by-country bibliography of reliable source materials is included.

______. "The Western Tradition of Human Rights in Comparative Perspective." *Comparative Juridicial Review* 14 (1977), p. 4. A valuable examination, in historical and philosophical terms, of the evolution of the great "liberal democracies"—Britain, France, and the United States—with emphasis on human rights elements in those nations' constitutions and legislation. Claude traces the stages of institutional development in the three countries structure and organization.

______, ed. *Comparative Human Rights*. Baltimore: Johns Hopkins University Press, 1976. An excellent collection of essays of human rights concerns. Emphasis is on public policy as a means of ensuring enjoyment of fundamental freedoms, and case studies echoing that view but dealing with a particular facet of human rights are included. Those contributions that may be of most interest in light of this study are annotated in Part B of the bibliography.

Cole, Sonia. *The Races of Man*. London: Trustees of the British Museum (National History), 1965. Illustrated summary providing background material on racial classification. The emphasis is biological.

Coleman, Howard David. "The Problem of Anti-Semitism under the International Convention on the Elimination of All Forms of Racial Discrimination." *Revue des Droits de l'Homme* 2 (1969), p. 609. This essay examines the form of discrimination known as anti-Semitism; it defines the term, explains its scope, and demonstrates how racially based anti-Semitism falls within the ambit of the International Convention on the Elimination of All Forms of Racial Discrimination.

Columbia Law School. "Symposium on the Status of Women." *American Journal of Comparative Law* 20 (1972), p. 585. The text of this very valuable symposium contains surveys on the status of women in Great Britain, Sweden, Norway, France, the Soviet Union, and Israel. Also included is a study of "The Status of Married Women under Customary Law in Senegal."

Connor, Walker. "Nation-Building or Nation-Destroying?" *World Politics* 24, no. 3 (1972), p. 319. According to Connor, only 12 contemporary states can be considered ethnically homogeneous. In nearly a third of the cases (29.5 percent), the largest group comprises less than half of the state's population. In 53 states (40.2 percent), the population is divided into at least 5 significant ethnic groupings.

Cranston, Maurice. *What Are Human Rights?* London: Bodley Hoad, 1973. A basic philosophical treatment that helps clarify and define rights concepts.

Danelski, Davie J. "A Behavioral Conception of Human Rights." *Law in Transition Quarterly* 3 (1966), p. 63. An examination of human rights, with the thesis that in order for a person to be accorded basic rights and dignity, he must first be perceived as a person. Human rights are distinguished from civil rights, which attach merely because of the operation of law.

Das Basu, Durga. *Commentary on the Constitution of India.* 6th ed., rev'd and enlarged. Calcutta: S. C. Sarkar Ltd., 1973.

Das Gupta, Jyotirindra. "Nation, Region, and Welfare: Ethnicity, Regionalism, and Development Politics in South Asia." *Annals of the American Academy of Political and Social Science* 433 (1977), p. 125. General study of minority groups in South Asia, particularly India.

Das Gupta, S. K. "Racial Discrimination and Human Rights." *Journal of the Indian Law Institute* 15 (1973), p. 440. A short critique on the ineffectiveness of United Nations measures against racial discrimination. Nations are urged to implement and enforce policies of nondiscrimination.

Deutsch, Karl W. "The Political Significance of Linguistic conflicts." In *Multilingual Political Systems.* Québec: University of Laval Press, 1975, p. 7. The neglect of linguistic conflicts has had grave social consequences, which extend even to the physical loss of life. Deutsch sets forth several theories about language conflicts for consideration by the political community and suggests possible solutions for the development of effective language policies that will aid political science in fulfilling two of its major tasks; namely, the protection of human life and the defense of the autonomy and dignity of the individual.

Djordjevic, Jovan. "The Yugoslav Constitution and New Individual Rights and Freedoms." In *Scritti in onore di Gaspare Ambrosini*, volume 1. Milano: Edditore Milano, 1970, p. 595. A survey of the fundamental rights guarantees incorporated into the Yugoslav Constitution of 1963. Among the rights enumerated is the right of minority group members to use their own language and retain their own culture.

Doehring, Karl. "Non-Discrimination and Equal Treatment under the European Human Rights Convention and the West German Constitution with Particular Reference to Discrimination against Aliens." *American Journal of Comparative Law* 18 (1970), p. 305. In Article 3 of the West German Constitution, equal treatment of all persons is mandated with regard to all state activities; even when no fundamental or constitutionally enunciated right is involved, the West German is protected against arbitrariness by officials. The corresponding provision of the European Convention on Human Rights, Article 14, prohibits discrimination only where those rights guaranteed by the Convention itself are at issue. German constitutional practice has long permitted distinctions to be made on the basis of citizenship; the Human Rights convention, though, specifically imparts fundamental rights to all persons regardless of alienage or citizenship and indeed cites discrimination on the basis of citizenship or alienage as impermissible. Here Doehring compares and contrasts the texts of the German and European documents, paying special attention to protection of the rights of non-nationals.

Donneur, Andre P. "La Solution Territoriale au Probleme de Multi-linguisme." In *Multilingual Political Systems*. Québec: University of Laval Press, 1975, p. 209. There are two solutions to the problems created by the coexistence of several languages within a nation: the principle of personality and the principle of territoriality. Donneur makes a comparative study of Switzerland and Belgium, nations that chose territoriality, and Canada, which chose personality, in solving multilingual problems in the areas of public administration, education, private services, commerce, and work.

Dressler, Alfred. "Human Rights in Constitutional Theory." *Bulletin of Czechoslovak Law* 25, no. 8 (1967), p. 56. This analysis of the United Nations Universal Declaration of Human Rights focuses on its applicability to socialist states and points our that the socialist concept of the individual's *duty* to the state makes enactment of many of the declaration provisions (on freedom of emigration, for example) impracticable. A brief summary of Czech constitutional history is included, with an emphasis upon the historical importance accorded protection of linguistic and cultural minorities in this multi-ethnic state.

Dreyer, June Teufel. "Ethnic relations in China." *Annals of the American Academy of Political and Social Science* 433 (1977), p. 100. Through ethnic minorities comprise only 6 percent of China's population, they inhabit some of China's most strategically valuable and resource-rich lands. This article traces historically the ways in which the Chinese government, from the beginning of the twentieth century to the present day, has perceived and treated such minorities.

Dryden, P. K. "Annotated Bibliography of Political Rights of African Women." *African Law Studies* 7 (1972), p. 27. A valuable source for sociologically oriented studies of the role of African women in their states. Law reviews are sadly underrepresented in this bibliography, which concentrates on sociological and political science articles and monographs. United Nations materials relating to women's rights are also included, but most of these date back to the early 1950s, and their present authority can be called into question.

Duchacek, Ivo D. *Power Maps: Comparative Politics of Constitutions*. Santa Barbara, Calif.: A. B. C.-Clio, 1973. A useful summary of comparative data on the world's constitutions in a limited number of selected areas. Breakdowns are provided on such topics as preambles, powers to declare and conduct wars, emergency powers, and so on. There are also data on different kinds of parliaments and presidential systems, a comparison between rigid and flexible constitutions, and other useful materials. It is only of secondary value, however, in a study of racial, religious, and sex discrimination.

______. *Rights and Liberties in the World Today: Constitutional Promise and Reality*. Santa Barbara, Calif.: A. B. C.-Clio, 1972.

Dunn, James A., Jr. "The Revision of the Constitution of Belgium: A Study in the Institutionalization of Ethnic Conflict." 17 *Western Political Quarterly* 27 (1974), p. 143. A brief but excellent history of the Flemish-Walloon conflict and the movement toward federalization of Belgium along ethnic and linguistic lines. Recent revision of the national constitution to satisfy demands for decentralization by the Flemish and the problems inherent in the designation of Brussels as a bilingual city are discussed.

of Indigenous Minorities." *Australian Yearbook of International Law* vol. 68 (1975), pp. 83-84.

Falch, Jean *Contribution à l'Etude du Statut des Langues en Europe.*" Centre International de Recherches sur le Bilinguisme, Québec: Les Presses de l'Université Laval, 1973 (In French). This volume provides comparisons between various nations on linguistic matters. For example, it compares the laws of the Western states of Belgium andSwitzerland with those of the socialist states of Czechoslovakia and Yugoslavia.

It distinguishes between countries that have several official languages and those which do not make this distinction. It also explains the difference between language protection via constitutional provisions and those that relegate language matters to statute.

Faruki, Kemal A. *The Evolution of Islamic Constitutional Theory and Practice.* Karachi: National Publishing House, 1971. This volume discusses the influence of *shar'ia* (religious law) upon governments of Muslim secular rulers from Islam's beginnings in the seventh century to the 1920s. The title is somewhat misleading, as national constitutions are discussed only peripherally.

Fischer, Georges. "Les Etats Multiraciaux." *Human Rights Journal* 5 (1972), p. 535. Written in French, this article explores the basic problems of selected multiracial states. It begins with several definitions, then attempts to classify types of groups. The body is devoted to the situation in the United States, India, England, and Malaysia. The reader, however, questions the choice since the situation in the West is so different from that of the Asian countries which are also discussed.

Fishman, Joshua A., and Haya Fisherman. "The 'Official Languages' of Israel: Their Status in Law and Police Attitudes and Knowledge Concerning Them." In *Multilingual Political Systems.* Québec: University of Laval Press, 1975, p. 497. An official language is one that is used by a government and promoted through the power of the state, but it is not necessarily the national language. Prior to 1948 the official languages in what is now Israel were English and Arabic, though Arabic was increasingly ignored. The authors document the past and present statutory law and, in a survey of police, show the confusion created by the differences in theory and practice.

Fisk, Winston, M. "The Constitutionalism Movement in Yugoslavia: a Preliminary Sruvey." *Slavic Review* 30 (1971), p. 277. An introduction to the Yugoslav Constitution, unique among Communist constitutions because of the provisions it makes for a federalist system. In Yugoslavia the provinces exercise an extraordinary degree of self-determination—the point is made that profound ethnic sentiments of the Croats, Serbs, and other ethnic minorities played a part in influencing the establishment of such a system.

Friedrich, Carl J. *Limited Government: A Comparison.* Englewood Cliffs, N. J.: Prentice-Hall, 1974. Aspects of constitutionalism, discussed by one of America's leading authorities. Chapter six is devoted to constitutional aspects of human rights protection.

______. "The Politics of Language and Corporate Federalism." In *Multilingual Political Systems*. Québec: University of Laval Press, 1975, p. 227. A philosophical paper on the relationship of language to nationality, the role of federalism in multilingual societies, cultural autonomy, and the principles of territoriality and personality. Austria-Hungary, Yugoslavia, and Estonia are cited as models.

Galanter, Marc "The Abolition of Disabilities—Untouchability and the Law." In *The Untouchables in Contemporary India*, edited by J. Michael Mahar. Tucson: University of Arizona Press, 1972., p. 227.

______. "Equality and Preferential Treatment: Constitutional Limits and Judicial Control." *Indian Yearbook of International Affairs* 14 (1965), p. 257. An important article describing the judicially imposed limitations on the overly broad language on special preferences in Articles 15 and 16 of the Indian Constitution.

Galizia, Mario. "The Declarations of Rights and Their Place in the History of Italian Constitutional Law." In *Associazione Italiano di Diritto Comparato: Italian National Reports to the Nineth International Congress of Comparative Law*. Tehran and Milano: Edditore Milano, 1974. p. 33. A limited historical sketch of the influence of the French and American declarations of rights on Italian sympathies and political ideals. The constitutions of Italian nation-states that were adopted as a result of the 1848 ferment and the impact of fascism with respect to constitutional rights provisions are discussed.

Gaur, Santosh Kumar. "Safeguards to Stateless Linguistic Minorities." *Lawyer* 2 (1970), p. 61. Many of India's component states contain members of various language groups within their borders but recognize and grant official status only to the tongue spoken by the majority of their citizens. Those who speak other languages are thereby disadvantaged in education and employment, and state governments do little to assist them in adjusting to life in a linguistically foreign community. Gaur suggests that the various state governments address themselves to the problems presented by the stateless linguistic minorities and that they champion the rights of such peoples by giving special subsidies and encouraging cultural and educational independence. Harking back to the India-Pakistan partition, Gaur warns of the bitterness and strife that may ensue if the needs and rights of these neglected peoples are not tended to.

Ghouse, Mohammad. "Judicial Control of Protective Discrimination." *Journal of the Indian Law Institute* 11 (1969), p. 371. Discussion of the definitions of "socially backward classes" and caste, within the meaning of Article 15 (4) of the Indian Constitution. Since "backward class" is nowhere defined in the Constitution, defining it is a matter of governmental policy; each state has the power to define "backward class," which would trigger with respect to such persons the special protection provisions of Article 15 (4).

______. "Minority Rights under the Indian Constitution." *Supreme Court Journal* 36 (1967), p. 67. A discussion of Articles 29 and 30 of the Indian Constitution. These articles guarantee the educational and cultural rights of linguistic and ethnic minority groups, including the rights to establish and administer educational institutions.

Glayden, J. "The Transnational Protection of Ethnic Minorities." *Canadian Yearbook of International Law* 13 (1974), p. 25. A discussion of ethnicity from a sociological and policy viewpoint; examples of ethnic consciousness are taken not only from Canada but from Europe, Africa and Asia. The work of the United Nations in this area is briefly discussed.

Glickman, H., "Traditional Pluralism and Democratic Process in Mainland Tanzania." *Journal of Asian and African Studies* 165 (1969).

Goitein, S. D., "Minority Self-Rule and Government Control in Islam." *Studia Islamica* 31 (1970), p. 106.

Gotlieb, Allan, ed. *Human Rights, Federalism, and Minorities*. Toronto: Canadian Institute of International Affairs, 1970. An important collection of essays by political leaders (including Pierre Trudeau) and distinguished scholars (Tarnopolsky, John Humphrey) concerning the protection of human rights in the federalist system of Canada. Emphasis is upon the cultural and language rights of the French-speaking Canadian and, indeed, several of the articles are in French.

Goy, R.H.M., "The International Protection of the Cultural and National Heritage." *Nederlands Yearbook of International Law* 117 (1973). This work examines treaty derived protections of certain minorities.

Graefrath, Bernhard, *The Economic, Social and Cultural Human Rights in the German Democratic Republic*. Berlin: Publications of the GDR Committee on Human Rights, 1970. Summary of economically and culturally based human rights enjoyed by citizens of the German Democratic Republic. An appendix places the United National International Covenant on Economic, Social and Cultural Rights and East German constitutional provisions and statutes side-by-side in order to demonstrate the latter's compliance with the declarations and goals of the former.

Grove, D. John. *The Race vs. Ethnic Debate: A Cross-National Analysis of Two Theoretical Approaches*. Denver, Colo.: Center on International Race Relations, 1974. Monograph contrasting the assimilation and pluralistic theories of multi-ethnic societies. Heavily laden with statistics; also good for its summarization of current work in the field.

Guggenheim, Malvina. "Re: Human Rights." *New York University Journal of International Law and Politics* 6 (1973), p. 427. This brief article concerns itself with the procedures of the Economic and Social Council on the Human Rights Commission and the Subcommission on Prevention of Discrimination and Protection of Minorities. The scope of its authority and the remedies suggested are limited.

Haksar, Urmila. *Minority Protection and International Bill of Human Rights*. Bombay: Allied Publishers, 1974. Concerned exclusively with the problem of minority protection in its relation to the International Bill of Human Rights. United Nations protection of minority rights is seen as extension of minorities problems going back to World War I and beyond.

Harris, George S. "Ethnic Conflict and the Kurds." *Annals of the American Academy of Political and Social Science* 433 (1977), p. 112. This article discusses the predicament of the Kurds, an ethnic minority spread throughout Turkish, Iranian, and Iraqi lands. The inability of the Kurds to establish their own state and their impotence as a force of power in states in which they are a statistically significant minority are analyzed here.

Henkin, Louis. "National and International Perspectives in Racial Discrimination." *Revue des Droits de l'Homme* 4 (1971), p. 263. Racial discrimination is a common practice, it is conceded here, and Professor Henkin of Columbia University attempts to explain the failure of international efforts to halt such discrimination by pointing out that governments rarely act with positive force against inequality. Indeed, he notes racial or ethnic discrimination can be a cornerstone of national policy (citing South Africa and Cyprus as examples). It is suggested that most governments are particularly loath to enforce racial equality by outlawing private discriminatory actions and that values of national autonomy often operate to discourage concerned nations from interfering in the affairs of states whose policy it is to discriminate.

Hewitt, Christopher. "Majorities and Minorities: A Comparative Survey of Ethnic Violence." *Annals of the American Academy of Political and Social Science* 433 (1977), p. 150. A comparative study of ethnic divisions that have escalated into open rioting or warfare and an analysis of the cause of such violent outbreaks.

Hingorini, L. "Minorities in India and Their Rights." *Revue des Droits de l'Homme* (1972), p. 479. A brief look at Indian constitutional treatment of minorities; it forms an excellent accompaniment to the many outstanding full-length studies in this area.

Horowitz, Donald. "Cultural Movements and Ethnic Change." *Annals of the American Academy of Political and Social Science* 433 (1977), p. 6. General discussion of ethnicity in the 1960s and 1970s with reference to African and European unrest and ethnic conflict.

Horrell, Muriel. *Legislation and Race Relations.* Johannesburg: South African Institute of Race Relations, 1971. With mimeographed supplementary materials. Supplementing constitutional provisions on racial separation, this book summarizes important legislation and regulations that affect race relationships. It is broken down by topic.

Imam, Mohammed, ed. *Minorities and the Law.* Bombay: Indian Law Institute, 1972. This collection of some thirty papers consitutes the best work on the problem of the plural society that is India. The theme is that the interests of minorities and backward classes must not be sacrificed in the interests of a unified central government. Emphasis is placed upon the scope and extent of constitutional and legal safeguards provided to the minorities. These papers were presented and discussed at a seminar on the topic organized by the Indian Law Institute in New Delhi in April 1971.

Joncic, K. *The Yugoslav Constitution and Relations Between the Nationalities.* Belgrade: Editor Medjunrodna Stampa-Interpress, 1967. Attempts to explain the treatment of nationalities in Yugoslavia under various constitutional arrangements.

Kloss, Heinz. *The American Bilingual Tradition.* Rowley, Mass.: The Newbury House Publishers, 1977. A detailed study of American immigration policy and its implications for the rights of nationality group members. Laws to protect and promote ethnic group rights are examined in a historical context. The organization and distribution of minority groups is delineated. An appendix provides a statistical survey of linguistic groups by state.

Koopmans, T., ed. *Constitutional Protection of Equality*. Leyden: Nijhoff, 1975. A useful treatment somewhat lacking in focus.

Kunstadter, Peter, ed. *Southeast Asian Tribes, Minorities and Nations*. 2 volumes. Princeton, N.J.: Princeton University Press, 1967. This is an important contribution to an explosive minority problem. It is an anthropologically oriented study of minority, ethnic, and tribal groups in India, China Malaysia, Thailand, and Indochina. Several of the contributions discuss how governments in Asia deal with minority groups and minority group concerns.

Kuper, Leo. *The Pity of It All: Polarization of Racial and Ethnic Relations*. Minneapolis: University of Minnesota Press, 1977. Following an introductory note on the problem, "From Reformism to Genocide," four case studies are analyzed: Algeria, Burundi, Rwanda, and Zanzibar.

______. *Genocide* (New Haven: Yale University Press, 1982). Kuper provides the first systematic study of genocide with historical detail and chilling accuracy.

Kyriakides, Stanley. *Cyprus: Constitutionalism and Crisis Government*. Philadelphia, 1968. This constitutional history of Cyprus focuses primarily on post-World War II constitutional plans and the adopted Constitution of 1960. Much attention is drawn to summary and analysis of the perpetual strain between Greek and Turkish Cypriots and the inevitable eruptions into violence that have ensued. Blame is placed on the 1960 Constitution for failing to avert alienation and frustration of the Turkish minority, since the constitutional guarantees of minority participation in government have been largely ignored or exploited by the Greek Cypriots. The author rejects the proposed solution (which has since become a reality) of a divided state.

Lador-Lederer, J. Josef. *International Group Protection: Aims and Methods in Human Rights*. Leyden: Sijthoff, 1968. Historical and sociological analysis of international human rights concerns with an emphasis on the protection of linguistic and ethnic minorities.

Lambert, Richard D., ed. Martin O. Heisler, special ed. *Ethnic Conflict in the World Today. Annals of the American Academy of Political and Social Science* (September, 1977) 433. Invaluable survey of ethnic trouble spots; the articles include general studies on ethnicity and minorities.

Lannung, Hermod. "The Rights of Minorities." In *Melanges Offerts a Polys Modinos*. Paris: A. Pedone, 1968, p. 181. Review of international efforts to protect the rights of minorities, especially the European Convention on Human Rights.

LaPonce, J. A. *The Protection of Minorities*. Berkeley: University of California Press, 1960. The earlier treatment of the subject of minority rights. Some of it is still provocative. Some of it is quite outmoded.

______. "Relating Linguistic to Political Conflicts: The Problem of Language Shift in Multilingual Societies." In *Multilingual Political Systems*. Québec: University of Laval Press, 1975, p. 185. According to the author's theory, languages become specialized in the mind of a multilingual person according to roles and stratified according to knowledge and preference; within society, men specialize in their roles, and stratify their power relationships. LaPonce suggests that political scientists study the effects of language shifts on the individual's self-esteem, social effectiveness, and position in the political structure in order to find the best solution for a multilingual state that wishes to both maintain linguistic diversity and reduce ethnic-linguistic conflicts.

Lerner, Nata *The Crime of Incitement to Group Hatred.* New York: World Jewish Congress, 1965. Worldwide survey of constitutional provisions and legislation that make criminal the incitement of racism, anti-Semitism, or other prejudices. Included also in the discussion are United Nations documents on human rights and racial tolerance.

Lieberson, Stanley, and James F. O'Connor. "Language Diversity in a Nation and Its Regions." In *Multilingual Political Systems.* Québec: University of Laval Press, 1975, p. 161. This study expands on a previous one by the same authors; it is, like the other, an attempt to reduce to mathematical terms data about the distribution of the mother tongues in a nation and its political subdivisions. They believe that such studies will show the probabilities of maintaining a multilingual nation and its potential for splintering into two or more separate countries.

Lillich, Richard B. "The Problem of the Applicability of Existing International Provisions for the Protection of Human Rights to Individuals Who Are Not Citizens of the Country in Which They Live." *American Journal of International Law* 70 (1976), p. 507. A brief editorial commentary explaining how the topic of alien rights was brought under the jurisdiction of the United Nations Sub-Commission on the Prevention of Discrimination and Protection of Minorities.

Linz, Juan J. "Politics in a Multi-Lingual Society with a Dominant World Language: The Case of Spain." In *Multilingual Political Systems.* Québec: University of Laval Press, 1975, p. 367. The language which is commonly called Spanish the world over is actually Castilian, one of the four languages of Spain. The Spanish government has never given serious thought to the issue of multilingualism, and official census or other statistical data have never included information on language use. Linz explores the history of multilingualism in Spain, with an emphasis on regional stirrings for greater recognition of the Catalan, Galician, and Basque languages. He suggests that in the future Spain will be forced to consider its language problems.

McDougal, Myres, S. "Human Rights and World Public Order: Principles of Content and Procedure for Clarifying general Community Policies." *Virginia Journal of International Law* 14 (1974), p. 387. Inquiry into the possibility of improving the intellectual procedures for the clarification and specification of the substantive content of human rights in particular instances of application. Although this article is primarily concerned with procedure and theoretical perspective, it also assists in obtaining an understanding of present human rights documents. The appendices are especially valuable; they provide a veritable checklist of human rights provisions for national or international documents.

McDougal, Myres S., Harold D. Lasswell, and Lung-Chu Chen. "Freedom from

Discrimination in Choice of Language and International Human Rights." *Southern Illinois University Law Journal* 1 (1976), p. 1151. One of series of articles by these authors, this essay concerns itself with the deprivations imposed upon certain peoples because of their linguistic identity. It is international in scope and outlook.

______. "Human Rights for Women and World Public Order: The Outlawing of Sex-Based Discrimination." *American Journal of International Law* 69 (1975), p. 497. A look at the creation and present status of certain international prescriptions intended to forster equality between women and men.

______. "The Protection of Aliens from Discrimination and World Public Order: Responsibility of States conjoined with Human Rights." *American Journal of International Law* 70 (1976), p. 432. An excellent article, which concerns itself with "the deprivations . . . imposed upon individuals on the ground that they do not possess the 'nationality' of the imposing state. By nationality we refer to the 'characterizations' states make of individuals for the purpose of controlling and protecting them . . .

______. "The Right to Religious Freedom and World Public Order: The Emerging Norm of Nondiscrimination." *Michigan Law Review* 74 (1976), p. 856. An excellent study of the problems and laws relating to religious freedom and toleration on both the international and domestic levels. It deals extensively with documentary (including constitutional) expressions on the subject.

______. "The Protection of Respect and Human Rights: Freedom of Choice and World Public Order." *American University Law Review* 24, 919 (1975). Refines and categorizes claims made on behalf of respect for individuals. Because the article deals with the sharing of respect in aggregate terms, it frequently touches upon group rights according to sex, religion, language, ethnicity, and race. Slavery and race relations are given detailed attention.

Mackey, William F. "Puissance, Attraction et Pression des Langues en Contact: Modeles et Indices." In *Multilingual Political Systems*. Québec: University of Laval Press, 1975. p. 119. The examples of India and Ireland in attempting to legislate language policy form the backdrop for this study. Mackey seeks to identify and measure the elements of linguistic power and to show what happens, in statistical terms, when two or more languages conflict. He feels that empirical data concerning demography, global dispersion of languages, mobility, economy, idealogy, and culture will be most valuable in future legislation.

Mackey, William F., and Albert Verdoodt. *the Multinational Society.* Rawley, Mass.: Newbury House Publishers, 1975. A collection of essays of varied quality and interest. Although there is little agreement on definitions, some of the articles were originally papers delivered at Ljubljana, Yugoslavia, seminar.

McRae, Kenneth D. "The Concept of Consociational Democracy and its Application to Canada." In *Multilingual Political Systems*. Québec: University of Laval Press, 1975, p. 245. A philosophical discussion of "segmented pluralism" or "consociationalism" as practiced in the Netherlands, Austria, Belgium, and Switzerland, where there exist a combination of strong social fragmentation and political efficiency and stability. The author suggests that "consociationalism" might be a solution to Canada's language problems.

Martin, O. "Managing Ethnic Conflict in Belgium." *Annals of the American Academy of Political and Social Science* 32 (1977). Historical summary of ethnic division between Flemish and Walloons in Belgium. Religious and linguistic bases for such division are discussed and analyzed.

Means, G. P. "Special Rights as a Strategy for Development." *Comparative Politics* 5 (1972), no. 29. A thoughtful analysis of an ill-studied subject.

Mensah-Brown, A. K. ed. *African International Legal History*. New York: United Nations Institute for Training and Research, 1975. Ethnic problems are intelligently analyzed in chapter 3, a legal and historical survey by Antony Allott on boundaries in Africa. The author points out how colonial-based boundaries disregarded tribal and ethnic considerations.

Micaud, Charles A. "Bilingualism in North Africa: Cultural and Socio-Political Implications." *Western Political Quarterly* 27 (1974), p. 92. Discussion of language in Tunisia, Morocco, and Algeria, where Arabic has been deemed the official tongue but where facility in French is considered vital for social and economic advancement. The point is made that, among young people, Arabic is falling into disuse and French is becoming the language of choice.

Mickenberg, Neil H. "Aboriginal Rights in Canada and the United States." *Osgoode Hall Law Journal* 9 (1971), p. 119. This article summarizes leading Canadian and American cases that have grappled with the question of aboriginal land title. Since both nations share a common colonial heritage, the manner is which Indian rights have been addressed by these governments is remarkably similar. Both nations recognize the aboriginal peoples right to possess land, but both also hold that this possessory right is inferior to any claims upon the land made by the sovereign.

Minority Rights Group. *Reports*. London: Benjamin Franklin House, 36 Craven Street, WC2N 5NG. A series of excellent monographs, each dealing with another of the world's minority groups and its problems. A list of the reports follow:

1. Religious minorities in the Soviet Union.
2. The two Irelands: the double minority—a study of intergroup tensions.
3. Japan's minorities: Burakumin, Koreans, and Ainu.
4. The Asian minorities of East and Central Africa.
5. Eritrea and Southern Sudan: aspects of wider African problems.
6. The Crimean Tatars, Volga Germans, and Meskhetians: Soviet treatment of some national minorities.
7. The position of blacks in Brazilian society.
8. The Africans' predicament in Rhodesia.
9. The Basques and Catalans.
10. The Chinese in Indonesia, the Philippines and Malaysia.
11. The Biharis in Bangladesh.
12. Israel's Oriental immigrants and Druzes.
13. East Indians of Trinidad and Guyana.
14. The Rom: the gypsies of Europe.
15. What future for the Amerindians of South America?
16. Problems of a displaced minority: the new position of East Africa's Asians.

17. India and the Nagas.
18. The Montagnards of South Vietnam.
19. The Namibians of South-West Africa.
20. Selective Genocide in Burundi.
21. Canada's Indians.
22. Race and law in Britain and the United States.
23. The Kurds.
24. The Palestinians.
25. The Tamils of Sri Lanka.
26. The untouchables of India.
27. Arab women.
28. Western Europe's migrant workers.
29. Jehovah's Witnesses in Central Africa.
30. Cyprus.
31. The original Americans: U.S. Indians.
32. The Armenians.
33. Nomads of the Sahel.
34. Indian South Africans.
35. Australian policy towards the Aborigines.

Mittal, J. K. "Right to Equality in the Indian Constitution." Part 1: 1970 *Public Law* 36 (1970); Part 2: *Public Law* 232 (1972). A comprehensive analysis of all forms of equality under the Indian Constitution. Part 1 traces the background of the equality provisions. Part 2 discusses the principles laid down by the Supreme Court and examines recent cases.

Moskowitz, Moses. *The Politics and Dynamics of Human Rights*. Dobbs Ferry, N.Y.: Oceana Publications, 1968. This discussion of human rights in a global and nationalistic context contains chapters on "Pluralism and Diversity," "The Rights of Man and the Fate of Minorities," and "The International Color Bar." Constitutional provisions dealing with human rights concerns are used to illustrate the author's presentation.

Mubako, Simi B. "Racialism and the Erosion of the Rule of Law in Rhodesia." *Eastern Africa Law Review* 4 (1971), p. 191. Constitutional, legislative, and administrative efforts by the Smith government to consolidate the power of the white minority in Rhodesia are discussed. It is noted that the 1969 Rhodesian Constitution ties suffrage and legislative representation to income and wealth, thereby barring the vast majority of black Rhodesians from the franchise.

Nair, V. Narayanan. "Protective Discrimination—the Supreme Court Retreats?" *Supreme Court Journal* 42 (1969), p. 33. A discussion of Article 15 (4) of the Indian Constitution, which permits special protections for persons who are socially and educationally backward. Though caste may be one element in determining backwardness, it is not in itself determinative of that status. Court cases concerning the reservation of a special number of places in universities and professional schools for members of the so-called backward classes are summarized.

Nanda, Ved P. "Racial Discrimination and the Law: Recent Legislation in Great

Britain, Canada, and the United States." In *Comparative Human Rights*, edited by Richard Claude. Baltimore: Johns Hopkins University Press, 1976, p. 214. An excellent survey, but no longer accurate in view of changes in the laws.

Palley, Claire. "Constitutional Devices in Multi-Racial and Multi-Religious Societies." *Northern Ireland Legal Quarterly* 19 (1968), p. 377. Sociologically oriented examination of institutions and practices utilized by multi-ethnic states in order to concentrate or decentralize political power. Various types of governmental structure—the federation, the confederation, the centrist—are examined, as is the effect of such structures on minority rights and interests. The constitutional provisions of such multi-ethnic states as Cyprus, Belgium, and the United States are scrutinized.

Paradis, Jerome B. "Language Rights in Multicultural States: A Comparative Study." *Canadian Bar Review* 48 (1970), p. 651. Constitutional provisions dealing with language use in Switzerland and Belgium are studied. The two European states are examined with an eye toward the future of Canada, where the Québécois have pressed for greater recognition of the French language and for protection of the language rights of French-speaking citizens. The author stresses that, just as the linguistic preference of Canada's French-speaking people must be respected, so must the rights of Québéc's English-speaking minority be rigorously protected.

Patel, Brundaban. "The Scope and Meaning of the Right to Freedom of Religion under the Indian Constitution." *Modern Review* 127 (1970), p. 370. Explication of the free exercise clause of the Indian Constitution. Religious exercise is deemed to be subject at all times to considerations of "public order, morality, and health," thus investing the state with much power to control and regulate religious practice.

Patra, Atul Chandra. "Multilingual Legislation." *Journal of the Indian Law Institute* 10 p. 661 (1968). A summary of the official language legislation of the Indian states. The constitutional provisions of other multilingual nations (Switzerland, Canada, and so on) are discussed as well. There is an interesting section on the evolution from Latin to French to English as the language of legal practitioners and the courts in England.

Pescatore, Pierre. "The Protection of Human Rights in the European Communities." *Common Market Law Review* 9 (1972), p. 73. This communication was written for the Parliamentary Conference on Human Rights organized by the Council of Europe on October 18-20, 1970. It was submitted on behalf of the Court of Justice of the European Community in order to give a concise outline of the Court's attitude on the problem of the protection of human rights.

Plamenatz, John. "Diversity of Rights and Kinds of Equality." In *Equality. . . Nomos IX*. J. Rolland Pennock and John W. Chapman eds., New York: Athenia Press, 1967, p. 79. This article and the entire volume, deal with equality from the theoretical and ethical standpoints exclusively.

Plourde, Gaston. *Options Politiques Fundamentales de L'Etat Plurilingue*. Québec: Les Presses de L'Universite Laval, 1972. Concerned primarily with linguistic rights. Various political arrangements for protecting linguistic and cultural groups are surveyed, with interesting comments on colonial and dependency status and the significance of that status on implementation of such rights.

Plural Societies. Published by the Foundation for the Study of Plural Societies, P.O. Box 3566, The Hague, The Netherlands. Quarterly. A leading journal that seems useful, but also reflects a South African bias in presentation.

Potocny, Miroslav. "The Principle of Self-Determination of Peoples (Article 1 of the International Covenants on Human Rights)." *Bulletin of Czechoslovak Law* 25, no. 8 (1967), p. 310. A discussion of the principle of self-determination as reflected in United Nations documents and as espoused in conclaves of the nonaligned countries.

Radvanova, Senta. "Protection of Matrimony, Maternity and Family." *Bulletin of Czechoslovak Law* 25, no. 8 (1967), p. 184. An examination of constitutional and legislative protection of women and the family unit. As in all socialist states, the right to day care for children is constitutionally guaranteed.

Rakowska-Harmstone, Teresa. "Ethnicity in the Soviet Union." *Annals of the American Academy of Political and Social Science* 433 (1977), p. 73. Agitation for change among non-Russian Soviet citizens forms the basis of this report. The author points out the long-standing domination of every aspect of Soviet society by persons of Russian descent and contrasts this with the current impetus toward ethnic self-assertion by other Soviet peoples.

Rappard, W. E. *La Constitution Fédèrale de la Suisse*. Neûchatel: Editions de la Baconnière, 1948. The definitive work on the Constitution of Switzerland.

Read, James S. "Bills of Rights in 'the Third World': "Some Commonwealth Experiences." *Verfassung und Recht Ubersee* 6 (1973), p. 21. Comparative analysis of bills of rights enacted by Asian and African Commonwealth nations during the 1960s. Emphasis is placed on the judicial enforceability of civil and political rights guarantees provided for in the constitutions and legislative enactments of these Third World states.

Retzlaff, Ralph H. "The Problem of Communal Minorities in the Drafting of the Indian Constitution." In *Constitutionalism in Asia*, edited by R. N. Spann. Bombay: Asia Publishing House, 1964, p. 55. A good brief survey of the legislative history behind India's failure to solve the Muslim problem through constitutional means.

Rigo, Sureda, A. *The Evolution of the Right of Self-Determination: A Study of United Nations Practice*. Leyden: Sijthoff, 1973. This study concentrates on United Nations responses to agitation on the part of colonies or ethnic groups within nations for a greater measure of self-determination. Discussion is organized by country for ready reference. United Nations support of the concept of self-determination is analyzed.

Roome, K.P.S. "Discrimination in By-Laws." *South African Law Journal* 86 (1969), p. 319. An examination of discriminatory statues passed by South African provincial legislatures.

Rosenne, Meir. "Some Legal Aspects of the Struggle for the Rights of Jews in the Soviet Union." *Israel Law Review* 9 (1974), p. 588. A brief essay commenting on the Soviet Union's discriminatory treatment of Jews, particularly with respect to emigration.

Roussillion, C. "Cultural Pluralism, Equality of Treatment, and Equality of Opportunity in Lebanon." *International Labour Review* 98 (1968), p. 225. A brief history of the immigrations of the peoples into the area that is now Lebanon is coupled with a discussion of the constitutional provisions that reflect the plural nature of Lebanese society. Emphasis is placed on the delicate balance between Christian and Islamic sects and the inevitable power struggles that accompany such a situation.

Roy, W. T. "Hostages to Fortune (A Socio-Political Study of the Anglo-Indian Remnant in India." *Plural Societies* 5, no. 2 (1974), p. 55. Brief introduction to the Indian "marginal man" resulting from British-Indian miscegenation. This is a subculture discriminated against both by the British and the Indians.

Rozenbaum, I. A. "Separation of Church from State in the USSR." *Soviet Law and Government* 11 (1972), p. 154. Analysis of the place religion holds in the Soviet system. It is emphasized here that the government of the USSR guarantees freedom of religious thought to all its people but must also retain an attitude of neutrality where religion is concerned (nothing must be done to foster or encourage the practice of religion). Religious activity is subject, however, to any legitimate exercise of the state's police power.

Rubenstein, Anunon. "Law and Religion in Israel." *Israel Law Review* 2 (1967), p. 380. The extent to which religion permeates secular aspects of life in Israel is examined in this essay. It is pointed out that even though jurisdiction over marriage, divorce, and inheritance is vested in religious bodies, Israel has managed to remain a secular nation and has been justly proud of its guarantee of religious freedom to all its citizens.

Rustow, Dankwart A. "Language, Nations, and Democracy." In *Multilingual Political Systems*. Québec: University of Laval Press, 1975, p. 43. The ideal of linguistic nationalism is to have political boundaries that coincide with language boundaries. This paper is an overview of the development of modern languages and modern states from precolonial times through today's modern era. Rustow concludes with some examples of nations which are trying to solve the problem of linguistic statehood and a plea for more comparative study of devices that they have used.

Rycroft, W. Stanley. "The Protestant Churches and Religious Freedom in Latin America." *Journal of Church and State* 8 (1966), p. 264. A former Protestant missionary in Latin America notes the dramatic increase of non-Catholic Christian denominations on that continent during the last half century. It is noted, however, that a state's guarantee of religious freedom may extend only to belief and may not include a corresponding guarantee of freedom to worship. In several nations—Chile, for example—religious toleration has come years or decades after a constitutional provision recognizing the right of religious freedom had been adopted.

Savard, Jean-Guy and Richard Vigneault, eds. *Les ÉtatsMultilingues, Problèmes et Solutions/Multilingual Political Systems, Problems and Solutions*. Publications of the International Center for Research on Bilingualism. Québec: University of Laval Press, 1975. This collection of twenty papers, presented at a Round Table of the International Political Science Association at Laval University in 1972, explores language and the political process in multicultural, multiracial, and multilingual societies in general philosophical terms, in statistical sociolinguistic studies, and finally, in specific case studies. Contributors include members of political science, language, and sociology faculties from universities in the United States, Canada, England, Germany, Lebanon, Israel, and Uganda. Most of the articles are well documented and contain basic bibliographies. Annotations to the most valuable of the articles appear in Part B.

Schacter, Oscar. "How Effective Are Measures against Racial Discrimination?" *Revue des Droits de l'Homme* 4 (1969) nos. 2-3, pp. 293-310. This excellent study contains no materials on constitutional measures to combat discrimination; it examines generally, however, the phenomenon of race discrimination. The psychological and cultural effects of discrimination upon minority group members and those in the majority are discussed and analyzed.

Schreiber, Anna P. "The Status of Women in the United States and the Scandinavian Countries." In *Comparative Human Rights*, edited by Richard Claude. Baltimore: Johns Hopkins University Press, 1976, p. 251. Review of social and economic factors that lead to unequal status between men and women in the United States, Norway, and Sweden. Emphasis is placed on the still-strong impact of the traditional wife-mother role as a factor in women's lower economic and occupational status, although it is noted that such concepts are changing, particularly in the United States.

Schreuer, Christoph. "The Impact of International Institutions on the Protection of Human Rights in Domestic Courts." *Israel Yearbook of Human Rights* 4 (1974) p. 60. An examination of the effect of international rights pronouncements (particularly the Universal Declaration of Human Rights) upon matters before the domestic courts of signatory states. It is pointed out that many governments look upon the Universal Declaration as a statement of goals and ideals rather than as a document with the force of law. West Germany is cited as having relied heavily on the Declaration in several court decisions involving construction of its own constitution. The international reaction to the incident is also discussed.

Shelton, Dinah. "Human Rights within Churches." *Revue des Droits de l'Homme* 6 (1973) pp. 487-563. Though not concerned directly with constitutions, this general study of the means by which organized religious groups discriminate on racial or sex grounds is excellent.

Sigler, Jay Adrian. "Research Resources on Comparative Rights Policies." In *Comparative Human Rights*, edited by Richard Claude. Baltimore: Johns Hopkins University Press, 1976, p. 286. Survey and review of scholarly literature in the field of human rights.

Simon, Walter B. "Occupational Structure, Multilingualism and Social Change." In *Multilingual Political Systems*. Québec: University of Laval Press, 1975, p. 87. Language conflicts that are but one facet of class and cultural conflicts have increased with the urbanization and industrialization of society. Simon believes that their importance has been underrated by social scientists, and he proposes a detailed outline for a study of the relationships between social class, language conflicts, and political ideology.

Smith, Alan H. "Prevention of Discrimination under Kenya Law." *International and Comparative Law Quarterly* 20 (1971), p. 136. The Kenyan Constitution prohibits discrimination on racial or tribal grounds, but elaborate constitutional distinctions are made between the rights enjoyed by Kenyan citizens, citizens of British Commonwealth nations, and aliens. This commentary briefly examines the relevant articles of the Kenyan Constitution and discusses recent cases that have dealt with the construction and effect of such constitutional provisions.

Spann, R. N., ed. *Constitutionalism in Asia*. Bombay: Asia Publishing House, 1964. A series of seminar papers in which much emphasis is placed on the problems of communal minorities.

Subba Rao, Shri K. "The Philosophy of the Indian Constitution." *Eastern Journal of International Law* 4, 173 (1972). A good introduction to the Indian Constitution, particularly as it relates to fundamental rights and protection of the backward classes. The author is the former chief justice of the Supreme Court of India, and he prefaces his discussion of fundamental rights concerns with an analysis of Indian federalism.

Szabo, Imre. *Cultural Rights*. Leiden: A. W. Sijthoff, 1974. Translated from the original Hungarian, this volume, by a member of the Hungarian Academy of Sciences, suffers from Eastern European overemphasis on word definitions. It is extraordinarily dull. What it does do however, is to provide some insights on Eastern European thinking that are absent from most of the literature on human rights.

Touret, Barnard. *L'Amenagement Constitutionnel des États de Peuplement Composite.* Québec: Les Presses de L'Universite Laval, 1973. A quite useful analysis of factors causing cultural heterogeneity. Race, language, ethnicity, and religion are seen as differentiating forces. Solutions to conflicts created by these forces, particularly territorial solutions, are examined. The book advocates greater regional autonomy and guarantees of collective rights for certain groups.

Tripathi, P. K. "Secularism: Constitutional Provision and Judicial Review." *Journal of the Indian Law Institute* 8, no. 1 (1966). A discussion of Articles 25 and 26 of the Indian Constitution. India wanted to avoid the American trend toward complete toleration in permitting nonconforming religious practice. The result: the present Indian Constitution guarantees religious freedom, but religious *practice* is at all times subject to state scrutiny and regulation.

UNESCO. *Cultural Rights as Human Rights*. Paris, UNESCO, 1970

______. *Four Statements on the Race Question*. Paris, UNESCO, 1969. A compilation of UNESCO's 1950, 1951, 1964, and 1967 statements on race and race prejudice. In all the statements the economic and social causes and consequences of racism are stressed. The unifying theme of all four statements—that racial differences are, ultimately, irrelevant—is brought forth clearly in this brief volume.

______. *Study of the Problem of Discrimination against Indigenous Populations*. Report of Jose R. Martinez Cobo. Geneva: E/CN 4/Sub. 1/622. July 1975. Every study on indigenous populations necessarily involves questions of racial discrimination. The indigenous populations are, for the most part, victims of white colonialism. Indians throughout South America, the Maoris of New Zealand, the Lapps of Finland, and so on, are all in this category. This is a rather disjointed report, but it does have a useful collection of data, enriched by reports and comments from various governments that have minority indigenous populations.

______. *Women, Education, Equality: A Decade of Experiment.* Paris, UNESCO Press, 1975. Report on the progress of three UNESCO-sponsored programs (in Upper Volta, Nepal, and Chile), all aimed at promoting educational and employment opportunities for women.

United Nations. *Human Rights: A Compilation of International Instruments of the United Nations.* New York: United Nations, 1973. Consolidation of all Human Rights documents issued under the aegis of the United Nations in the quarter century since the promulgation of the Universal Declaration of Human Rights.

______. "Law and the Status of Women: An International Symposium." New York, 1977. *Columbia Human Rights Law Review* 8, no. 1 (1977), p. 1. Following an introductory chapter, fifteen articles, each discussing law and the status of women in a different country, are set forth. Some of the nations profiled include Sweden, France, Egypt, Kenya, Peru, and Iran.

______. *Protection of Minorities: Special Protective Measures of an International Character for Ethnic, Religious or Linguistic Groups.* New York: United Nations, 1967. (Sales no. E. 67. XIX.3).

______. *Racial Discrimination.* By Special Rapporteur Hernan Santa Cruz. New York: United Nations, 1971. (Sales No. E. 71. XIV 2). Revised and Updated Version, 1976, New York: United Nations, 1977. (Sales No. E. 76. XIV.2). E/CN 4/Sub. 2/307/Rev. 1.

______. *Report on Slavery.* By Special Rapporteur Hans Egen. 19 UN ESCOR, Annexes (Agenda Item 8), UN Doc. E/2673 (1955). A concise summary of information supplied by both member and nonmember governments in an attempt to get a clear view as to the extent to which slavery and practices resembling slavery exist in the world today. Slavery, serfdom, debt bondage, exploitation of children, and purchase of wives are among the topics explored.

______. *Report on Slavery.* By Special Rapporteur Mohamed Awad. New York: United Nations, 1967. E/4168. Revised. This update of the 1955 report consolidates information received from governments, specialized agencies, and nongovernmental organizations on the subject of slavery. These data frequently make reference to Constitutional revisions and statutes on the subject. The report is particularly useful with regard to women's rights, since under United Nations definitions marriage arrangements without consent of both parties and marriage of very young girls are considered to be forms of involuntary servitude.

______. *Report on Slavery.* By Special Rapporteur Mohamed Awad. United Nations, New York, 1971. E/CN 4/Sub 2/322. Another update of an earlier report. Focus of this study is upon measures that might be taken to implement and enforce international conventions on the abolition of slavery. The possibility of cooperation by police and security forces of member nations in helping combat slavery is also examined.

______. *Seminar on the Promotion and Protection of the Human Rights of National, Ethnic, and Other Minorities.* Ohrid, Yugoslavia, 25 June—8 July, 1974. New York: United Nations, 1974. This pamphlet is not nearly so valuable as the title would indicate. While the participants are all able and knowledgeable, Eastern European and Yugoslavian problems are overemphasized. Nonetheless, attention was drawn to the fact that many constitutions profess human rights, including those of minorities, but that such principles are often violated in actual practice.

______. *Study of Discrimination in the Matter of Religious Rights and Practices.* By Arcot Krishnaswami. New York: United Nations, 1960. E/CN 4/Sub 2/200/Rev. 1. While this text does not furnish any statistical or systematic information on religious freedoms and practices in the different countries of the world, it provides the valuable function of defining the dimensions of religious practices. It discusses the scope of freedom to maintain or change religion, the scope of freedom of manifest religion, and the scope of permissible limitations upon freedoms. There is also a good philosophical discussion on individual and collective aspects of freedom.

The United Nations and Human Rights. Eighteenth Report of the Commission to Study the Organization of Peace. Dobbs Ferry, N.Y.: Oceana Publications, 1968. Review of existing United Nations Human Rights documents with an emphasis on the Universal Declaration of Human Rights. Included is an analysis of the documents by Professor Louis B. Sohn; the documents themselves are appended to the text. A good general introduction to the efforts of the United Nations in the context of human rights protection.

United States Department of State. *Country Reports on Human Rights Practices.* Reports submitted to the Committee on International Relations, U.S. House of Representatives, and Committee on Foreign Relations, U.S. Senate, February 3, 1978. Washington, D.C.: Superintendent of Documents, 1978. These reports were prepared for Congress in accordance with sections of the Foreign Assistance Act of 1961. There is a brief summary of human rights practices of roughly 100 of the 160 countries of the world. For some reason not explained in the report, South Africa, Argentina, Chile, and Brazil are among those omitted. While the reports are very brief, they do make references to the status of women and occasionally to matters of religious practice.

______. *Human Rights and U.S. Policy: Argentina, Haiti, Indonesia, Iran, Peru, and the Philippines.* Reports submitted to the Committee on International Relations, U.S. House of Representatives, December 31, 1976. 94th Congress, 2d Session. Department of State report on human rights in six selected nations.

______. *Human Rights in the International Community and in U.S. Foreign Policy, 1945-1976.* Prepared for the Subcommittee on International Organizations of the Committee on International Relations, U.S. House of Representatives, July 24, 1977. 95th Congress, 1st Session. Study examines evolution of international human rights and considers U.S. foreign policy and its relationship to human rights.

______. *The Status of Human Rights in Selected Countries and the U.S. Response.* Prepared for the Subcommittee on International Organizations of the Committee on International Relations, U.S. House of Representatives, July 25, 1977. 95th Congress, 1st Session.

Van Boven, Theodor C. "Some Results on Special Problems Relating to Human

Rights in Developing Countries." *Revue des Droits de l'Homme* 3 (1970), p. 383.

Van den Berghe, Pierre. *Race and Racism: A Comparative Perspective*. New York: John Wiley and Sons, 1967. Case studies of Mexico, Brazil, the United States, and South Africa as multiracial societies. Social factors that militate for or against racial integration are examined, as are historical and cultural biases. Governmental institutions are scrutinized for the parts they play, intentionally or not, in encouraging racist sentiments.

Van Dyke, Vernon. "One Man, One Vote, and Majority Rule as Human Rights." *Revue des Droits de l'Homme* 6 (1973), p. 447. Outline of some of the ways in which various countries restrict voting and majority rule and as a consequence discriminate against some of their citizens. Particular attention is paid to South Africa and Rhodesia.

Van Niekerk, Barend. "The Dream of Liberty—Bills of Rights for the Bantustans." *South Africa Law Journal* 90 (1973), p. 403. An examination of the idea, expressed by Chief Gatsha Buthelezi, of entrenching in "constitutions of liberty" basic human and civil rights for South Africa's Bantu peoples and possible ways of achieving this goal.

Van Maaseveen, H. Th. J. F., and G.F.M. Van Der Tag. *On Written Constitutions.* (Dobbs Ferry, N.Y.: Oceana Press, 1981).

Vasil, R. K. "Communalism and Constitution-Making in Fiji." *Pacific Affairs* 45 (1972), p. 21. Constitutional history of Fiji, from its last years of dependency upon Britain to its first years as an independent state. Discussion centers upon the division of legislative seats among members of the three major ethnic groups—Indians, native Fijians, and persons of European descent. Though Indians constitute a majority of Fiji's population, a constitution that enabled political power to be entrenched in the hands of the Fijians and the Europeans was ultimately adopted.

______. "Ethnic Discrimination in Fiji: An Indian View." *Veenhoven,* Volume two, p. 191.

Veenhoven, Willem A., ed. *Case Studies of Human Rights and Fundamental Freedoms: A World Survey*. 5 volumes. The Hague: Nijhoff, 1975.

Veiter, Theodor. "Commentary on the Concept of 'National Minorities.' " *Revue des Droits de l'Homme* 7 (1974), p. 273.

Wagley, Charles, and Martin Harris. *Minorities in the New World.* New York: Columbia University Press, 1958. Somewhat dated historical examination of six minority groups in the Western Hemisphere—Indians in Mexico and Brazil, blacks in Martinique and the United States, the French in Canada, and American Jews. The study was sponsored by UNESCO.

Watts, R. L. "Asian Multicultural Federations." In *Multilingual Political Systems.* Québec: University of Laval Press, 1975, p. 561. Federal political systems would seem to be the solution for the problems of integration and separatism in multilingual, multicultural societies. This comparative study of the treatment of central institutions, political parties, and official language policies shows how the theory has succeeded or failed in India, Pakistan, and Malaysia.

Wenner, Manfred W. "The Politics of Equality Among European Linguistic Minorities." In *Comparative Human Rights*, edited by Richard Claude.

Baltimore: Johns Hopkins University Press, 1976. p. 184. A study of minority groups in the multilingual nations of Europe and examination of efforts to guarantee to such minorities the right to function in their own tongue. Constitutional provisions in such nations as Belgium and Switzerland that evidence concern for minority linguistic groups are studied.

Wood, James E., Jr., "Religious Liberty in Ecumenical and International Perspective." *Journal of Church and State* 10 (1968), p. 421. In this essay, written in celebration of the twentieth anniversary of the United Nations Universal Declaration of Human Rights, it is noted that true religious freedom has become possible only within the last two centuries. Recent United Nations and ecumenical documents supporting the principle of religious freedom are summarized and discussed.

Index

About The Authors

JAY A. SIGLER is Professor of Political Science at the Camden campus of Rutgers University in New Jersey. He is the author of eight other books, including *American Rights Policies*, *Understanding Criminal Law*, *Double Jeopardy*, and *The Legal Sources of Public Policy*. He has also authored numerous articles on human rights and constitutional law for scholarly journals.

JAMES B. MULDOON is Professor of History at Rutgers University. He has specialized in medieval canon law and has published a number of books, including *The Expansion of Europe: The First Phase* and *Popes, Lawyers and Infidels*.